National and Global Responses to the COVID-19 Pandemic

A. S. Bhalla

National and Global Responses to the COVID-19 Pandemic

Do Leaders Matter?

palgrave
macmillan

A. S. Bhalla
Commugny, Switzerland

ISBN 978-3-031-29520-1 ISBN 978-3-031-29521-8 (eBook)
https://doi.org/10.1007/978-3-031-29521-8

This Palgrave Macmillan imprint is published by the registered company Springer Nature Switzerland AG.
The registered company address is: Gewerbestrasse 11, 6330 Cham, Switzerland

To the frontline health workers around the world in the hope that their enormous sacrifices to save human lives are not in vain, and that political leaders and public as well as private institutions will reward them with greater recognition, better treatment and financial benefits in the post-pandemic era

Also by A.S. Bhalla

Asia's Trouble Spots: The Leadership Question in Conflict Resolution
Blending of New and Traditional Technologies (Co-editor)
Buddhist Art in Asia
Economic Transition in Hunan and Southern China
Employment, Environment and Development (Editor) (Also in Portuguese)
Facing the Technological Challenge
Glimpses of Medieval Switzerland
Globalization, Growth and Marginalization (Editor) (Also in French)
Imperial India: A Pictorial History
In Search of Roots
Market or Government Failures? An Asian Perspective
Monuments, Power and Poverty in India: From Ashoka to the Raj
New Technologies and Development (Co-editor)
Poverty Among Immigrant Children in Europe (Co-author)
Poverty and Exclusion in a Global World (Co-author) (Also in Japanese)
Poverty and Exclusion of Minorities in China and India (Co-author)
Poverty and Inequality Among Chinese Minorities (Co-author)
Regional Blocs: Building Blocks or Stumbling Blocks (Co-author)
Royal Tombs of India
Small and Medium Enterprises: Technology Policies and Options (Editor)
Switzerland Then and Now

Technology and Employment in Industry (Editor) (Also in Spanish)
Technological Transformation of Rural India (Co-editor)
The Employment Impact of China's WTO Accession (Co-author)
Towards Global Action for Appropriate Technology (Editor)
Uneven Development in the Third World: A Study of China and India

Preface

Hardly a day passes when something is not written on the COVID-19 pandemic. Despite the plethora of literature, one rarely comes across a systematic analysis of the role of leaders, institutions (public and private) and people's behaviour in explaining the differences between successes and failures in fighting the COVID-19 pandemic. Even less studied is the *relationship* of consensus and cooperation, or competition and conflict between the key players.

Permission to publish preliminary research on COVID-19 without peer review, or open access publishing, largely explains the explosion of the literature on the coronavirus pandemic. Most of the scientific papers are concerned with such issues as the origin of the virus, its mutants, genome sequencing, clinical trials of vaccines and their efficacy particularly for different groups such as children, women and the elderly. The social sciences literature on COVID-19 can be grouped under three main categories: (1) the economic and social impact, (2) risk and uncertainty and human behaviour and (3) politicization of the pandemic, blunders of governments and governance failures.

If much has already been written on the coronavirus pandemic, why yet another book on the subject? Although literature exists in abundance under all the above categories, it is surprising that very little of it deals specifically with leadership failures at different levels, which is the core of the book. And to the best of our knowledge, hardly any literature exists on the relationship, *collaborative or conflictual,* between key actors in the pandemic, namely leaders, agents and followers. This book is a modest attempt to fill this gap.

As the book demonstrates, most political leaders, particularly in the West, lacked the foresight and prescience of Lawrence Wright, the author of the *End of October*, who wrote the thriller about a deadly virus, a world in lockdown that predicted the shape of things to come in the form of the coronavirus pandemic.

Several policy lessons for the future are worth noting: need for global cooperation, greater role for government, strengthening of public health care and safety nets, and global sharing of COVID-19 data and vaccines, besides a change in human behaviour, working habits and lifestyles.

The pandemic has exposed the myth of Western exceptionalism and the limitations of such conventional divides as North and South, advanced and developing, rich and poor, democratic and authoritarian. It has also exposed the myth of robustness and superiority of Western governance and healthcare systems. Traditionally, good performance has been associated with the West which enjoys the benefits of well-equipped and well-funded healthcare systems and services. But the scorecard on COVID-19 has shown how false this assumption has become.

The Coronavirus pandemic has attacked all countries rich and poor, small or large, and of different political ideologies without any discrimination. The success and failure to fight the virus also cuts across these divides. Both rich and poor countries, those from the North and South and democratic as well as authoritarian ones have coped well or poorly in controlling the virus.

I owe a debt of gratitude to a number of scholars. Professor Colin Mackerras of Griffith University, Brisbane, Australia, provided useful comments on earlier drafts of all chapters. He contributed a section on Sino-American Relations of Chap. 5; Professor Alan Lindsay Greer, Director, Research Relations for Physical Sciences and Technology, University of Cambridge, made various scientific inputs to Chaps. 1 and 7; David Bloom, Clarence James Gamble Professor of Economics and Demography, T.H. Chan School of Public Health, Harvard University, gave valuable suggestions on an earlier draft of the manuscript besides supplying written material and publications; Professor Archie Brown, Emeritus Professor of Politics, University of Oxford, gave generously of his time to discuss leadership issues, besides offering valuable comments and suggestions; Professor Shujie Yao, Deputy Dean, Social Sciences Faculty and Chueng Kong Special Chair of Economics, Chongqing University, gave useful comments on early drafts of Chaps. 2, 4, and 7. The drafting of Chap. 6 on Global and Regional Action and the international management of health benefited from discussions with Dr. Keith Bezanson, former President, International Development Research Centre (IDRC), Ottawa, and former Director, Institute of Development Studies (IDS), Brighton; and Imre Hollo, World Health Organization (WHO) Geneva. Dr. Nguyen Van Quang, Vice-Dean, School of Economics, College of Economics, Technology and Fisheries, Bac Ninh Province, Vietnam, contributed local primary material and reviewed drafts on Vietnam's response to COVID-19. I have also benefited from useful discussions on national and global public health issues and responses with Dr. Simon Deakin, Director of the Economic and Business Research Centre, University of Cambridge, and with Dr. Didier Wernli, Director of the Geneva Transformative Governance Lab, Global Studies Institute of the University of Geneva. Statistical estimates for Chap. 2 were undertaken by Ms. Jing Fang of Chongqing University. However, a usual disclaimer is in order: all errors of omission or commission remain my sole responsibility.

A. S. Bhalla

About the Book

It is surprising that very little existing literature discusses the vital role of relations between leaders (political, scientific, industry and academic), public and private institutions (public health departments, centres for disease control, educational and scientific institutions and multilateral organizations) and followers (citizens, public and local community) in tackling the COVID-19 pandemic. Yet, the relationship between these key stakeholders is crucial in determining the outcomes of responses to the coronavirus pandemic. Synergy between the stakeholders can ensure their success, whereas conflict can undermine efforts to control the pandemic. Followers' trust and confidence in their leaders and governments is the key to good performance. The book's review and assessment of 16 political leaders and relevant national institutions offer several policy lessons for the future, notably the need for greater global cooperation, a more *effective* role for government, strengthening of public health care systems, and global sharing of COVID-19 data and vaccines. The pandemic has resulted in changes in human behaviour, working habits and lifestyles, which raises numerous issues. The conventional approaches to leadership underestimate or ignore the importance of these issues. This book is a modest attempt to fill the gap.

Special features of the book include a historical review of previous pandemics, coverage of the COVID situation across different geographical regions and an analysis of the reasons for Southeast Asia's success in controlling the spread of COVID-19 while the West failed, barring a few exceptions. Initial conditions such as healthcare spending and infrastructure are important features contributing to a country's preparedness in coping with a pandemic, and leadership plays a critical role. The book unveils the limitations of existing global action to control the present and future pandemics.

Praise for *National and Global Responses to the COVID-19 Pandemic*

"Bhalla's skills underlying his previous books shine through in this wide-ranging, sometimes brutally incisive, analysis of responses to the COVID pandemic. Framing his arguments in terms of Leaders, Agents and Followers, he probes the multiple interactions of politics, governance, science and commerce. It is shocking that leaders were so badly prepared for a pandemic that was so widely anticipated. Bhalla's historical perspective, and his assessment of comparative national responses to the pandemic, highlight many lessons to which too many leaders will continue to be deaf."

—Lindsay Greer, *Professor, Director of Research Relations (Physical Sciences and Technology), University of Cambridge; former Head of the School of Physical Sciences*

"This is an important book which deserves to be widely read. It provides a compelling account of the role of leadership in framing the political response to a global problem. This and the data which it presents will make an important contribution to an on-going debate. If at points the argument and its conclusions are challenged, that itself will be useful contribution to our understanding of a subject on which public fear has too often got in the way of clear thinking."

—James Mayall, *Emeritus Professor of International Relations, University of Cambridge; Fellow of the British Academy*

"When it comes to pandemics, Ajit Bhalla understands the vital importance of leadership in mitigating impacts and exiting from disasters and near disasters. Whether in communities, countries, or on the global stage, and in whatever historical period, the power of science and technology is not enough. Leaders need to build trust and human understanding if the scientific breakthroughs are to be truly beneficial."

—Dame Sandra Dawson, *Professor Emerita, University of Cambridge; former Director, Cambridge Judge Business School*

"Bhalla's book makes a significant contribution to the understanding of COVID-19 by focusing on the relationships between political leaders, governments and people. It convincingly demonstrates that countries which enjoyed synergy between the three stakeholders as well as public trust and confidence in government fared much better in their fight against the pandemic."

—Prem Chauhan, *former Union Health Secretary, Government of India*

"This most comprehensive study emphasizes the important roles of leadership, medical professionals and the public to fight COVID-19. The lack of or weak leadership in some advanced countries is mainly responsible for the failure to tackle the contagion, which had serious consequences on economies and people's well-being. A major contribution of the book is its suggestions for coping strategies against future public health disasters."

—Shujie Yao, *Deputy Dean, Social Sciences and Cheung Kong Special Chair of Economics, Chongqing University, China*

"The book is a fascinating read for those interested in the intersection of leadership styles and political systems in managing situations that are fraught with uncertainties. It offers an impressive overview of the global response to the COVID-19 pandemic, where policy responses were highly contextual, while covering a wide canvas of the rich and poor, north and south."

—K Sujatha Rao, *Former Union Health Secretary, Government of India*

"Hindsight brings clarity, and we know that leadership was the key differentiator between countries that successfully managed COVID-19 as well as the vaccine roll-out, and those that did not. Ajit Bhalla's timely contribution explores all facets of leadership during the pandemic, and is written in a logical and easily accessible manner."

—Marie Kirsten, *Project Coordinator for South Africa's COVID-19 Country Report, National Treasury, Government of South Africa*

"Dr Bhalla provides an analytical, balanced and comprehensive account of leadership (or absence of it) during the COVID-19 pandemic with lessons for the future. Highly readable and evidence-based, the book transcends the boundaries of any one specialty, and must be read by individuals from different areas of interest. While it answers many questions, it will also spark debate and public discourse on the topic, and that, in my opinion, will be its biggest contribution to the handling of future epidemics and pandemics."

—Chandrakant Lahariya, *a leading public policy and health systems expert; formerly with the World Health Organization; co-author of Till We Win: India's Fight against the COVID-19 Pandemic*

"Dr Ajit Bhalla has written a timely book looking into the political dimensions of the public health response, and how politics inevitably influence the reaction of our institutions to the pandemic. Leadership is important on a national and global level, and this book dissects the different types of leadership and their impact during the pandemic. These questions of leadership remain pertinent in guiding health policy for the present pandemic and for future public health emergencies."

—Alexander So, *Honorary Professor of Medicine, University of Lausanne*

"Going through more than two and a half years of COVID-19 pandemic, we cannot underestimate the importance of leadership for tackling human health crises. Ajit Bhalla traces the importance of the history of pandemics, discusses challenges confronting national and global leaders, and proposes what could be done better to prepare for future pandemics."

—Thu Anh Nguyen, *Country Director, Woolcock Institute of Medical Research in Vietnam and Clinical Senior Lecturer, University of Sydney Central Clinical School, Australia*

"This stimulating book offers food for thought on the relationship between leadership styles, populism, and the effectiveness of the response to the COVID-19 crisis. All these themes are of great interest even to those involved in a deeper study of political psychology."

—Gilda Sensales, *Associate Professor of Social and Political Psychology, Sapienza University of Rome*

Contents

About the Author

A. S. Bhalla is former Fellow, Sidney Sussex College, Cambridge, UK and former Special Adviser to the President of International Development Research Centre (IDRC), Ottawa. He was Hallsworth Professorial Fellow, Manchester University, Research Associate, Yale University, New Haven, and Research Officer at the University of Oxford. He is the author of several books on different subjects including *Asia's Trouble Spots: The Leadership Question in Conflict Resolution* (2019).

Abbreviations

A3PCON	Asia Pacific Policy Planning Council
AaH	All about Health (Netherlands)
ACT	Access to COVID-19 Tools-Accelerator
AIDS	Auto-Immune Deficiency Syndrome
AJPH	American Journal of Public Health
AMC	Advance Market Commitment
ASEAN	Association of South-East Asian Nations
BAME	Black, Asia, Minority Ethnic
BBC	British Broadcasting Corporation
BIVD	Bank for Investment and Development of Vietnam
BJP	Bharatiya Janata Party
BMC	Bio Medic Central
BMJ	British Medical Journal
BRI	Belt and Road Initiative (China)
CAA	Chinese for Affirmative Action
CARES	Citizens Assistance and Relief in Emergency Situations Fund (India) and Coronavirus Aid, Relief and Economic Security Act (US)
CCP	Chinese Communist Party
CDC	Centres for Disease Control
CEPI	Coalition of Epidemic Preparedness
CEPR	Centre for Economic Policy Research
CGD	Center for Global Development
CHUV	*Centre Hopitalier Universitaire Vaudois*, Switzerland
CIGI	Centre for International Governance Innovation
CMAJ	Canadian Medical Association Journal
CNN	Cable News Network

COBRA	Cabinet Office Briefing Room (UK)
COVAX	COVID-19 Vaccines Global Access Facility
CRS	Congressional Research Service
DARPA	Defence Advanced Research Projects Agency (US)
DELVE	Data Evaluation and Learning for Viral Epidemics
DRC	Democratic Republic of Congo
ECDC	European Centre for Disease Control
EGHRIN	European Global Health Research Institutes Network
EMA	European Medicines Agency
EPA	European Policy Analysis
ERF	Emergency Response Framework
EUROPP	European Politics and Policy
EWARS	Early Warning, Alert and Response System
FDA	Food and Drug Administration (US)
FDI	Foreign Direct Investment
FEMA	Federal Emergency Management Agency
GAVI	Global Alliance for Vaccines and Immunization
GERM	Global Epidemic Response and Mobilization
GHSI	Global Health Security Index
GISAID	International Repository of Viral Genetic Information
GLO	Global Labour Organization
GOI	Government of India
HERA	Health Emergency Preparedness and Response Authority
IAVI	International AIDS Vaccine Initiative
ICC	International Chamber of Commerce
ICU	Intensive Care Unit
IFDC	International Fertilizer Development Center
IFR	Infection Fatality Ratio
IHME	Institute of Health and Metric Evaluation (US)
IHR	International Health Regulations
ILO	International Labour Office
IMF	International Monetary Fund
IPPPR	Independent Panel for Pandemic Preparedness and Response
IPT	International Pandemic Treaty
JAMA	Journal of American Medical Association
JEET	Joint External Evaluation Tool
JEM	Journal of Experimental Medicine
LERU	League of European Universities
LSE	London School of Economics and Political Science
LSHTM	London School of Hygiene and Tropical Medicine
MERS	Middle East Respiratory Syndrome
mRNA	Messenger Ribonucleic Acid

MSF	*Médecins sans frontières*
NAFTA	North American Free Trade Area
NATO	North Atlantic Treaty Organization
NBER	National Bureau of Economic Research
NCAER	National Council of Applied Economic Research
NGO	Non-Governmental Organization
NHS	National Health Service (UK)
NPR	National Public Radio
NRI	Non-Resident Indian
PAVM	Partnership (EU-Africa) for Vaccine Manufacturing
PLOS	Public Library of Science
PPE	Personal Protective Equipment
RD	Public Health Responsibility Deal (UK)
RIS	Research and Information Systems
SAARC	South Asian Association for Regional Cooperation
SAGE	Scientific Advisory Group for Emergencies (UK)
SARS	Severe Acute Respiratory Syndrome
SDR	Special Drawing Rights (IMF)
SEWA	Self-employed Women's Association
SSRN	Social Science Research Network
TRIPS	Trade Related Aspects of Intellectual Property Rights
UNICEF	United Nations Children's Fund
UN OCHA	United Nations Office for the Coordination of Humanitarian Affairs
WDR	*Westdeutscher Rundfunk* (North Rhine Westphalia Broadcasting Station)
WEF	World Economic Forum
WHA	World Health Assembly
WHO	World Health Organization
WMO	World Meteorological Organization
WTO	World Trade Organization

List of Tables

PART I

History and Context

CHAPTER 1

Viruses and Leadership in a Historical Perspective

The winners of past wars were not always the armies with the best generals and weapons, but were often merely those bearing the nastiest germs to transmit to their enemies.
—Jared Diamond, *Guns, Germs and Steel*

Germs and viruses have been known to mankind for thousands of years. They caused infectious diseases such as smallpox, cholera, influenza, malaria and tuberculosis, which were transmitted to humans through domestic animals. Diamond (2005, pp. 207–8) describes three stages of evolution of diseases. The first stage refers to the diseases that human beings pick up directly from domesticated and wild animals. The second stage involves the direct transmission between human beings of a pathogen originating from an animal. In the third stage, these human diseases become well established and may end up being lethal.

For centuries there have been striking similarities between the nature of viruses and germs. Generally, the responses of governments and political leaders in hiding bad news have been virtually identical, and people's anger against their governments and political discontent become rampant (Pamuk, 2020, April 23; 2021). This denial or downplaying of epidemics and serious diseases has occurred throughout history. Descriptions of the plague,[1] for instance, have strikingly similar themes such as "carelessness, incompetence and selfishness" of the authorities, and public anger,

A. S. Bhalla, *National and Global Responses to the COVID-19 Pandemic*, https://doi.org/10.1007/978-3-031-29521-8_1

misinformation and falsehoods, leading to rumour mongering, myths and charlatans offering magical cures. An inevitable outcome of a pandemic was panic, fear of death, sense of insecurity in the face of human suffering and the resulting feelings of loneliness and helplessness.

Has anything changed since those ancient times? It does not seem so when observing how populist leaders and right-wing media in countries like the United States have been spreading false information in an effort to dilute or contradict honest scientific information. Threats to Dr. Fauci and Bill Gates in the United States for seeking or speaking the truth are a consequence of such actions. The fake news, alternative truths and conspiracy theories of today are no different from ancient myths and superstitions. Trump's recommendation to the American people to ingest or inject disinfectants and drink bleach to cure COVID virus is no less dangerous than the voodooism or sorcerers' recipes of ancient times.

While the earlier pandemics were *localized* or *regional,* the coronavirus pandemic is truly *global.* It is affecting the entire humanity, which is how a pandemic is generally distinguished from an epidemic. Spectacular developments in the fields of information technology and communication systems distinguish today's world from the distant past. But as discussed in the subsequent chapters, this process of globalization and interconnectedness is a double-edged sword. While it enables scientists to share and exchange knowledge and ideas and learn from past experiences and best practices, it also allows the rapid spread of falsehoods far and wide.

The stock of knowledge has become vast thanks to a large body of scientists and engineers, and valuable past experiences and best practices are available to learn from. Finally, the world is facing a public health crisis, an economic crisis and a food crisis all at once, which is unprecedented.

Previous Viruses

Below we examine a selected number of previous viruses to assess their characteristics as well as parallels with COVID-19.

Russian Flu (1889–1890)

This virus, first reported in St Petersburg in the Russian Empire, quickly spread throughout the northern hemisphere thanks to the existence of rail, road and sea transport. The growth in population was also responsible for its rapid spread to almost all major cities of Europe: from Poznan to

Vienna, London, Paris, Lyon and to other places. The disease afflicted the rich and famous as well as the poor. The public health authorities closed all schools and isolated the elderly. Charity organizations played their part. The virus spread to the United States in 1890 when few Americans believed it could cross the Atlantic! It was transmitted throughout the world in several waves, lasting from October 1889 to December 1890, killing about a million people.

In this pre-virology period, the British Local Government Board undertook two epidemiological surveys, which established that the Russian flu was very infectious with a short incubation period of 2–3 days, and that it led to deaths due to respiratory disease. A proper public health response was not provided despite these findings. The consequence was avoidable deaths of a large number of people.

Great Influenza (1918)

The 1918 influenza, like COVID-19, was a respiratory virus which killed millions of people. It was deadlier than the current coronavirus. There are remarkable parallels between the 1918 pandemic and COVID-19 in terms of the apathy displayed by the leadership, the responses of the public health authorities and the scientific community, as well as the economic fallout.

The Great influenza (Spanish Flu) originated in an army camp in the United States (US) and may have been an unintended consequence of the US preparations for World War I. Barracks and training camps, which were overcrowded with soldiers, were an ideal breeding ground for the virus, as they did not meet even the minimum public health standards. As infected soldiers moved between camps, so did the virus. In addition, soldiers were sent to hospitals to attend to the sick, which spread the disease to civilian patients.

Later, American troops carried it to Europe during World War I. The epidemic killed over 100 million people worldwide, that is more people in 24 weeks than HIV/AIDS killed in 24 years, more in a year than the Black Death killed in a century in the Middle Ages.

Voluntary lockdowns, stay-at-home instructions and closure of department stores, small shops and schools and universities were not strictly observed by the public, which did not trust the national and local governments. Barry (2018, p. 175) concludes: "The public could trust nothing and so they knew nothing. Society is, ultimately, based on trust; as trust broke down, people became alienated not only from those in authority, but from each other."

Despite the widespread epidemic, the government single-mindedly focused on the war in Europe and not on the war against the disease. President Wilson did not recognize the disease. According to Barry (2018, pp. 460–61): "From neither the White House nor any other senior administration post would there come any leadership, any attempt to set priorities, any attempt to coordinate activities, any attempt to deliver resources."

US state governors and mayors begged for help in providing more doctors and nurses, but with barely any response from the federal government. Mayors and local authorities were left to fend for themselves. Some even kidnapped nurses from other states! Few volunteered when the Council of National Defence created a Volunteer Medical Service to enlist doctors.

Many states distorted facts about the influenza or failed to report the severe effects of the disease. Fear spread among the population, with people even afraid to be treated in hospitals or by a doctor. They would try all sorts of "folk medicine" or fraudulent remedies such as gargling with disinfectants or wearing camphor balls and garlic around their necks.

There were shortages of drugs and medical supplies. Hospitals could not cope with the number of patients coming in, and doctors and nursing staff were overwhelmed. Prolonged lockdowns, necessitated due to delays in timely action, resulted in mental stress amongst people who missed social interaction.

Some Americans blamed the poor and immigrants for the disease. For example, Denver Health Commissioner blamed "foreign settlements of Italians" in the city for its difficulties with influenza. Historians of epidemics argue that the powerful blamed the poor for their suffering and stigmatized and isolated them (Barry, 2020, March 17).

Asian Influenza (H2N2) (1957)

This influenza originated in Guizhou in southwest China and spread to neighbouring areas (Yunnan and Hong Kong) before reaching India, the United Kingdom and the United States. The total number of deaths worldwide were estimated to be one to two million people. A vaccine was rapidly developed, which helped control the spread of the virus.

It was the first major pandemic since the 1918 influenza and displayed similar pathogens and distribution patterns.[2] There were also similar waves that spread across the world from February to May, October and December. Just as it was believed to be controlled, a new wave occurred in February 1958 when most American deaths of about 70,000 occurred.

Government responses to the Asian flu in advanced countries such as the United Kingdom and the United States were passive. The pandemic was allowed to take its course, and tackling it was left to local medical officers. Meanwhile, the health authorities did not introduce border checks or strict isolation measures.

Hong Kong Influenza (H2N2) (1968–1969)

This influenza spread rapidly to Singapore and Vietnam. By September, 1968 infection cases were diagnosed/confirmed in Australia, the Philippines and Europe. The returning American troops from Vietnam brought the virus to California in December 1968. The second wave of the virus was deadlier than the first, displaying a more lethal strain of seasonal flu. It killed one to four million people worldwide, according to the *Encyclopaedia Britannica*. A vaccine was found within months, which may have controlled the spread of the virus from developing into new waves.

The governments in the United Kingdom, the United States and elsewhere did not take the pandemic seriously. As in the case of the 1957 Asian flu, no public health measures were undertaken to contain the virus. Even its discovery and early cases of infection were first reported by the media instead of by government agencies, according to the scientist who was responsible for fighting the disease (Honigsbaum, 2020).

HIV/AIDS (Human Immunodeficiency Viruses/Auto-Immune Deficiency Syndrome) (1985)

Little was known or understood about HIV/AIDS when it was first officially recognized. The symptoms of the disease were equated with some sort of cancer or pneumonia. It took several years for the medical profession to discover that it was a sexually transmitted disease, prevalent initially and mainly among homosexual men. Women infected with HIV/AIDS could transmit the disease to their newborn babies. It could also spread through blood transfusion and contaminated needles/syringes.

At the beginning, it was mistakenly believed that a crew member from a Canadian airline (who died of the disease) brought it to the United States from Canada. Actually, it originated in Zaire (present-day

Democratic Republic of the Congo), spread to the Caribbean and then on to the United States. Since the start of the epidemic in 1985, over 84 million people worldwide were infected and over 40 million died (UNAIDS Fact sheet). Many were young and healthy who died for lack of any curative drugs which took more than a decade to develop, manufacture and distribute. The poorest regions of Africa remain the most affected even today. Despite all efforts to create a vaccine for HIV/AIDS, none has been developed so far despite decades of intensive research.

As with other viruses, the devastating impacts of HIV/AIDS were initially downplayed and even considered insignificant. It is only when deaths among gay celebrities (including Hollywood star, Rock Hudson, a friend of President Ronald Reagan) occurred that the US president decided to finance research on a cure. National governments failed to respond quickly. Global institutions such as the WHO were equally negligent: it took 6 years to launch a campaign against HIV/AIDS.

In 2002, a Global Fund for AIDS, Malaria and Tuberculosis was created with a secretariat in Geneva. Its major contributors are governments, the private sector and the Bill and Melinda Gates Foundation. It is an innovative example of multilateral funding from a central secretariat directly to governments, private institutions, research institutes and universities; most other similar funds, channelled grants through national governments. Indeed, the Global Fund offers a model for global research funding for COVID-19 (see Chap. 6).

SARS (Severe Acute Respiratory Syndrome) (2002)

SARS was first discovered in Foshan (Guangdong, China). It soon spread to 26 countries and territories, including Canada, Hong Kong, Singapore, Taiwan and Vietnam. Over 8000 people were infected, of which about 1000 died. The outbreak lasted about a year before it could be controlled.

China took four months to announce the SARS outbreak to the WHO. Taiwan was also slow and non-transparent in reporting SARS cases. WHO's Global Outbreak Alert and Response Network, an early warning system, detected SARS, which led to a globally coordinated effort among existing institutions to prevent the rapid and widespread transmission of SARS infections.

China's slow response to SARS needs to be examined in the light of post-Mao economic liberalization under which healthcare services were partially privatized and decentralized. Public funds from the centre to county and local hospitals, for example, were reduced, since these institutions were expected to become partly self-financing. In 2002, China's public health system and the Centres for Disease Control were weak and understaffed compared to what they are today. In two decades, China has made remarkable progress in public health, having learnt lessons from its experience with SARS (Nkengasong, 2020, January 27). When the SARS health crisis and China's failure to report it triggered international condemnation, the Chinese authorities were quick to recentralize SARS management (Schwartz & Evans, 2007). The Health Minister and the mayor of Foshan were dismissed, and the disease was brought under control in less than six months.

Outside China, the virus hit Singapore and Vietnam. Both countries took proactive measures to control it. For example, Singapore was the first country to employ thermal scanners for tracing patients and for the strict enforcement of isolation and quarantine measures (Menon & Goh, 2005; Jin et al., 2006).

SARS infections also spread to Canada, in particular, Toronto and Vancouver. The authorities in Toronto were slow in their response, showing poor leadership and with no communication to the public about the virus and the risk involved. It challenged the WHO's advisory regarding travel restrictions and lifted them prematurely, which may have led to a relapse of SARS. According to nurses, hospital administrations and officials dismissed their early warning about the deadly disease as an "overreaction" (Menon, 2006, p. 365). On the other hand, despite being exposed to daily arrivals from China and Hong Kong, the authorities in Vancouver were more successful in controlling SARS through prompt action, including preparedness by local health officials and hospitals, and timely public health alerts to the local population.[3]

SARS is a type of coronavirus whose symptoms are similar to those of seasonal influenza, namely fever, headache, dry cough and shivering. But being less infectious, it proved to be less severe in terms of the number of cases and deaths. Therefore, it was also easier to control especially since the international community and the WHO had joined forces in a coordinated response.

Some work was undertaken (particularly in China) to develop a SARS vaccine, according to some scientific publications dating from 2003. But a vaccine was never tested or commercialized because it was possible to contain the virus through public health measures instead (Skowronski et al., 2006).

Swine Flu (HlNl, 2009)

Swine flu is so called because it came from human contact with pigs. Later the virus spread through human-to-human transmission, mainly to children and young people. Older people may have been immune due to an earlier exposure to the virus. Women were also affected, particularly those who were pregnant or had underlying health conditions.

The virus was first detected in Mexico in February and March 2009. Confirmed cases of two children in Southern California were also reported, spreading rapidly to several other US states and to many other countries around the world.

It was brought under control by 2010. Some of its features were similar to those of the great influenza of 1918. The American Centers for Disease Control (CDC) estimated deaths due to swine flu at around 300,000 worldwide out of a total of 700 million infections. Deaths occurred due to respiratory failures.

Swine flu is a seasonal virus which keeps recurring mainly in the winter season, such as in India in 2015. A vaccine now exists to treat the virus, particularly among those who are seriously ill.

Experience of the swine flu in Asia suggests that the countries in the region were unprepared despite the lead time they enjoyed and their earlier experience with SARS. Governments and public health authorities were overwhelmed, and they were unable to rapidly increase the supply of ICU-beds and ventilators in hospitals. While China, Hong Kong and Singapore coped with the swine flu aggressively, countries in South Asia did not.

The US response to the swine flu was quicker than its response to COVID-19. Communication by the government to the American public and the rest of the world was honest, rapid and accurate, and the CDC was active and effective in containing the virus. The government sought scientific advice on a regular basis. President Obama invited scientific experts, who had helped tackle the 1976 swine flu, to figure out what went wrong then and what went right.

MERS (Middle East Respiratory Syndrome) (2012)

MERS was first discovered in Saudi Arabia and Jordan. Between 2012 and 2019, nearly 2500 cases and about 850 deaths were reported worldwide. Originally, the virus was limited to the Middle East region as its name indicates. Over 85 per cent of the confirmed cases were found in Saudi Arabia alone. Later, it spread across Asia, Europe and North America through international travel.

It is generally more severe in people with underlying health conditions. It is also more common among males than females. Unlike SARS, it continues to circulate and spread intermittently and in community clusters. There is a risk of it spreading globally. For example, human-to-human transmission of the MERS virus was reported in Jordan in 2014, in South Korea in 2015 and in Saudi Arabia in 2018.

Although MERS-CoV has had a consistently high mortality rate in humans, no specific vaccine has been developed for it. The MERS-CoV spike (S) protein is a key target for development of a MERS vaccine (Zhou et al., 2018).

The government's response to MERS was slow despite a large number of cases and deaths. The international scientific community, which offered help, complained of a lack of government accountability, poor communications between different agencies, namely hospitals, laboratories and government health departments, and a failure to learn from their past mistakes during the SARS epidemic.

Ebola (2014)

Ebola was originally named Zaire 1976, since its clinical description was recorded near the Ebola River in Zaire (today's Democratic Republic of the Congo). Its outbreak in West Africa affected several countries such as Guinea, Liberia and Sierra Leone. A few cases of the virus infection were also recorded outside Africa.

The virus was transmitted primarily from animals to humans through direct contact and between humans through body fluids. Its spread was relatively limited considering that only about 29,000 suspected cases and over 11,000 deaths were recorded.

Governments in affected countries failed to mobilize manpower (e.g. local clinicians) and medical resources quickly. This is understandable as they are very poor with few resources and little or no local capacity for early warning or for coping with diseases such as Ebola without external help. Medical supplies and personnel could be mobilized thanks to the efforts of *Médecins sans Frontières* (MSF). In part, global efforts by the WHO and the UK and US governments also helped to contain and eventually control the virus.

The virus was brought under control in a little less than two years. The first vaccine for it was developed in December 2016. The WHO's experience in controlling Ebola since through its Global Outbreak Alert and Response Network (cited above) is relevant for COVID-19. But the network secretariat is understaffed and underfunded. Besides, a system developed for Ebola may not be suitable for a more infectious disease such as COVID-19.

An independent panel's report pointed out significant leadership failures at both the national and global levels (including poor early response from the WHO) in coping with Ebola (*The Lancet*, 2015). But there are some positive features of recent WHO action in Guinea and the Democratic Republic of Congo (DRC). In February 2021, Guinea announced an outbreak of Ebola, which occurred for the first time since the end of the previous outbreak in 2016. A swift response mounted by the national authorities with the support of the WHO, which supplied 24,000 Ebola vaccine doses, resulted in close to 11,000 high-risk people and about 3000 frontline workers being vaccinated. In April 2022, the DRC announced a third outbreak of Ebola in the north-western Equateur Province following a previous outbreak in 2018. The WHO responded with the recruitment of a large contingent of local African staff for contact testing and tracing. The personal involvement of the WHO Director-General (an African) on the ground and timely involvement of other UN agencies engaged in different aspects of humanitarian work are noteworthy. It is worth pointing out that African responders with a knowledge of local languages, culture and customs are more likely to be trusted than foreigners (Maxmen, 2019, September 11).

During the Ebola outbreak, Bill Gates (2015) warned that no global system existed to meet the challenges of a pandemic, but that one needed to be developed through concerted global efforts that should involve the G7, NATO, the WHO and the UN.[4]

How Different Is COVID-19 (2019)

The viruses described above were quite different from COVID-19, in terms of both epidemiology of the disease and the health systems.

Firstly, they were more limited in geographical coverage, being regional or sub-regional, whereas COVID-19 has already reached nearly 200 countries in all the regions of the world.

Secondly, with the exception of the 1918 influenza and HIV/AIDS, they were less lethal judging from the much smaller number of deaths. The 1918 flu affected the younger age group between 20 and 40 years, but not the older group, while COVID-19 affected people over 60 years of age who were more vulnerable than the young and children. There is no clear-cut scientific explanation for this anomaly, but three hypotheses have been advanced: (1) older people may have been affected by an earlier flu virus, which may have given them immunity; (2) their earlier exposure may have harmed, more than helped, immune responses later; (3) the stronger immune systems of the young may have overreacted, the so-called Cykotine storms! However, the resilience of new variants, which affected both young (including children) and old, raises doubts about the validity of these explanations.

Thirdly, the previous viruses were less infectious. The new COVID variants, particularly Delta and Omicron, seem highly transmissible, much more so than Alpha or Beta.

Fourthly, they did not spread at an alarming *speed* and *magnitude* with which COVID-19 has affected humanity worldwide. Such factors as globalization, rapid urbanization, growth of mega cities and urban slums accompanied by population growth have contributed to the rapid spread of the new virus. Globalization has also threatened it through connectivity, faster air travel and communications (Goldin & Mariathasan, 2016).[5]

Fifthly, COVID-19 has exposed the weaknesses and limitations of national healthcare systems, services and infrastructure, even of high-income countries. These health systems, considered robust and well-funded unlike those in poor developing countries, were under severe strain, and in some countries, they were barely able to cope. Medical and healthcare personnel were unable to treat regular patients on top of those with COVID-19, leading to *indirect* or excess deaths unrelated to the virus (see Chap. 2).

Sixthly, the speed of development of COVID vaccines seems unprecedented (see below). Yet it is ironical that a country like the United States with abundant supplies of the vaccines has been unable to fully vaccinate its population and/or share its supply of vaccines equitably with poor countries whose people are desperate to be inoculated. Many unused vaccines were wasted instead of being shared with low-income countries. Vaccine hesitancy, partisanship and political dysfunction, besides health illiteracy, are some of the major stumbling blocks to raising the vaccination rates (see Chap. 4).

COVID-19 is different from normal seasonal flu, although many symptoms are similar: fever, aches and headaches, running nose and sore throat. But one striking difference, which sets COVID-19 apart, is a sudden loss of sense of smell, and in rare cases, even memory loss, loss of consciousness, breathing difficulties, blood clots and brain damage.

The development of COVID-19 vaccine in less than a year (while no vaccines have been developed against AIDS after several decades of research) is another unique legacy of the pandemic. But many issues and hurdles remain. A report of the Royal Society's DELVE (Data Evaluation and Learning for Viral Epidemics) Initiative (Callaway, 2020; Callaway et al., 2020; Delve Initiative, 2020) has suggested that a vaccine may reduce the severity of disease but not infection and its transmission. There may be serious side effects (such as blood clots that developed among people who received the AstraZeneca and Johnson and Johnson vaccines) which may reduce or destroy public confidence. This is particularly true in low- and middle-income countries such as South Africa, where demonstrations took place against some clinical studies for allegedly exploiting local populations (Ibid.). The efficacy of clinical trials is more likely to occur in most-affected large countries such as Brazil, South Africa and the United States. Other countries, where the proportion of affected populations is quite small, trials are likely to be much less effective. Vaccines thought to be effective during trials may turn out to be not so when used on a mass scale due to margins of error. A *partially* effective vaccine (such as influenza vaccines) may either not be effective in particular groups, such as children and older people, or it may require a higher level of protection in a given population through delivery of multiple doses and boosters to raise the immunity level of an individual or a group of the population.

Current efforts for vaccine development are focused on preventing COVID-19, not on stopping the transmission of SARS-CoV2, the virus that causes COVID-19. This latter *indirect* effect is equally important, but has not received the attention it deserves. New variants keep emerging for which new vaccines may need to be developed.[6]

Lack of standardization of clinical trials and data collection during trials limits scientists' capacity to study comparability of the effectiveness of different vaccines. Different laboratories have employed different methods of study design and measurements which make an evaluation of vaccines very difficult. Moreover, there has been no *coordination* among different bodies to determine which vaccines should be tested first as a matter of priority and urgency, on the basis of which criteria and how the effectiveness of different efforts can be measured and compared.

Besides vaccines, drugs against COVID-19 (*molnupiravir* and *Paxlovid*), which are cheaper and easier to administer (especially in poor countries), have also been developed (Nolan, 2021; Robbins, 2021). However, their effectiveness against COVID-19 is open to question. A recent Israeli study (based on a sample of 109,000 patients) concluded that these oral medicines are not effective for young adults (between 40 and 64 years) (Perrone, 2022). However, they do provide relief to those who are older than 65 years (Ronen et al., 2022).

There are geopolitical differences as well, for example, between SARS and COVID-19. During the SARS epidemic, the international community quickly coordinated a joint response to control the disease. In contrast, in the case of COVID-19, there was a serious lack of a global response or leadership (Bildt, 2020, May 20). Unlike the previous viruses, COVID-19 has had unimaginable global health consequences: for the first time in human history, it shut down the global economy. Prolonged shutdowns brought about a global economic collapse, which for once has not resulted from a financial crisis or an economic recession. National leaders cannot successfully meet this monumental challenge without global cooperation and concerted coordination.

Some Unknowns

There are other unknowns for which further scientific research is needed.

Firstly, will several waves of the virus spread over time? Will they reappear in quick succession as the economies gradually reopen, or will they take their time and be staggered over several years? Most countries have already experienced several waves (see Chap. 2). What determines when one wave ends and a new wave begins? An answer to the wave question will depend on the way in which virus infections are measured. One indicator used is the R discussed below. Another is the number of new cases per 100,000. Countries which had undertaken widespread testing enjoyed the momentum of an early start and learned how to tackle the virus may postpone or even avoid the onset of successive waves.

What is the reproduction rate of the virus? The contagion rate of a virus is measured by what is known as the basic reproduction number, Ro, that is, how many people an infected person will infect. If Ro is 1, it means that one other person will be infected. If it is 23, which was considered to be the infection rate of COVID-19, it would mean infecting two to three persons. However, a Harvard study suggests that Ro might be closer to five or six persons (Shaw, 2020). This means that controlling the spread of the virus through such public health measures as social distancing, hand-washing, isolation and quarantine may be much harder than was originally assumed.

Secondly, what is the effect of the virus on children? Some scientists and epidemiologists believe that children are less affected by COVID-19 than adults. One Chinese study of 36 children in Ningbao and Wenzhou, two cities in Zhejiang province, showed that children were less susceptible (*The Economist*, 2020a, May 2). The study has the limitation of using a very small sample size, but a larger study of contact survey data for Wuhan and Shanghai confirms this conclusion. However, another study of 391 cases and 1286 of their close contacts for Shenzhen showed that the rates of infection were similar in both children and adults (Bi et al., 2020; Qiu et al., 2020; Zhang et al., 2020). A review of 45 scientific papers suggests there are fewer and milder diagnosed cases and very few deaths among children (Ludvigsson, 2020). Other studies in Australia, Germany and the Netherlands confirm the Chinese data. One of the reasons for children's capacity to fight COVID-19 better than adults may be their stronger innate immune system, especially against unfamiliar pathogens. The immune system of adults tends to weaken with age, which increases their vulnerability to infections. It is also plausible that children have fewer occasions to get infected, particularly if they are mass tested and their classrooms are properly ventilated.

Thirdly, what effect does weather have on the speed at which the virus spreads and on its reach? It is generally believed that hotter and drier climates limit the transmission of the virus. However, opinions differ on this point. A Canadian study, backed by Swiss researchers, shows that variations in heat and humidity had little or no effect on the spread of coronavirus, but such public health interventions as social distancing and school closures had a stronger effect (Juni et al., 2020). An MIT study showed mixed results, suggesting that climate had some effect (Hao, 2020). Still others suggest that the warm weather, humidity and sunshine in tropical Asia may be one explanation for the lower death rates there (WMO, 2021). Data used by the above-cited studies suffer from several limitations since little is known on how COVID-19 mutates and evolves or its reproduction numbers and its direct and indirect transmissions.

Fourthly, is the coronavirus airborne, that is, carried by tiny aerosols besides being transmitted through droplets on surfaces? An increasing number of scientists now believe that this is indeed the case, but many questions still remain unanswered. For example, how significant is airborne transmission, how long do the aerosols linger in the air, and how significant is long-range transmission by aerosols?

Fifthly, COVID-19 shows much wider symptom variations than those observed during the 1918 influenza or SARS epidemics, which has puzzled scientists and medical professionals alike. A major symptom diagnosed was the virus's attack on the lungs, as in pneumonia, which delayed its identification. With the spread of the virus, more symptoms came to light: it was observed to attack the heart with normal breathing and without temperature, as well as the kidneys, guts, blood vessels and the nervous system. It is unclear whether cardiac inflammation found in many COVID-19 patients is actually caused by the virus.

Finally, the origin of COVID-19 is still a mystery. It is associated with China, but may have actually originated across the border in Myanmar, Laos and/or Vietnam which are also home to China-like bats and viruses. According to Dr. Daszak, Head of EcoHealth Alliance, nobody had been looking for the virus in those countries. He believes "quite likely that bats in Myanmar, Laos and Vietnam carry similar SARS-related coronaviruses" (*The Economist*, 25 July 2020b). If this is true, one wonders why, for instance, Vietnam (which has a border with China) did not suffer much from COVID-19 during the first six months following its detection in China. Vietnam may enjoy a generalized immunity from the current virus because similar viruses have been prevalent there for several years.

One of the major issues, even in the most advanced high-income countries, is the lack of common and uniform standards and definitions across states/regions, besides an absence of accountability. Reliable and comparable information is needed not only for better knowledge but also for more informed and effective action. A glut of data about the virus may exist, but they are neither comparable nor backed by intelligence about the risks involved and how communities should deal with them. Such basic data as the average hospital stay of patients or rates of hospitalization are not easily available on a comparable basis.

Concluding Remarks

Further scientific research is needed before there can be any conclusive answers to the above questions. But scientists have also found out a good deal about the new virus within a very short period of time. For example, Dr. Ramakrishnan (2020, May 18), Nobel laureate in Chemistry and President of the Royal Society, observes that the virus has been identified and sequenced, the biology of the virus is being understood, as well as "the infectivity and routes for development for vaccines and therapeutics." Thus, given time and adequate resources, scientists will be able to find answers to the questions raised above.

So much for science and scientists. As for leadership, one thing is already known, that is, the major powers (e.g. France, Russia, the United Kingdom and the United States) which won wars launched by human beings against one another through *hard power* have failed to win a war which nature has launched against humanity. The main reason for this fundamental failure is to be found in a lack of *soft power* (organization, leadership, capacity to plan and prepare and command public trust and confidence).

Indeed, one common element in the response of leadership to the previous pandemics is the lack of preparation and failure to recognize the damage the viruses cause in terms of loss of life, as well as economic and social well-being. With the exception of the 1918 influenza and HIV/AIDS epidemics, other pandemics such as SARS, swine flu and Ebola turned out to be milder and less deadly than expected. The geographical spread of these pandemics was also more *regional* than *global*. This outcome was due to pure luck and not to a timely government response.

Most countries were complacent and unprepared for COVID-19, just as they were for the 1918 flu, despite having the benefit of the available experiences of SARS and Ebola to fall back on (see Chaps. 2 and 4). A variant of the 1918 influenza emerged in 1920, which was also lethal, but hardly any policymaker responded to it. Instead, many countries lifted most restrictions in the midst of high cases and even deaths (Barry, 2022, January 31). Similar reactions are being observed with COVID-19, showing that most countries have failed to learn lessons from the handling of previous pandemics.

A large number of high-income Western countries were overconfident about the robustness of their national health systems, services and infrastructure. As discussed in Chap. 2, many had underinvested in health following the 2008 financial crisis. In contrast, low-income countries were fully conscious of the limitations of their health systems. They did not have adequate resources to provide the much-needed healthcare to their citizens even in the pre-pandemic period, unlike high-income countries. But even with limited national resources, countries such as India could have given a much higher priority to health services and primary healthcare. During the past three decades, Amartya Sen (2011), Nobel laureate in Economics, and several others have stressed the need for a greater emphasis on primary healthcare and education, but to almost no avail (Bhalla, 1992, 1995; Drèze & Sen, 1989, 1995).

The WHO and national governments had developed surveillance systems in 2003, which would alert the spread of SARS. There were advance warnings by experts and prescient scholars, historians and philanthropists. In a thriller, Lawrence Wright (2020), a staff writer for the *New Yorker*, predicted a deadly virus and a world in lockdown. Notwithstanding these dire warnings, governments of many high-income countries initially downplayed the severity of the COVID-19 virus. They were very slow in their response, despite the successful early experiences of many Asian and Pacific countries, such as China, South Korea, New Zealand and Vietnam.

Notes

1. Other plague novels are Defoe (1972), Manzoni (1972), and Thucydides (2010).
2. Barry (2018, p. 394) mentions the case of "Typhoid Mary" Mallon, an Irish immigrant who was imprisoned for 25 years, noting that "if she had been of another class, the treatment of her might well have been different."
3. Private communication with Dr. Alexander So, Emeritus Professor of Medicine, University of Lausanne and Lausanne University Hospital (CHUV).
4. For a discussion on lessons from HINI influenza for pandemic preparedness and response, see Fineberg (2014) and Fisher et al. (2011).
5. For a detailed discussion of globalization and health risks, see Goldin and Mariathasan (2016).
6. For a discussion of different properties of new variants, see Callaway and Ledford (2021); Ledford (2021); Maxmen (2021); Prillaman (2022).

References

Barry, J. (2018). *The great influenza: The story of the deadliest pandemic in history.* Penguin Books.

Barry, J. (2020, March 17). The single most important lesson from the 1918 influenza. *New York Times.*

Barry, J. (2022, January 31). What we can learn from how the 1918 pandemic ended. *New York Times.*

Bhalla, A. S. (1992). *Uneven development in the Third World: A study of China and India.* Macmillan Press.

Bhalla, A. S. (1995). *Uneven development in the Third World: A study of China and India.* Macmillan Press.

Bi, Q., Wu, Y., Mei, S., Ye, C., Zou, X., Zhang, Z., Liu, X., Wei, L., Truelove, S. A., Zhang, T., & Gao, W. (2020, March 27). Epidemeology and transmission of Covid-19 in Shenzhen, China: Analysis of 391 cases and 1,286 of their close contacts. *medRxiv.*

Bildt, C. (2020, May 20). Why this time was different. *Project Syndicate.*

Callaway, E. (2020, April 30). Scores of corona virus vaccines are in competition—How will scientists choose the best? *Nature.*

Callaway, E., & Ledford, H. (2021, December 2). How bad is Omicron? What scientists know so far. *Nature.*

Callaway, E., Ledford, H., & Mallapaty, S. (2020, July 3). Six months of coronavirus: the mysteries scientists are still trying to solve. *Nature.*

Defoe, D. (1972). *A journey of the plague year (1664).* Printed for E. Nutt and the Royal Exchange.

Diamond, J. (2005). *Guns, germs and steel: A short history of everybody for the last 13,000 years.* Vintage.

Drèze, J., & Sen, A. (1989). *Hunger and public action.* Oxford University Press.

Drèze, J., & Sen, A. (1995). *India: Economic development and social opportunity.* Oxford University Press.

Fineberg, H. V. (2014, April 3). Pandemic preparedness and response—Lessons from the H1N1 influenza of 2009. *New England Journal of Medicine.*

Fisher, D., Hui, D. S., Gao, Z., Lee, C., Oh, M. D., Cao, B., Hien, T. T., Patlovich, K. and Farrar, J. (2011). Pandemic response: Lessons from influenza H1N1 2009 in Asia. *Respiratory, 16.*

Gates, B. (2015, April 9). The next epidemic: Lessons from Ebola. *New England Journal of Medicine.*

Goldin, I., & Mariathasan, M. (2016). *The butterfly defect: How globalization creates systemic risks, and what to do about it.* Princeton University Press. (Third printing, paperback edition). Chapter 6 on 'Pandemics and Health Risks.

Hao, K. (2020, March 19). Warmer weather could slow the spread of coronavirus. *MIT Technology Review.*

Honigsbaum, M. (2020, May 25). Revisiting the 1957 and 1968 influenza pandemics. *The Lancet.*

Jin, Y., Pang, A., & Cameron, G. T. (2006). Strategic communication in crisis governance: Singapore's management of the SARS crisis. *Copenhagen Journal of Asian Studies, 23*(1).

Juni, P., Rothenbühler, M., Bobos, P., Thorpe, K., Bruno, M., da Costa, R. Fisman, D., Slutsky, A., & Gesink, D. (2020, May 8). Impact of climate and public health interventions on the Covid-19 pandemic: a prospective cohort study. *Canadian Medical Association Journal (CMAJ).*

Ledford, H. (2021, December 17). How severe are Omicron infections? *Nature.*

Ludvigsson, J. F. (2020). Systematic review of Covid-19 in children shows milder cases and a better prognosis than adults. *Acta Paedratica, 109*(6).

Manzoni, A. (1972). *The betrothed (1827).* Penguin Books.

Maxmen, A. (2019, September 11). Behind the frontlines of the Ebola wars. *Nature.*

Maxmen, A. (2021, December 16). Omicron blind spots: why it is hard to track coronavirus variants. *Nature.*

Menon, K. U. (2006). SARS revisited: Managing "outbreaks" with communications. *Annals Academy of Medicine Singapore, 35*(5).

Menon, K. U., & Goh, K. T. (2005). Transparency and trust: Risk communications and the Singapore experience in managing SARS. *Journal of Communication Management, 9*(4).

Nkengasong, J. (2020, January 27). China's response to a novel coronavirus stands in stark contrast to the 2002 SARS outbreak response. *Nature Medicine.*

Nolan, S. (2021, October 18). Will new Covid treatments be as elusive for poor countries as vaccines? *New York Times.*

Pamuk, O. (2020, April 23). What the great pandemic novels teach us. *New York Times.*

Pamuk, O. (2021). Nights of Plague. in Turkish; English edition expected in October 2022.

Perrone, M. (2022, August 26). Israeli study shows Pfizer Covid pill of no benefit in younger adults. *The Times of Israel.*

Prillaman, M. (2022, July 21). Prior Omicron infection protects against BA.4 and BA.5 variants. *Nature.*

Qiu, H., Wu, J., Hong, L., Luo, Y., & Song, Q. (2020, March 25). Clinical and epidemiological features of 36 children with coronavirus disease (Covid-19) in Zhejiang, China. *The Lancet.*

Ramakrishnan, V. (2020, May 18). Trust in science during the coronavirus (Covid-19) pandemic. *Royal Society of the UK, Blog.*

Robbins, R. (2021, October 11). Merck applies for emergency authorization for what would be the first pill to treat Covid. *New York Times.*

Ronen, A., Wolff Sagy, Y., Hoshen, M., Battat, E., Lavie, G., Sergienko, R., Friger, M., Waxman, J.G., Dagan, N., Balicer, R., & Ben-Shlomo, Y. (2022, August 24). Nirmatrelivir use and severe Covid-19 outcomes during the Omicron surge. *New England Journal of Medicine.*

Schwartz, J., & Evans, R. G. (2007). Causes of effective policy implementation: China's public health response to SARS. *Journal of Contemporary China, 16*(51).

Sen, A. (2011, May 12). Quality of life: India versus China. *New York Review of Books.*

Shaw, J. (2020, May 13). Covid-19 may be much more contagious than we thought. *Harvard Magazine.*

Skowronski, D. M., Petric, M., Daly, P., Parker, R. A., Bryce, E., Doyle, P. W., Noble, M. A., Roscoe, D. L., Tomblin, J., Yang, T. C., & Krajden, M. (2006). Coordinated response to SARS, Vancouver Canada. *Emerging Infectious Diseases, 12*(1).

Stiglitz, J. (2019). *People, power and profit.* New York: W.W. Norton.

The Delve Initiative. (2020, October 1). SARS-CoV-2 vaccine development and implementation; scenarios, options, key decisions. *Report no. 6.*

The Economist. (2020a, May 2). Covid-19 infections: Think of the children.

The Economist. (2020b, July 25). Covid-19, the bat signal—The hunt for the origins of SARS-Cov-2 will stretch beyond China.

The Lancet (2015, November 22). *Will Ebola change the game? Ten essential reforms before the next pandemic.* The Report of the Harvard-London School of Hygiene and Tropical Medicine (LSHTM) Independent Panel on the Global Response to Ebola.

Thucydides. (2010). *The history of the plague of Athens (1859).* Kessinger Legacy Printing of Rare Books.

WMO (World Meteorological Organization). (2021, March 18). Review of meteorological and air quality factors affecting the Covid-19 pandemic. *First Report of the WMO Covid-19 Task Team.*

Wright, L. (2020). *The end of October.* Transworld Publishers.

Zhang, J., Litvinova, M., Liang, Y., Wang, Y., Wang, W., Zhao, S., Wu, Q., Merler, S., Viboud, C., Vespignani, A., & Ajelli, M. (2020, April 29). Changes in contact patterns shape the dynamics of the Covid-19 outbreak in China. *Science.*

Zhou, Y., Jiang, S., & Du, L. (2018, August 9). Prospects for a MERS CoV spike vaccine. *Expert Review of Vaccines, 17*(8).

CHAPTER 2

State of National Healthcare and the Pandemic

People stood at their windows or on their doorsteps to applaud them (nurses, doctors and caregivers). They are the saints next door … they are the antibodies to the virus of indifference … With some exceptions, governments have made great efforts to put the wellbeing of their people first, acting decisively to protect health and to save lives … Yet some groups protested to keep their distance, marching against travel restrictions—as if measures that governments must impose for the good of their people constitute some sort of political assault on autonomy or personal freedom.

—Pope Francis

Coronavirus pandemic is a national as well as a global health crisis to cope with which countries need adequate and robust health systems and services. Was the pre-pandemic state of healthcare strong enough to meet the challenge of COVID-19? What would be an appropriate response to expand/redeploy required health resources (e.g. medical and health staff, medical supplies, hospitals and hospital beds) to meet critical shortages? These questions are not easy to answer. But it is safe to say that most national healthcare systems and services even in high-income countries of the West were ill-equipped and ill-prepared to cope with the coronavirus pandemic. This is the result of several years of neglect of public healthcare.

A. S. Bhalla, *National and Global Responses to the COVID-19 Pandemic*, https://doi.org/10.1007/978-3-031-29521-8_2

Low priority to health sectors resulted from a false dichotomy between health and economy. Health of workers contributes to economic growth and well-being. The economics of good health is now well-known. Yet, the significant contribution of human health to development is worth repeating: gains in worker productivity, better use of human assets, improved utilization of natural resources, better education and reduction in costs of medical care. Therefore, more expenditures on health need not be in conflict with development objectives.

Some countries (e.g. the United States) have relied on markets to supply health services and insurance, while others have relied on public healthcare systems. Stiglitz (2019, pp. 211–12), Nobel laureate in Economics, has argued that America's greater economic/social inequalities and unequal opportunity of access to healthcare have been accompanied by declining life expectancy unlike in European countries with similar income levels.

Access to healthcare cannot be attributed entirely to favourable *public* policies and programmes and their effective implementation. Private demand for healthcare services and products, the nature of income distribution and the extent of economic and social inequalities, spatial distribution of health services, the efficiency with which they are organized at the local level and absence of delivery systems to reach the poor also explain inequality in access and opportunity to avail of the available healthcare (Bhalla, 1992, 1995).

The literature on COVID-19 is concerned with several issues. First, there are *studies which analyse the economic impact* on national and the global economy. In this category belong such works as those by the IMF estimating the loss of economic output by countries, regions and the global economy resulting from the pandemic; that commissioned by the International Chamber of Commerce, which makes an economic case for global vaccinations; and a Chicago University study which estimates that expansion of vaccine supply can provide global benefit of over $17 trillion. It makes an economic case for investing more now to expand vaccine capacity (Camakli et al., 2021; Hanushek & Woesmann, 2020).

Other studies estimate the true numbers of confirmed cases of COVID-19 as well as of actual and excess deaths (Wolf et al., 2020), determine the social and psychological impact on victims (Crayne & Medeiros, 2020), examine the negative consequences of the politicization and subsequent blunders committed by governments (Abassi, 2020), deal with the worsening of inequalities disproportionately hurting ethnic minorities as a result of COVID-19 (Blundell et al., 2020) and investigate such scientific topics as genome sequencing and side effects of vaccines (e.g. Agus et al., 2021; Oldenberg et al., 2021).

A few studies deal specifically with leadership issues such as effectiveness of leaders, followers' trust in government and strength of public health agencies (e.g. Lenton et al., 2022). A *Special Issue* of the *Leadership* journal on leadership and COVID-19 (Tourish, 2020) contains three case studies on New Zealand, the United Kingdom (UK) and the United States (US) which were written in the very early phase of the pandemic and have long been overtaken by subsequent events. Another quantitative study examines the leadership role in managing COVID-19, which is based largely on leaders' weekly statements in the first few weeks of the pandemic (Madeiros et al., 2022). Using a content analysis, the authors show that a charismatic leadership style is associated with higher infections, whereas a pragmatic style with fewer infections in the long term. But the leaders' statements alone are insufficient. They may reflect pure rhetoric, or at best intent, which may or may not be backed by any timely or effective policy response (see Chaps. 3 and 4). The sample of the study is also too small to enable any generalization.

To the best of our knowledge, no study deals with the nature of *relations* (consensual or conflictual) that exist between leaders, agents (institutions) and followers, the three key players. This is the central theme of the book. We argue that difficulty in isolating a leader's performance stems partly from an underestimation of the nature of his relations with other key players (public and private agents and followers) which can be critical.

Below we examine the implications of the healthcare capacity and preparedness for the containment and control of COVID-19. This is done by testing the following hypotheses:

1. *Leaders*, who gave a high priority to the health sector in the past, created solid *initial conditions* which would ensure later preparedness. The current pandemic has exposed the failures of past governments and political leaders to determine a good balance between sectoral priorities between, for example, defence industry and social sectors such as healthcare. Other things being equal, countries with well-funded and well-staffed healthcare sectors are likely to be more successful in the fight against a health pandemic. This hypothesis is tested in this chapter in the following sections and in Chap. 4.

2. Countries in which a sizeable proportion of the population is old and suffers from pre-existing conditions (cancer, diabetes, obesity, tuberculosis) are likely to be more vulnerable to COVID-19 than those with young populations, which are less affected by these conditions. The following cross-country and in-country regression analyses suggest that this hypothesis is valid.
3. Countries with bigger government (public expenditure as a proportion of GDP), inter alia, would be more successful than those with smaller governments. To test this hypothesis, Table 2.1 presents data on total government expenditure as percentage of GDP as an indicator of the size of government. As discussed below, only some countries used government resources effectively to manage COVID-19.
4. Health issue such as a pandemic and its containment/mitigation is a *leadership* issue par excellence. Bold and visionary leaders, who are prepared to take calculated risks, are more likely to succeed than are cautious and risk-averse leaders. This hypothesis is tested in Chap. 4.
5. Related to the above, leaders who set an example of probity and personal adherence to the social objectives are more likely to succeed than those who flout their own rules and are guided mainly by self-interest. In Chap. 4, we discuss 16 specific leaders' performance within an integrated framework (developed in Chap. 3) to answer this question.
6. For personal health matters, leadership is *necessary* but not *sufficient* on its own. A consensual *relationship* between "leaders", "agents" and "followers" (citizens, public, local communities) is a precondition for the successful management of the health crisis (Bhalla, 2021). We discuss the political leadership role side by side with that of leaders in public health (public and private agents such as Health Ministers) and followers (citizens and communities) for the same countries to draw some qualitative conclusions about respective roles of each stakeholder.

Pre-pandemic Healthcare Status

We examine cross-country data for the following indicators, namely (1) health expenditure and government expenditure as a proportion of GDP, (2) health expenditure per capita and (3) health and education expenditure as a proportion of military expenditure, and (4) physicians and hospital beds per 10,000 people (Table 2.1).

Table 2.1 Indicators of national healthcare and government expenditure

Country	*Health expenditure*			*Physicians*	*Hospital beds*	*Government expenditure*
	% of GDP (2019)	*PPP per capita (current international $) (2019)*	*Health/ education exp. as% of military exp. (2010–2017)*	*Per 10, 000 people (2010–2018)*	*Per 10,000 people(2010–2019)*	*As % of GDP (2020)*
Australia	9.9	5294	6.9	36.8	38	30.3
New Zealand	9.7	4439	13.3	35.9	26	36.6
United States	16.8	10,921	6.2	26.1	29	32.9
Canada	10.8	5521	13.1	26.1	25	29.0
Denmark	10.0	6015	15.5	40.1	26	39.6
Finland	9.1	4710	11.4	38.1	36	41.2
Norway	10.5	7217	11.4	29.2	35	45.8
Sweden	10.9	6223	17.6	39.8	21	35.1
Germany	11.7	6739	13.4	42.5	80	32.9
Netherlands	10.1	6248	13.6	36.1	32	43.2
Portugal	9.5	3518	7.7	51.2	35	44.7
Switzerland	11.3	8532	25.4	43.0	46	19.7
Austria	10.4	6134	21.7	51.7	73	50.9
Belgium	10.7	5847	18.3	30.7	56	44.3
United Kingdom	10.1	5087	8.4	28.1	25	47.2
France	11.1	5492	–	32.7	59	52.1
Italy	8.7	3988	9.5	39.8	31	50.6
Spain	9.1	3984	11.6	38.7	30	41.8
Ireland	6.7	6011	33.5	33.1	30	25.8
Japan	10.7	4587	14.9	24.1	130	23.7
Greece	7.8	2419	–	54.8	42	58.5
Poland	6.4	2206	5.8	23.8	65	41.3
Hungary	6.3	2156	11.6	34.1	70	44.2
Czech Republic	7.8	3477	12.7	41.2	66	38.4
Turkey	4.3	1187	–	18.5	29	34.0
Russia	5.6	1704	1.7	40.1	71	35.4
Argentina	9.5	2199	17.0	30.9	50	25.6
Brazil	9.6	1498	11.1	21.6	21	39.2
Chile	9.3	2424	7.4	25.9	21	26.3
Mexico	5.4	1111	18.8	23.8	10	22.4
Peru	5.2	712	7.2	13.0	16	26.9
Ecuador	7.8	934	5.2	20.4	14	26.6
Colombia	7.7	1204	3.7	21.8	18	36.4
Cuba	11.3	2599	7.1	84.2	53	–
Jamaica	6.1	598	11.5	13.1	17	29.8
South Africa	9.1	1187	13.6	9.1	23	38.4

(*continued*)

Table 2.1 (continued)

Country	*Health expenditure*			*Physicians*	*Hospital beds*	*Government expenditure*
	% of GDP (2019)	*PPP per capita (current international $) (2019)*	*Health/ education exp. as% of military exp. (2010–2017)*	*Per 10, 000 people (2010–2018)*	*Per 10,000 people(2010–2019)*	*As % of GDP (2020)*
Nigeria	3.0	162	–	3.8	–	–
Senegal	4.1	145	4.6	0.7	3	19.8 (2018)
Algeria	6.2	750	2.8	17.2	19	–
Morocco	5.3	424	3.4	7.3	10	28.8
Egypt	4.7	582	3.8	4.5	14	30.2
Saudi Arabia	5.7	2789	1.1	26.1	22	34.9
Jordan	7.6	797	2.4	23.2	15	28.2
Israel	7.5	3326	2.8	46.2	30	42.4
China	5.3	880	–	19.8	43	–
South Korea	8.2	3521	4.6	23.6	124	29.8
Singapore	4.1	4102	2.1	22.9	25	26.0
Iran	6.7	868	4.0	15.8	16	19.6
Thailand	3.8	731	5.4	8.1	–	22.1
Vietnam	5.2	559	4.1	8.3	32	–
India	3.0	211	3.1	8.6	5	15.7

Sources: World Bank database for health expenditure; UNDP (2021), *Human Development Report*; for health and education expenditure as percentage of military expenditure, physicians and hospital beds; IMF, *Government Finance Statistics Yearbook* for total government expenditure; World Bank and OECD data for GDP estimates

Taking health expenditure first, in general, Nordic countries (Denmark, Norway and Sweden) and Western European countries (e.g. France and Germany) spend more than Southern Europeans such as Italy, Portugal and Spain. These countries spend between 10 and 12 per cent of GDP on health. However, in terms of per capita health expenditure, Switzerland is the leader followed by Norway, Germany and the Netherlands. Nordic countries (except Sweden) and Germany have also done well in containing the coronavirus and in mitigating its adverse effects, especially during the first waves. Italy and Spain were the badly affected countries, which spend relatively low amounts on health. Each spends per capita on health an amount which is about half of that spent by the above-mentioned countries. The United Kingdom's health expenditure is no more than that for Argentina (a little over 9 per cent) and much lower than that for Germany and Switzerland. The United Kingdom's COVID performance was poorer than that of the Nordic countries and Germany.

Current leaders of many *Western European countries* (especially the United Kingdom) may have inherited the aftermath of earlier leadership failures. Political leaders in the past, especially the conservative UK governments, drastically cut expenditures on social sectors especially following the 2008–2009 economic and financial crisis. Austerity measures, introduced by many other countries following the crisis, had similar adverse consequences for healthcare services.

The above situation contrasts sharply with that in Europe following World War II when political leaders decided that the State should ensure access of all to healthcare. Perhaps the United States was "the only major advanced country not to recognize access to medical care as a basic human right." (Stiglitz, 2019, p. 13).

Paradoxically, the United States is an outlier, which records the highest health expenditure as percentage of GDP (17%) and large health expenditure per capita (nearly PPP $11,000). Yet it is one of the worst-affected countries, which has so far failed in the fight against COVID-19. What explains this paradoxical situation? The US health systems and services, based largely on profit-driven private sector (with the exception of Medicaid for the poor), are inefficient, uncoordinated and inequitable. Most of the health expenditure on *private* health insurance benefits mainly the rich and middle-income groups (see Chap. 4).

That low priority is accorded to health and education is shown by the ratios of health and education expenditures to military expenditures. Among the high-income countries, the ratios are the lowest for Australia, Portugal, the United Kingdom and the United States. *European countries* (e.g. Nordic ones except Sweden and Switzerland), which were relatively more successful in fighting COVID-19, register much higher ratios. Austria, Germany and the Netherlands have even higher ratios. Austria has the highest ratio and scores well in fighting the pandemic. *Germany* has abundant resources and well-funded and well-staffed health system. The country has the highest number of intensive-care beds per 100,000 patients in Europe. It has more nurses per capita than most other European countries. But as discussed in Chap. 4, even Germany found it difficult to manage the surges in cases and hospitalizations.

In *Eastern Europe and Russia*, apart from the Czech Republic, countries do not spend much on health. The national per capita health expenditure is less than half of that spent by Western European countries.

Russian ratios are even lower. Russia along with the Czech Republic, Hungary and Poland failed to control COVID-19.

Australia and New Zealand spend nearly 10 per cent of GDP on healthcare, a ratio similar to that of Finland, Germany, Sweden and the United Kingdom. Yet these two countries along with Finland have been much more successful in their fight against COVID-19. This situation may be explained by their effective and dedicated leaders (who were better prepared) and to a lesser extent, by their geographical location. While Finland is physically very close to Russia, a traditional enemy, the other two are quite remote.

In *Latin America and the Caribbean*, Argentina, Brazil and Chile spend over 9 per cent of their GDP on health, but Mexico and Peru only a little over 5 per cent. The per capita expenditure of Brazil and Mexico is half or even less than that of Western European countries. According to Fiocruz, a public-sector research institute in Brazil, the fragmented public health system is in a state of collapse especially for serious COVID-19 patients. In 25 out of 27 states, more than 80 per cent of intensive-care beds were occupied at the end of March 2021. According to the federal health ministry, in six states, oxygen supplies were extremely low, and several states suffered from shortages of drugs (*The Economist*, 2021b, March 27). The second wave, caused largely by the new variant (P.1), caused serious strain on public health departments since the available vaccines were less effective. The private health sector, which accounts for half the country's ventilators and intensive-care beds, serves mainly the rich population. Cuba spends over 11 per cent of GDP on health. Its per capita expenditure on health is higher than that of Argentina and Chile.

In *Asia*, with the exception of China, Singapore and South Korea, countries spend very low proportions of their GDP on health. Their per capita expenditure on health is also very low.

In *Africa and the Middle East*, South Africa spends over 9 per cent of its GDP on health, which is higher than what Ireland, Italy and Greece spend. Other countries such as Jordan, Morocco, Nigeria and Senegal spend very little.

We examine two physical indicators of health *quality*, namely the number of physicians per capita and the number of hospital beds per capita. These two indicators are similar in Canada and the US as well as in Australia and New Zealand. But wide variations are noticeable within Europe. Austria, Denmark, Germany, Portugal, Sweden and Switzerland have far more physicians per capita than do, for example, Finland, France, Ireland, the Netherlands and the United Kingdom. The former group of countries have also been more effective in coping with COVID-19 than the latter, judging from the lower number of cases and deaths per capita (see Table 2.4).

Despite reasonably high physician-population ratios, *Italy and Spain* performed poorly, presumably for lack of proper planning and preparedness (see Chap. 4). There are wide variations also in the number of hospital beds per capita: ranging from 83 in Germany, 76 in Austria, 65 in France and 44 in Finland, to lows of 28 in Ireland and the United Kingdom, 26 in Sweden and 25 in Denmark.

In *Eastern Europe*, the number of physicians per capita ranges from 41 in the Czech Republic to 34 in Hungary and only 24 in Poland. The number of hospital beds ranges between 65 and 70.

In *Latin America and the Caribbean*, with the exception of Argentina and Cuba, and to some extent Chile, the number of physicians per capita is quite low. Argentina has five times as many hospital beds per capita as Mexico and more than twice as many as Brazil, Chile and Peru. These ratios are much higher in Cuba than in any of the above mentioned countries. The number of COVID-19 cases per capita and mortality rates are also the lowest in Cuba.

In *Asia*, the numbers of physicians per capita are quite similar in Japan, South Korea and Singapore, but not the number of hospital beds per capita. Japan has the highest number of hospital beds per capita in the world (130) followed by South Korea (124). The figures are very low for other poor Asian countries such as India.

In *Australia and New Zealand*, the numbers of physicians and hospital beds per capita are low compared with those in most European countries. But they are about the same or slightly higher than those in Canada and the United States.

In *Africa and the Middle East*, the numbers of physicians and hospital beds per capita are woefully low except in Israel, Jordan and Saudi Arabia.

The next question to be considered is whether countries with bigger governments (higher government expenditure as % of GDP) are more successful in fighting COVID-19 than those with much leaner government and diminished role of the state. In Austria, Belgium, France, Greece and Italy, government expenditure as a share of GDP is 50 per cent or more. But among these, only Austria and Greece have been relatively more successful in managing COVID-19. Others such as Finland, Hungary, Ireland, Norway, Poland, Portugal, Spain and the United Kingdom spend between 45 and 50 per cent. Most among these, with the exception of Finland and Norway, performed poorly. The UK government's expenditure is higher than that of Finland, Germany and Norway, yet its performance in tackling COVID-19 was much worse, which suggests that other factors are at play such as *leadership* failures, inefficient use of public funds, lack of preparedness and spreading of false information about the severity of the pandemic (Chap. 4).

The size and role of government raise broader issues of governance and effective use of public funds. It is not just the *size* of government but also its *quality* and effectiveness that matters.

Finally, the *context and environment* in which the leaders operate are also highly relevant. The robustness or lack thereof of the pre-pandemic national healthcare systems and services is a concrete example of such a context. Two countries, both with similarly strong and well-funded healthcare (e.g. France and Germany), showed very different outcomes for COVID-19 containment and mitigation. The reasons for this divergence need to be sought in the relative failure of French leadership to act quickly and the followers' failure to fall in line behind their leader (see Chap. 4).

The Coronavirus Pandemic: Cases, Deaths and Vaccinations

There are several health (vaccination rates, cases, hospitalizations and deaths, infection-fatality ratios) and economic (GDP loss, loss of incomes and jobs) indicators to measure success and failure of COVID responses across countries. However, association between vaccination rates and COVID outcomes is not so clear-cut. Many countries have recorded large spikes in cases despite a high vaccination rate. Economic indicators may also pose problems of isolating the specific impact of COVID response. Country responses can also be measured in several other ways: (1) total number of COVID-19 cases and deaths per capita, (2) monthly averages of these numbers (see Table 2.2) and (3) daily new deaths per capita (see Fig. 2.1). We prefer to consider deaths per capita for inter-country comparisons since the case numbers are sensitive to differences in the rates of testing across countries besides variations of definition and coverage. These data are also more easily available.

Table 2.2 shows that of the top 20 worst performers, a large number are from North America (the United States), Eastern Europe (Bulgaria,

Table 2.2 Coronavirus deaths (total and 28-day averages), infections and infection-fatality ratios (IFR)

Region/country	*Total no. of deaths*	*No. of deaths per million*	*28-day average no. of deaths*	*28-day average deaths per million*	*Adjusted infections per 1000*	*IFR ratios*
North America						
United States	970,806	2946	34,795	106	545	4.55
Canada	37,183	978	933	24	346	4.51
Eastern Europe						
Bulgaria	36,266	5230	1293	186	613	3.85
Hungary	44,961	4611	1895	194	540	3.52
Czech Republic	39,352	3678	1212	113	531	2.65
Poland	114,087	3006	4578	121	469	3.95
Slovakia	19,073	3494	872	160	166	9.31
Romania	64,625	3351	2302	119	709	3.51
Ukraine	112,459	2548	1470	33	503	2.54
Russia	356,327	2473	19,253	134	1165	4.06
Western Europe						
Belgium	30,510	2640	590	51	397	5.61
Italy	157,607	2646	5011	84	273	5.88
United Kingdom	164,099	2441	3153	47	374	6.31
Greece	26,847	2505	1664	155	154	4.84
France	141,869	2105	4421	66	376	3.83
Portugal	21,408	2077	649	63	255	7.26
Spain	101,703	2148	3705	78	284	7.02
Sweden	18,053	1744	1201	116	368	5.00
Austria	15,344	1721	807	90	151	5.44
Germany	126,871	1524	5665	68	188	6.34
Netherlands	22,388	1284	350	20	344	5.95
Ireland	6638	1329	221	44	261	5.87
Turkey	97,077	1151	5167	61	606	3.29
Denmark	5386	924	1100	189	166	6.21
Finland	2783	503	506	91	204	4.85
Norway	2169	403	621	115	311	1.42
Latin America/Caribbean						
Peru	211,751	6422	2641	80	674	10.36
Brazil	657,098	3091	13,758	65	648	4.15
Argentina	127,439	2808	2377	52	887	4.31
Colombia	139,415	2740	1546	30	539	4.43
Mexico	321,806	2496	7208	56	777	6.65
Chile	44,339	2319	3272	171	420	5.98
Ecuador	35,348	2004	243	14	797	6.33
Cuba	8504	751	20	2	235	2.32

(*continued*)

Table 2.2 (continued)

Region/country	*Total no. of deaths*	*No. of deaths per million*	*28-day average no. of deaths*	*28-day average deaths per million*	*Adjusted infections per 1000*	*IFR ratios*
Africa & Middle East						
Tunisia	28,065	2375	690	58	1016	4.87
South Africa	99,829	1692	1531	26	789	7.40
Morocco	16,050	435	180	5	665	5.53
Saudi Arabia	9025	259	44	1	356	7.72
Egypt	24,277	237	645	6	834	6.30
Senegal	1964	117	6	0.4	590	4.22
Kenya	5647	105	14	0.3	491	3.90
Uganda	3595	79	13	0.3	217	5.07
Nigeria	3142	15	0	0.0	328	2.74
Ghana	1445	47	12	0.4	230	3.06
Asia-Pacific						
Iran	139,478	1661	4871	58	621	4.53
Malaysia	34,244	1058	1968	61	436	5.27
Sri Lanka	16,422	749	473	21	182	4.38
Indonesia	153,411	561	7367	27	516	5.27
Philippines	57,999	529	2590	24	351	3.60
Vietnam	41,740	429	2382	24	67	8.15
India	516,352	374	5051	4	706	4.01
Myanmar	11,101	354	4	0.06	279	6.75
Thailand	24,162	346	1568	22	152	3.30
Singapore	1191	209	254	45	59	0.68
Australia	5722	223	844	33	18	4.18
Bangladesh	29,114	177	183	1	690	2.41
Japan	26,952	214	5485	43	67	7.05
South Korea	12,101	234	4747	92	28	3.24
Pakistan	30,328	137	352	1	796	4.85
New Zealand	144	28	91	18	3	3.61
China	10,037	7	5142	4	1	4.33
World Total	6,070,904	782	199,406	26	433	

Sources: Based on Johns Hopkins University COVID-19 database (19 March, 2022). Infections per capita and IFRs are taken from "Pandemic preparedness and COVID-19: an exploratory analysis of infection and fatality rates, and contextual factors associated with preparedness in 177 countries, from January 2020 to 30 September 2021, *The Lancet,* 1 February 2022. They are based on cumulative infections for 1 January 2020 to 30 September 2021. IFRs are calculated by applying 9-day lag as there is a delay between infections and deaths. IFRs are cumulative deaths divided by lagged infections

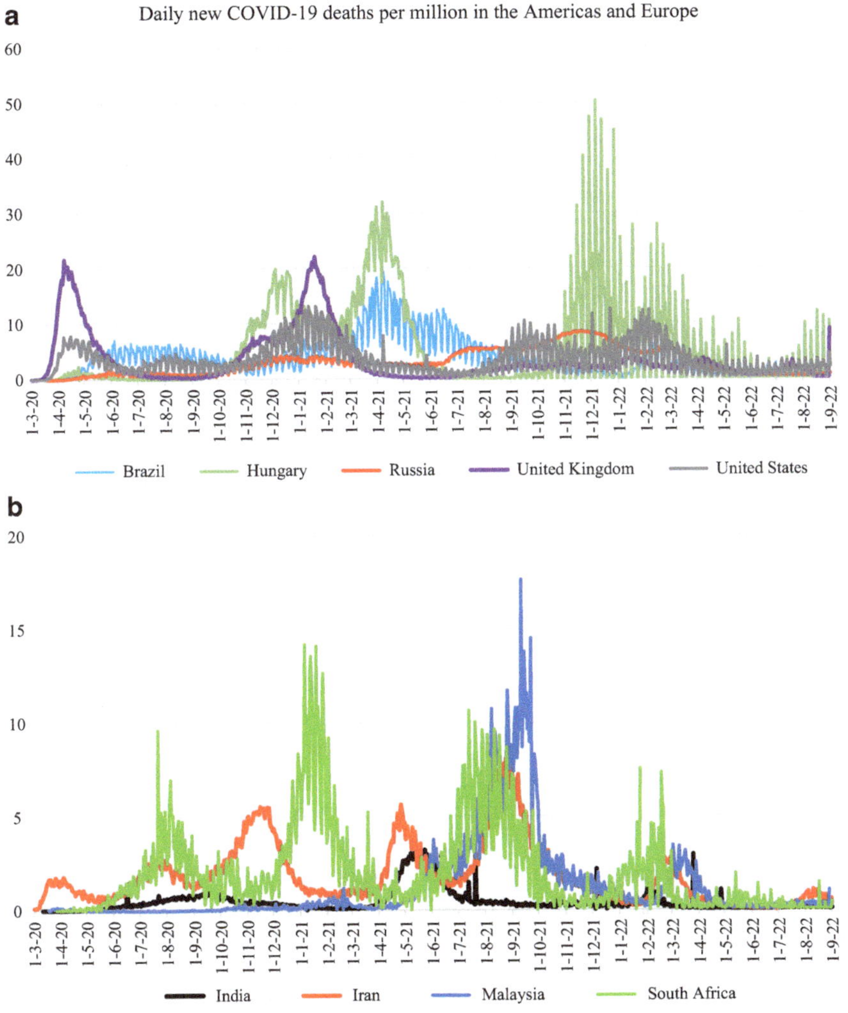

Fig. 2.1 (**a**) Daily new COVID-19 deaths per million in the Americas and Europe. (**b**) Daily new COVID-19 deaths per million in selected developing countries in Asia and Africa. (Note: The abscissa indicates the date in DDMMYY format. Source: Johns Hopkins University database on COVID-19)

Hungary, Poland, Romania, Russia, Slovakia, and Ukraine), Western Europe (Belgium, France, Greece, Italy, the United Kingdom) and Latin America (Argentina, Brazil, Colombia, Ecuador, Mexico and Peru). The Nordic countries (Denmark, Finland and Norway) are more successful in terms of low death rate per capita. Overall, the best performers are from Asia and the Pacific.

If one examines the monthly averages of deaths, the ranking of poor Western performers becomes worse. For example, the United States moves up from ninth rank to fourth rank, and Greece from 17 to 2.

Estimates of COVID infections per capita and infections-fatality (IFR) ratios (cumulative deaths to lagged infections) (*The Lancet*, 2022; IHME, 2022)[1] show wide variations across countries. The age profile of a country is the single most important factor explaining these variations. Measures of people's trust in the government (discussed in Chaps. 3 and 4) were significantly correlated with lower standardized infection rates. Other studies also show that high-trust countries and regions within a country can reduce COVID deaths by reducing mobility (during prolonged lockdowns and quarantines) (Bargain & Aminjonov, 2020). A regression analysis shows that one standard deviation increase in confidence is associated with 351 fewer predicted deaths per million inhabitants (Adamaecz-Völgyi & Szabo-Morvai, 2021).

Figure 2.1 presents daily new COVID-19 deaths for five badly-affected countries from 31 January 2020 to 31 August 2022. Most of these countries are governed by populist/nationalist leaders such as Bolsonaro, Johnson, Orban and Trump, who failed to control the pandemic. One of the distinguishing features of the current pandemic is the populist/nationalistic sentiments which have deeply influenced how several governments have responded to COVID-19. These forces were much weaker especially during the 2009 pandemic of H1N1.

Most figures of confirmed cases are underestimated since many countries include only those cases which were admitted to hospitals. They often leave out infections in public or private care homes or those taking place in the community. Many patients may simply be reluctant to go to overcrowded hospitals or may not enjoy access to them. Some countries include care home patients but do not cover community infections that occur outside. Apart from differences in coverage, the procedures for data collection also vary across countries.

Underreporting of data has been a subject of debate. For example, Balmford et al. (2020) estimated excess deaths (difference between the total number of COVID and other observed and expected deaths during a given period) for OECD countries, which also show wide variations. These estimates capture only the beginning of COVID-19 when deaths were quite low for most countries. Our estimates (for January 2020 to 31 December 2021 based on IHME data) of the ratio of excess deaths to COVID-19 deaths in Table 2.3 show wide differences between high-income and low-income countries as well as within countries. As discussed in Chap. 4, both sets of countries have used underreporting of COVID-19 cases and deaths as a political strategy and a disinformation campaign.

Table 2.3 Excess deaths, observed deaths and COVID-19 deaths

	Observed deaths (January 2020–31 Dec. 2021)	*Excess deaths*	*Ratio of observed deaths to excess deaths (%)*	*Excess deaths per million*	*COVID deaths per million (31 Dec. 2021)*	*Ratio of excess deaths to COVID-19 deaths*
North America						
United States	824,612	979,023	84	2971	2503	1.19
Canada	30,395	36,315	84	956	800	1.19
Eastern Europe						
Bulgaria	30,892	66,016	47	9521	4455	2.14
Hungary	39,145	44,701	87	4585	4015	1.14
Slovakia	16,619	22,558	74	4132	3044	1.36
Romania	58,734	94,901	62	4921	3045	1.62
Poland	96,472	170,537	56	4494	2542	1.77
Ukraine	101,901	143,411	71	3249	2309	1.41
Russia	650,235	650,235	100	4512	2100	1.00
Western Europe						
Belgium	28,327	28,840	98	2496	2451	1.02
Italy	137,555	216,122	64	3629	2310	1.57
United Kingdom	173,167	173,841	100	2586	2576	1.00
Greece	20,758	21,379	97	1995	1937	1.03
France	121,833	133,544	91	1982	1808	1.10
Portugal	18,957	34,621	55	3359	1840	1.83
Spain	99,231	138,445	72	2924	2096	1.40
Sweden	15,363	15,835	97	1529	1484	1.03
Austria	13,730	16,234	84	1821	1540	1.18
Germany	111,702	162,255	69	1949	1342	1.45
Netherlands	21,367	39,974	53	2292	1225	1.87
Ireland	5939	5939	100	1189	1189	1.00
Turkey	82,287	157,089	52	1863	976	1.91
Denmark	3266	9489	34	1627	560	2.91
Finland	1735	7355	24	1330	314	4.24
Norway	1334	1334	100	248	248	1.00

(*continued*)

Table 2.3 (continued)

	Observed deaths (January 2020–31 Dec. 2021)	*Excess deaths*	*Ratio of observed deaths to excess deaths (%)*	*Excess deaths per million*	*COVID deaths per million (31 Dec. 2021)*	*Ratio of excess deaths to COVID-19 deaths*
Latin America/Caribbean						
Peru	202,783	278,044	73	8433	6150	1.37
Brazil	619,426	685,889	90	3227	2914	1.11
Argentina	117,166	122,053	96	2690	2582	1.04
Colombia	129,944	145,777	89	2865	2554	1.12
Mexico	418,315	625,034	67	4848	3244	1.49
Chile	39,123	39,123	100	2047	2047	1.00
Ecuador	34,063	88,252	39	5002	1931	2.59
Cuba	8329	23,029	36	2033	735	2.76
Africa & Middle East						
Tunisia	25,573	57,499	44	4865	2164	2.25
South Africa	91,476	239,864	38	4044	1542	2.62
Morocco	14,849	110,476	13	2993	402	7.44
Saudi Arabia	8883	26,902	33	773	255	3.03
Egypt	21,736	203,987	11	1993	212	9.38
Senegal	1891	35,437	5	2116	113	18.74
Kenya	5377	173,658	3	3230	100	32.29
Uganda	3293	69,483	5	1519	72	21.10
Ghana	1293	36,642	3	1179	42	28.33
Nigeria	3033	164,021	2	796	15	54.09
Asia-Pacific						
Iran	131,589	203,439	65	2422	1567	1.55
Malaysia	31,481	52,066	60	1609	973	1.65
Sri Lanka	14,991	14,991	100	684	684	1.00
Indonesia	144,092	624,121	23	2282	527	4.33
Philippines	52,991	142,417	37	1300	484	2.69
Vietnam	32,257	73,427	44	754	331	2.28
India	489,145	3,030,817	16	2196	354	6.20
Myanmar	19,271	94,192	20	1731	354	4.89
Thailand	21,697	27,855	78	399	311	1.28
Singapore	848	848	100	149	149	1.00
Australia	2257	2257	100	88	88	1.00
Bangladesh	28,072	287,310	10	1745	170	10.23
Japan	18,388	88,026	21	700	146	4.79
South Korea	5593	5666	99	109	108	1.01
Pakistan	28,908	430,307	7	1948	131	14.89
New Zealand	69	69	100	14	14	1.00
China	4789	15,892	30	11	3	3.32
World Total	5,941,130	14,150,346	42	1823	765	2.38

Sources: Observed deaths and excess deaths (January 2020–31 December 2021) are from the IHME (2021) database, and COVID-19 deaths are from Johns Hopkins University database

COVID-19 deaths may be under-counted unintentionally especially in developing countries with an incomplete death registration system. But even in high-income countries, which do not undertake widespread testing/tracing of the population, deaths can be incorrectly recorded as non-COVID. This is more likely to be the case of deaths due to community transmission.

Table 2.4 presents vaccination rates for a sizeable number of countries, which show wide variations. For example, countries with the highest rates are Vietnam (92%), China (91%) and Chile (91%), perform much better

Table 2.4 COVID-19 vaccination rates in different countries

Region/country	*Total no. of doses per 100 residents*	*Fully vaccinated (%)*	*Partially vaccinated (at least one dose) (%)*	*Booster doses per 100 residents*
Europe & North America				
Hungary	171.3	63.7	65.9	44.2
Czech Republic	173.7	64.4	65.2	48.0
Romania	87.3	42.2	42.4	9.1
Greece	205.4	71.3	74.0	65.4
United States	197.0	68.1	79.8	34.9
Poland	152.2	59.6	60.2	39.9
United Kingdom	216.0	75.7	80.2	60.2
Italy	240.6	80.6	85.4	77.2
Belgium	255.9	79.3	80.2	100.1
Ukraine	71.8	34.3	35.7	1.7
Russia	127.2	54.5	60.8	13.5
Portugal	269.4	86.2	94.8	68.1
Spain	202.3	85.9	87.2	54.9
Austria	225.5	74.9	77.3	67.4
France	227.3	78.8	81.1	69.0
Sweden	245.4	73.7	75.5	93.3
Germany	228.7	76.3	77.9	77.2
Switzerland	191.1	69.6	70.6	55.8
Ireland	222.0	81.2	82.2	63.5
Netherlands	207.0	68.6	73.3	69.2
Denmark	226.0	81.7	82.3	62.8
Canada	253.1	83.5	91.0	78.6
Finland	237.6	78.6	81.8	77.2
Norway	226.4	75.5	80.8	69.6

(*continued*)

Table 2.4 (continued)

Region/country	*Total no. of doses per 100 residents*	*Fully vaccinated (%)*	*Partially vaccinated (at least one dose) (%)*	*Booster doses per 100 residents*
Latin America/Caribbean				
Cuba	376.6	88.3	94.6	76.5
Chile	327.5	92.6	94.6	143.4
Argentina	246.6	83.5	91.2	72.6
Brazil	225.9	82.3	88.7	57.7
Peru	262.4	86.1	91.5	84.7
Mexico	174.6	64.1.	76.8	44.2
Colombia	176.1	72.4	84.3	28.4
Africa & Middle East				
Tunisia	111.4	54.1	61.1	10.6
Morocco	150.0	63.7	67.8	18.7
Kenya	42.2	20.0	26.3	3.1
Gabon	25.7	11.6	14.0	0.1
South Africa	64.2	33.0	37.9	6.5
Egypt	98.5	39.1	52.5	9.6
Saudi Arabia	195.8	72.8	77.4	45.3
Asia-Pacific				
Iran	184.2	69.7	77.5	37.1
Malaysia	223.5	85.1	86.9	50.3
Sri Lanka	183.0	67.3	78.2	37.5
Indonesia	161.6	63.0	74.4	24.2
Philippines	154.3	67.3	71.4	19.2
Australia	247.5	84.3	86.6	76.7
South Korea	250.4	86.3	87.2	79.8
Thailand	204.3	77.3	82.2	46.1
Vietnam	271.9	87.6	92.8	58.9
India	159.4	68.9	74.4	16.1
New Zealand	234.4	81.3	84.5	69.3
Myanmar	118.6	50.6	63.9	4.1
Japan	291.8	81.9	83.1	126.8
Singapore	252.0	88.0	88.4	75.6
Cambodia	269.0	87.3	91.1	62.1
Bangladesh	203.3	76.3	90.6	27.1
Pakistan	136.9	59.9	63.2	36.8
China	247.1	90.9	93.2	58.2

Source: *The Financial Times* database, 23 December 2022

than many Western democracies. The second order of countries (rates between 85% and 90%) include Cambodia, Cuba, Malaysia, Portugal, Singapore, South Korea and Spain. The third group of countries, with rates varying from 75% to 85%, are Canada, Finland, Japan, New Zealand, Peru, Thailand. In other countries, the rates are even lower because of such factors as a lack of adequate supply of affordable vaccines and people's hesitancy to get vaccinated. The story of Waldemar Haffkine, who developed cholera vaccine in the Louis Pasteur Institute in Paris and applied it to people in Bengal in 1894, is quite revealing about the current scepticism about the COVID-19 vaccines (Gunter & Pandey, 2020). The initial reluctance of the British Indian government and the Indian public was soon replaced by wide acceptance by the Calcutta *bustee* residents when Haffkine inoculated himself with cholera vaccine in public. He proved that the vaccine was saving lives and hired Indian instead of British doctors.

A snapshot view of the status of the pandemic can be obtained by comparing Tables 2.2, 2.3, 2.4 and 2.5. Generally, countries with high hospitalization and death rates had relatively lower vaccination and booster rates (see Table 2.4). A comparison of Table 2.4 with Tables 2.3 and 2.5 bears this out. For example, high death rates in the United States and most East European countries are associated with relatively lower vaccination rates and booster doses per 100 residents. As of 30 June 2022, the target of 70 vaccination rate for each country was missed by about 131 countries. Only about 61 per cent of the world received two or more doses, according to *Our World in Data*.

COVID-19 Waves

During the first three years of the pandemic (2020–2022), the world witnessed several waves of COVID-19. Many scientists predict another such wave in the winter of 2023, given the spread of highly transmissible variants and subvariants.

There is no universal date for the start and end of different waves. Admittedly, the choice of date is arbitrary and varies from country to country. Bearing this in mind, we present data in Table 2.5 separately for different waves because their severity varied over time. While the first wave was quite mild in most countries, the subsequent waves were much more severe owing partly to the emergence of new more deadly variants like Delta and Omicron. The final wave (31 December–31 August 2022)

Table 2.5 Coronavirus mortality rates in different waves: A comparison between Europe (plus North America) and the Asia-Pacific (Number of deaths per million people)

	Deaths per capita				
	1st wave (2 July 2020)	*2nd wave (31 Jan. 2021)*	*3rd wave (8 Aug. 2021)*	*4th wave (31 Dec. 2021)*	*5th wave (31 Aug. 2022)*
Europe & North America					
	I. Cases of failure (deaths per capita *over 1000)*				
Hungary	60	1285	3080	4019	4870
Czech Republic	33	1524	2838	3377	3884
Romania	87	951	1779	3046	3451
Greece	18	541	1220	1940	3116
United States	391	1361	1872	2513	3105
Poland	39	980	1984	2557	3057
United Kingdom	604	1581	1940	2213	3051
Italy	585	1486	2153	2307	2964
Belgium	887	1917	2297	2451	2800
Ukraine	27	541	1266	2313	2678
Russia	67	500	1125	2100	2595
Portugal	154	1211	1695	1839	2415
Spain	599	1232	1732	1888	2371
Austria	79	866	1206	1540	2313
France	443	1129	1666	1837	2287
Sweden	523	1120	1416	1479	1893
Germany	108	687	1103	1347	1768
Switzerland	210	1103	1250	1415	1608
Ireland	348	662	1010	1184	1572
Netherlands	352	804	1026	1204	1296
Denmark	104	364	438	560	1183
Canada	236	549	707	804	1158
Finland	56	127	185	310	1007
	II. Cases of moderate success (deaths per capita *between 1000 and 200)*				
Norway	47	105	149	243	737
Asia-Pacific					
	I. Cases of failure (deaths per capita *over 1000)*				
Iran	132	690	1119	1567	1636
Malaysia	4	23	332	973	1079
	II. Cases of moderate success				
Sri Lanka	1	14	233	683	767
Indonesia	11	110	392	527	576
Philippines	12	98	266	470	543

(continued)

Table 2.5 (continued)

	Deaths per capita				
	1st wave (2 July 2020)	*2nd wave (31 Jan. 2021)*	*3rd wave (8 Aug. 2021)*	*4th wave (31 Dec. 2021)*	*5th wave (31 Aug. 2022)*
Australia	4	35	37	88	539
South Korea	5	28	41	109	519
Thailand	1	1	89	311	452
Vietnam	0	0	35	333	442
India	13	112	310	349	375
New Zealand	4	5	5	10	372
Myanmar	0	58	216	354	361
Japan			121	146	320
Singapore	5	46	7	146	292
	III. Successful cases (deaths per capita *below 200)*				
Cambodia	0	0	93	180	184
Bangladesh	12	49	138	170	173
Pakistan	21	53	108	131	132
China	3	3	3	3	4

Source: Based on Johns Hopkins University COVID-19 database

Note: (1) Countries in the two groups are ranked in the descending order of deaths per capita during the last wave (31 August 2022). (2) The dates in brackets refer to the day the Johns Hopkins data were reported

captured the effect of Omicron and its sub-variants. It significantly changed the ranking of countries. For example, compared with the earlier wave (31 December, 2021), countries such as the United States, Australia, Canada, Denmark, Greece, New Zealand and South Korea badly suffered.

Deaths per capita are divided into three categories of (1) failure, (2) moderate success and (3) success. The highest number of cases of failure (23) belong to the group of European and North American countries, followed by one case of moderate success in Norway. On the other hand, in Asia and the Pacific, Iran and Malaysia were the only two cases of failure. But their death rates along with that of India remained much lower than those of Hungary, Russia, the United Kingdom and the United States (see Table 2.5 and Fig. 2.1a and b). Twelve cases (including Australia and New Zealand) were of moderate success. Four countries were successful.

Moving from the fourth to the final wave, several countries in North America and Europe witnessed worsening of their ranking. Belgium, Italy, the United Kingdom and the United States remained among the top ten worst cases. Eastern European countries, namely Hungary, Czech Republic and Romania were the three worst performers. In Asia and the Pacific, the situation of Australia, Japan, New Zealand, South Korea and Vietnam worsened. The number of successful countries was reduced from nine to only four.

A comparison between the third and fourth waves highlights some interesting changes. First, the number of failed cases rose in North America and Europe with more countries from Eastern Europe (Romania, Ukraine and Russia) joining the ranks of failing cases. Although the average rates of vaccination in Europe as a whole are quite high (over 70%), those in the Eastern European countries are quite low. Secondly, although the Asian countries were also hit hard by the fourth wave, they still remained relatively far more resilient than Europe and the United States. In the Omicron wave, the mortality rates of Iran, Malaysia and India, considered to be badly affected cases, were much lower than those of Hungary, Russia, the United Kingdom and the United States (Table 2.5 and Fig. 2.1a and b). Thirdly, Thailand and Vietnam, which were successful cases during the third wave, moved into the moderately successful group.

Selected Country Experiences

Selected national experiences described below show that most countries underwent several waves of COVID-19. The threat of the virus was downplayed, and precious time was lost before "social distancing" measures were introduced.

The *United Kingdom* was very slow in its response, and when attacked for very slow testing, it gave exaggerated estimates of tests and testing kits. The second wave in September hit the country hard, and a new strain of virus caused further rise in infections and daily deaths. The vaccination campaign was successful in checking the virus in early 2021. But in the summer of 2021, the new Delta variant led to a spike in cases and hospitalizations despite a high rate of vaccinations. Although the arrival of Omicron at the end of 2021 forced the United Kingdom to adopt more restrictive measures (e.g. mask mandate), its strategy remained looser than in the rest of Europe: decision was taken not to introduce quarantine proposed by Scotland and Wales.

In the *United States*, lack of rapid preparation occurred because of the prevailing environment—disdain for science and scientists, promotion of untruths and conspiracy theories, lack of tolerance for professional experts and priority to short-term political gains in an election year. During the second wave of the pandemic towards the end of 2020, hospital admissions and cases and deaths spiralled out of control. Despite abundant vaccine supplies, a substantial proportion of the population including many healthcare workers remained unvaccinated. The new Delta and Omicron variants in late 2021 led to a spike in cases, hospitalizations and deaths, mainly among the unvaccinated.

In *Italy*, COVID patients had to be flown to Germany and Switzerland for treatment. It is possible that the virus was circulating unnoticed long before the first case was confirmed on 31 January 2020. Very high cases of pneumonia (as in China) reported in the month of January may have actually been COVID-19 patients. Italy's second wave in winter was deadlier than the first, partly because of poor enforcement of public health measures. Low vaccine rates, vaccine hesitancy, pandemic fatigue and the spread of new Delta and Omicron variants contributed to the new waves in 2021 and 2022.

The Italian case is somewhat peculiar. The virus remained concentrated mainly in the north which has world-class healthcare facilities, in fact, better than those in most other European countries. It did not spread as much in southern Italy, which is much poorer and lacks adequate healthcare services. Notwithstanding North-South movements, COVID deaths generally remained lower in Southern Italy during the second wave (see Table A2.1).

Germany, which was successful in controlling the first wave, witnessed its highest daily death toll among elderly people in December 2020. Its death toll remained low in the first wave since its older population at high risk was protected. The bulk of the affected population, relatively young with stronger immune system, recovered quickly which may also explain the low death count during the first and second waves (Jonathan, 2020, April 4). But Germany, like most other countries, has not escaped the new waves due largely to the new variants which are much more infectious.

In *Eastern and Central Europe*, the first wave arrived late and was quite mild judging by the very low number of deaths per capita during the first wave. But the death rates increased exponentially in January 2021 due partly to a deadly new British variant which could not be controlled due to lack of strict quarantine measures and low rates of vaccination. In early

May 2021, Hungary and the Czech Republic were the two top countries ranked by deaths per capita (see Table 2.5). These two countries maintained their ranking in the latest wave (31 August 2022). Lax rules of public health guidelines and their poor enforcement, campaigns during regional elections and failure of the leaders to listen to scientists and experts or to follow their own rules, besides low vaccination rates, were responsible for high infections and deaths (Chap. 4; and Kottasova, 2021, March 1).

In the *African region*, one of the worst affected countries was *South Africa*, where new strains of the virus (Beta) similar to that in the United Kingdom (Alpha), and Delta which is much more contagious, significantly raised infections in the first half of 2021. The spike of COVID-19 at the end of 2021 was due largely to Omicron, a new variant, which was discovered there and in Botswana. The region's infection rates and deaths have been rising rapidly, given very low rates of vaccination and shortages of vaccine supplies. It was hoped that the production of Johnson and Johnson vaccine by a local manufacturer would raise availability, but the vaccines from the plant were exported to Europe! The decision by many rich countries to give booster shots to their populations despite WHO's call for a moratorium till December 2021 left fewer supplies for Africa and other poor countries. Besides vaccine shortages and vaccine scepticism, there are the logistical difficulties involved in their distribution and delivery.

Latin America and the *Caribbean* contain major hotspots, notably, Argentina, Brazil, Mexico, Peru and Chile. The virus arrived in the region later than in Asia, Europe and North America. It was an opportunity to plan and prepare, which was not seized. While such countries as *Chile, Ecuador, El Salvador* and *Peru* introduced strict measures (e.g. lockdowns, stay-at-home and self-isolation), the worst-hit ones like Brazil and Mexico were initially very slow to act.

In Asia, *India* was one of the worst-hit countries like the United States and Brazil in terms of the number of infections but not deaths. It underwent several COVID waves during which strict lockdowns were introduced and implemented. But the virus could not be controlled due to lack of preparedness and limited capacity of the healthcare system. However, despite lapses at the national level, the experience of Dharavi slum in Mumbai, India, the largest in Asia, is a remarkable case study of how COVID-19 was brought under control through innovative *community-based approaches* and *aggressive* action in highly unfavourable conditions (see Box 2.1).

Box 2.1 How COVID-19 Was Controlled in Dharavi, a Mumbai Slum

Strict lockdown of the type imposed in India is very difficult to enforce in a poor country with large families, cramped housing and high density of population. A congested and sprawling slum like Mumbai's Dharavi accommodates about a million people in an area no larger than 1 square mile. Social distancing, isolation and quarantine, and washing hands with soap, the typical public health measures, are impossible to enforce in such a densely populated area.

The Maharashtra state in which Dharavi is located recorded the highest number of confirmed cases in India of which more than half were in the slum alone. However, through aggressive action and ingenuity, the local leaders, agents and followers (community and residents) brought COVID cases under control. The first case was reported on 1 April 2020. By end of June, cases reached 2000 and deaths, 80. The number of cases were one-fifth of what it was in May; 80 per cent recovery rate was achieved.

The initial conditions in the Dharavi slum were most unfavourable. There were no beds or intensive care facilities inside the slum. Availability of water and soap was limited, and most residents had to use community toilets. A survey of 7000 tested slum dwellers in early July 2020 was conducted by *Niti Aayog* (India's Policy and Monitoring Commission, successor to the Planning Commission) and the Tata Institute of Fundamental Research (Cash & Patel, 2020; Lahariya et al., 2020). Rate of infection was found higher than elsewhere because of community sharing of toilets and lack of running water. The initial response by the authorities was to declare Dharavi a containment zone. This top-down approach failed to work because the urban slum dwellers did not trust the government and municipal corporation.

The virus was brought under control following a change in the Mumbai corporation's strategy.

The control of the virus despite the adverse conditions can be attributed to the joint and reinforcing efforts of local leaders,agents (the municipal corporation, doctors and NGOs), and followers (residents and the local community).The assistant municipal commissioner responsible for the slum and his team provided the leadership

(*continued*)

Box 2.1 (continued)

in designing a strategy under which health infrastructure (beds, ICU beds, masks and protective equipment) was developed from scratch, and volunteer doctors were mobilized. This people- and community-driven approach to COVID-19 achieved remarkable results. Besides providing treatment to patients, these doctors were employed to inspire confidence among the slum residents. Testing staff and health workers were hired, and a number of healthcare camps were established to provide free testing. During the first 10 days, 47,000 people were screened, and 400 symptomatic cases were tested. Of these cases, 20 per cent, who tested positive, were quarantined in private hospitals, a sports complex and a marriage hall. Community toilets were sanitized three times a day, and running water and soap were provided for regular and frequent hand washing.

An NGO (Acorn Foundation) and its relief workers distributed free meals and rations every day to the slum residents, mostly immigrant and informal workers who had lost their livelihood. Other charitable organizations, Bollywood actors, politicians and philanthropists financed the supply of PPEs, medicines and ventilators for the slum. The response of the followers, the slum residents, was also very positive. They showed up for tests voluntarily and would like treatment on any pretext. Besides, they observed public health measures which were recommended by the local government.

The above success story caught the attention of Western (*BBC, Los Angeles Times, Washington Post*) as well as Indian media (*Indian Express, The Hindu*) which extensively reported it (Masih, 2020, 31 July).

So far, only public health indicators have been discussed. But such economic indicators as real GDP growth were also adversely affected in most countries. According to the IMF estimates, most countries registered a decline in real GDP in 2020 except China, Egypt and Vietnam (see Table 2.7). Both China and Vietnam took restrictive public health measures and brought virus under control, which enabled quick economic recovery. Although real GDP growth was positive and generally high in most countries in 2021 except Japan and Thailand, it was expected to be much lower in 2022 and 2023, with its decline being most marked in Russia and in 2023, in Chile and Germany. Estimates for unemployment were made only until 2021, which also show significant increase between 2019 and 2021, especially in South Africa, Spain and the United Kingdom.

A Cross-country Regression Analysis[2]

We use the country data in Tables 2.1 and 2.2 to test the effect of age composition of population, urbanization, weather (warm climate) and the size of government on COVID-19. The following estimating equation is used:

$$\begin{aligned}\ln\left(deaths / pop\right)_j = {} & \beta_0 + \beta_1 \ln ageing_j + \beta_2 \ln urb_j + \beta_3 \ln gov_j \\ & + \beta_4 temp_j + \beta_5 G5_j + \beta_6 D4_j + \beta_7 EU_j \\ & + \beta_8 ASIAN_j + \beta_9 CHN_j + \varepsilon_j \end{aligned} \quad (2.1)$$

where the subscript *j* represents country *j*; $deaths/pop_j$ denotes COVID-19 deaths per million populations. $ageing_j$ denotes population over 65 (a demographic variable); urb_j denotes the urbanization rate. *Gov* denotes the share of government expenditure as % of GDP used to test the first two key actors of the institutional framework developed in Chap. 3, that is, leaders and public agents; $temp_j$ is a dummy variable indicating climate, which equals 1 when country *j* is located in the temperate zone; otherwise, it equals 0. It is used to test the second element noted above, namely dry heat in Asia.

In addition to the climate dummy variable, we further control several regional dummy variables. $G5_j$ refers to the G7 except for Japan and Canada. $D4_j$ refers to the BRICS except China. EU_j refers to EU countries except Germany, the United Kingdom, France, and Italy. $ASIAN_j$ refers to Asian countries except China and India. CH_j refers to China. These regional dummy variables are used to control fixed effects, including location, climate and so on.

Table A2.2 reports the results. *Ageing* is positively, though not significantly, associated with deaths per million. To some extent, these results support the hypothesis that a relatively young Asian population (compared to the United States and Europe) explains Asia's relative success in controlling the virus. The urbanization rate (*urb*) has a significant positive impact on deaths per million, implying that the higher the population density, the faster the spread of virus.

That bigger size of government can reduce COVID deaths weakly supports a positive role of leaders and public agents. Assessing the impact of climate on COVID-19 is complex. Our quantitative analysis does not capture a significant effect of *temp*. A WMO report (2021) points out that the virus survives longer under cold and dry conditions and frequently exhibits some form of seasonality, particularly in temperate climates. G5, EU and D4 countries have significantly higher deaths per million. The performance of Western countries is worse than Asian countries (except India and Iran) in terms of COVID-19 prevention and control. The significant negative relation between deaths and the share of elderly people suggests that the general ageing characteristics and ineffective policies of epidemic prevention and control in the Western countries may have caused more COVID-19 deaths, rather than the particular vulnerability of the elderly population. For example, earlier lockdowns (introduced in some Asian countries) would save lives even if they imposed greater immediate economic cost. On the other hand, later lockdowns (as in the United Kingdom) would cost many more lives.

We argue that these variations are explained largely by non-economic institutional factors such as poor leadership, low rule enforcement and public's lack of trust and confidence in leaders/governments. In other words, variations in deaths per capita in different countries depend on whether there is *cooperation, competition* or *conflict* between leaders, agents and followers. Below we show that most Southeast Asian countries were successful because the three stakeholders were in sync. On the other hand, in many Western countries, leaders failed in crisis governance and management, policy planning; agents in the design and enforcement of public health guidelines/rules and followers in compliance and change of behaviour (Chap. 3; Bhalla, 2021; Bhalla & Fang, 2022).

COVID-19 Deaths in Selected Indian States

There are wide inter-state variations in confirmed COVID cases and deaths (see Table A2.3). The states are listed in a descending order of deaths per capita. Although the number of Maharashtra's confirmed cases per capita is not the highest, it is still higher than most with the exceptions of Delhi, Andhra Pradesh and Kerala. The lowest number of deaths per million are in Bihar, Uttar Pradesh, Gujarat, Kerala and Madhya Pradesh.

We examine the influence of three causal factors for COVID-19, namely (1) proportion of the elderly population, (2) rate of urbanization and (3) per capita public expenditure on health. A larger proportion of people at

60 and above in a state does not appear as a significant factor. The states with the highest ratio of old people (e.g. Kerala, Andhra Pradesh, Tamil Nadu and West Bengal) have relatively low death rates compared to those with low proportion of old people or a high proportion of the young (e.g. Delhi). Despite the highest per capita expenditure on health, Delhi registered the highest number of deaths per million, which is explained mainly by a very high urbanization rate and high density of population.

The south of India (Andhra Pradesh, Karnataka and Tamil Nadu) was badly affected. Yet the two states, Andhra Pradesh and Karnataka, along with Kerala are perhaps the only states with well-developed primary healthcare systems. Both states have a large number of healthcare workers and high public health expenditure per capita (Table A2.3). Andhra Pradesh and Tamil Nadu present a rather peculiar picture of a lower incidence of mortality. A case study shows that mortality plateaued at ages of 65 and over "in contrast to observations in the United States." (Laxminarayan et al., 2020). This relatively lower incidence of the virus in older ages is explained by a number of factors, namely possible underestimation due to poor surveillance systems, higher socioeconomic status of older people and stringent stay-at-home orders for them, besides regular contact with community health workers. But the issue of poor surveillance systems also applies to the incidence of infections among the younger and older population groups.

If older age and expenditure on health do not explain a high mortality rate, it is plausible that a higher rate of urbanization (the two states show higher urbanization rate than many states although not as high as that of Kerala and Delhi) explains relatively higher number of deaths per million. But Kerala's rate of urbanization is second highest in the country after Delhi, but the number of its deaths per million is much lower than that of either Andhra Pradesh or Tamil Nadu. This suggests that there are other explanatory factors at work, for example, committed, technocratic and science-based leadership, better enforcement of public health rules and restrictions and more favourable response by agents and followers.

The Kerala state government drew lessons from its experience of the 2018 Nipah virus and conducted effective and extensive testing and tracing of cases and community mobilization to achieve a low mortality rate (Chathukalam & Tharamangalam, 2021). Andhra Pradesh and Tamil Nadu also initiated widespread testing and tracing, delineated 5-km zones and daily house-to-house surveillance but failed to reduce the mortality rate.

But Kerala's success was accompanied by several drawbacks as well, leading to successive waves of the virus, which the state government failed to anticipate. It did not foresee the existence of community transmission. On purely ideological grounds, the government kept out private hospitals on which 65–70 per cent of the population depends. It failed to recognize that the third wave was triggered largely by the NRI super spreaders coming from the Middle East. Active cases rose nine-fold, from 499 on 4 May to 4465 on 4 July 2020. The returning NRIs were not carefully tested or screened, which led to rapid spikes in infections. A political consensus between the ruling party and the Congress opposition was necessary but could not be achieved (Balsari et al., 2020; *The Lancet*, 2020). These failures question the widely held belief that governments will be more prepared to successfully control new waves of the virus because they will have better knowledge and more experience to cope with the virus.

WHO, some individuals from the state as well as the international media, prematurely celebrated the so-called Kerala miracle (WHO, 2020; Tharoor, 2020; *The Economist*, 2020a, May 9, 2021a, March 13). That half of new Delta infections in India were recorded in Kerala in July 2021 raises doubts about the so-called miracle.

Premature celebrations of Kerala's success had an unwanted consequence of complacency and poor enforcement of public health guidelines by the leaders, agents and followers. Political polarization between the Communists-led government and the Congress-led opposition did not help matters. Of course, traditionally, there has been a synergy between the state, society and individuals. But this synergy is highly exaggerated, considering protests by many villagers in coastal areas against such state interventions as testing and rapid spike of infections.

The northern belt in India (Bihar, Haryana, Rajasthan and Uttar Pradesh), with the exception of Punjab, appears to have performed relatively better. As shown in Table A2.3, cases and deaths per million are lower in these states. Two main factors seem to account for their relative success, namely low share of the population of elderly people (8 per cent compared to 12 per cent in Punjab) and low rates of urbanization. Rural areas tend to show lower rates of incidence of the virus. However, rural infections started rising in early May 2020 when trains brought migrants home from heavily infected urban areas of Delhi and other big centres. But this did not appear to affect the case and death ratios. In Bihar, an important source of migrant labour to various Indian urban centres such as Delhi, Kolkata and Mumbai, about 1.6 million workers returned to their homes during May and June, 2020. Apparently, they did not adversely affect the results for the following reasons. Random testing of returning workers was undertaken regardless of whether they were asymptomatic, young or old. The testing rate for returning workers was nearly 3 per cent (defined as the number of tests divided by the state's population), which is much higher than the average official testing rate of 0.1 per cent (Malani et al., 2020). A strict institutional quarantine policy was adopted under which the returning migrants were quarantined for 14 days.

Maharashtra was the worst case with the highest number of deaths per capita followed by Delhi and Karnataka. This situation may be explained by several factors: high rate of urbanization, congested urban public transport, high share of old people and low public expenditure per capita on health.

By comparing deaths per million in badly-affected Indian states (Table A2.3) with those in the American states (Table A2.4), we find that COVID-19 deaths per capita are generally much higher in the American states. For example, New York and New Jersey figures are more than four times those for the two worst-hit Indian states of Maharashtra and Delhi. Other bad performers such as Karnataka, Tamil Nadu and Punjab also show lower figures than those for Illinois, Massachusetts, Michigan and Pennsylvania (Laxminarayan et al., 2020).[3]

COVID-19 Deaths in the American States

The US COVID-19 data classify American states into two groups, namely (a) those led by Democrat governors and (b) others led by Republican governors. This grouping is intended to observe any possible differences of deaths due to a political factor in view of a high degree of politicization of the pandemic. We undertook regression analysis to examine possible influence of three explanatory variables on deaths.

The basic regression equation is as follows:

$$\ln\left(deaths / pop\right)_i = \beta_0 + \beta_1 \ln x_i + \beta_2 \ln y_i + \beta_3 \ln z_i + \varepsilon_i \tag{2.2}$$

where *deaths/pop* denotes COVID-19 deaths per million population, x denotes share of population over 65 (a demographic variable), y denotes urbanization rate (a spatial variable) and z denotes a dummy variable (political variable, where 1 represents states led by a Democrat governor and 0 states led by a Republican governor). The results of the regression are significant at 5% level (since the value exceeded 2.04) (see Table A2.5). Only the urbanization rate, *y*, is significant; the demographic and political variables are not.

The results show that state-level deaths per million in the United States are highly correlated with the urbanization rate and population density. Lack of statistical connection between deaths and the share of elderly people is surprising, but not entirely implausible. Only three American states (Florida, Maine and West Virginia) have 20 per cent of state population over 65 years. In most states, this share is about 15–16 per cent. COVID-19 may have affected the relatively younger population (as happened in Germany) which recovers quickly.

Although our results do not show a relation between the political variable and COVID deaths, a detailed study of the growth rate of new COVID infections shows a positive and significant correlation. The study shows that (1) although "the number of new cases per capita in March through May (2020) was much higher in the states with Democratic governors, states with Republican governors outstripped their Democratic counterparts as of the first week of June. Since then, the number of new cases per capita with Republican governors has been 30-40 per cent higher," and (2) seven out of ten good performers ranked in terms of control of the growth rate of new infections have Democratic governors (Akovali & Yilmaz, 2020). A more recent study (Patterson, 2022) concludes that Democratic governors are likely to be faster and more likely to adopt stay-at-home orders.

COVID-19 Deaths in Care Homes in the West

A significant proportion of COVID-19 deaths in the Western countries occurred in care home facilities because of the concentration of elderly people with pre-existing conditions among the residents. But that alone cannot explain much larger number of deaths there than in hospitals. Runaway COVID-19 infections, shortages of medical gear and lack of government attention are familiar stories concerning Western nursing homes. But *Belgium's* response offers a gruesome twist: Paramedics and hospitals sometimes flatly denied care to elderly people, even while hospital beds were unused (Stevis-Gridneff et al., 2020, 8 August). In *Spain*, the soldiers discovered elderly patients in retirement homes abandoned and, in some cases, dead in their beds. Presumably, the care staff left them there fearing for their own lives in the absence of adequate PPEs. The Defence ministry noted that the staff at some care homes left when COVID-19 was detected.

Sweden, once an enviable model of a welfare state and equality of health treatment, registered over 45 per cent of COVID-19 deaths occurring in its nursing homes. Like the United Kingdom and the United States, it had significantly lowered the scale of public health and other services during the 2008–2009 financial crisis. Other reasons for such large number of deaths include the privatization of nursing homes which increasingly rely on temporary, part-time and untrained staff to cut costs and maximize profits. Hospitals often refused to accept sick elderly people from homes. It is ironical that the elderly with pre-existing conditions who need care most were simply ignored. Some Swedish municipalities banned health-care workers from wearing masks and gloves "on the grounds that the people they cared for might feel offended." (*The Economist*, 2020b, 10 October). In general, more immigrants from Somalia and Syria died of COVID-19 than Swedes. The local authorities failed to provide official guidelines or other assistance to them in time.

In *France*, in a report (7 May, 2020) of a nationwide survey of 9513 nursing home facilities, 695,060 residents and 385,290 staff members, 4599 (48.3%) registered at least one case of COVID-19 and 12,521 deaths (Belmin et al. (2020). A retrospective cohort study was undertaken (from 1 March to 11 May 2020) of those homes in which staff members decided to self-confine themselves with residents voluntarily to prevent the spread of the virus.

In the *United Kingdom,* in England and Wales, at the peak period during the first wave, 75 per cent of all COVID deaths occurred in care homes and remaining 25 per cent in hospitals (Comas-Herrera & Hernandez, 2020; Holt & Butcher, 2020; Office of National Statistics, 2020a, 3 July). This was the time when many hospitals sent residents back to care homes (without testing them!) in order to free beds to cope with the surge in cases, which may partly explain such a high proportion of deaths in care homes. Hospitals in England and Wales were under greater pressures to make beds available by transferring patients to care homes than those in Northern Ireland and Scotland.

A similar pattern was observed in Northern Ireland where deaths were much higher in hospitals than in care homes until the middle of April 2020. But towards the end of April and beginning of May, care home deaths were far in excess of those in hospitals (McCormack, 2020). The shares of deaths in care homes and hospitals are the same in Scotland, that is, about 46 per cent of the total (Office of National Statistics, 2020b, 5 August). The remaining deaths occurred at home or in hospices. Such factors as crowded and unhygienic conditions, close contact between residents, lack of adequate healthcare and nursing staff, limited or no supplies of PPEs for the staff and inadequate funding were largely responsible for a high number of deaths.

It is difficult to hire permanent staff for care homes which offer lower salaries for similar work elsewhere, which results in a high turnover. A study by Public Health England, based on six care homes in London, found that temporary workers who are hired to replace permanent workers often move between care facilities and transmit the virus (Booth, 2020; Ladhani et al., 2020).

In the *United States*, over one-third of the total number of COVID-19 deaths were linked to long-term care facilities. There are wide variations in these deaths, however. In Table A2.6, the states are grouped into (a) those led by Democrat governors and (b) others led by Republican governors. In each of these two groups, states are ranked in the descending order of the share of care home deaths in the total state deaths. West Virginia accounts for 98 per cent of the state's deaths in care homes. Other states with more than 60 per cent deaths include Kansas, Pennsylvania and Connecticut. Nineteen states have deaths ranging between 40 and 60 per cent, and 12 states' death share below 30 per cent (Yourish et al., 2020, 11 May).[4]

Inter-state variations in cases and deaths may be due to several factors, namely varying rates of testing, availability of care homes, rate of urbanization and the proportion of elderly people. No connection between cases and deaths and political factors such as Democratic or Republican states is discernible. Both groups of states recorded high and low rates. Kansas led by a Democrat governor has 71 per cent share of deaths in care homes, and Vermont and Massachusetts, run by Republican governors, show respectively figures of 57 per cent and 55 per cent. Inter-state differences may also be attributed to the ethnic composition of the population. Generally, Democratic states consist of a larger proportion of minorities (African Americans, Hispanics and Asians) with pre-existing conditions than Republican states with majority white population. The latter also tend to be more rural than urban. One may, therefore, conclude that a high share of care home deaths in the states may be due to lack of health facilities and care workers and greater share of minorities, besides poor leadership.

In *Canada*, also there was greater incidence of COVID deaths in care homes than elsewhere. As in the United States, there were differences across provinces and territories. Those between Ontario and British Columbia were particularly striking. As of 10 September 2020, there were nearly 2000 deaths in Ontario care homes compared with only 156 in British Columbia (Liu et al., 2020).

Having discussed in detail the state of patients' health at different levels as well as institutions, we now turn to a review of the Global Health Security Index which turned out to be quite misleading. Our above results contradict the findings of this Index. Therefore, a brief review of the Index is in order.

Global Health Security Index, COVID-19 and Leadership

Johns Hopkins University and Nuclear Threat Initiative have developed a Global Health Security (GHS) Index to identify gaps in national capacity as a basis for allocating financial resources (Johns Hopkins University, 2019, 2021). Important components of the global index included early detection and reporting of an epidemic, rapid response, robust health sector and commitments to improving national capacity. The Index, which is a weighted average of six components, shows some startling results. Firstly, for the overall index the United States is ranked at the top, and the United Kingdom, close behind. These two countries are among the worst performers on COVID-19 as has been shown by the above empirical findings. Secondly, less than 7 per cent of the countries were prepared for preventing a pandemic; less than 5 per cent for a rapid response to it and only 19 per cent for its detection.

The authors of the Index were overoptimistic about the predictive power of the Index to warn against future epidemics besides identifying gaps in national health capacity. Even in its revised form in 2021, the Index failed to provide early warnings or to measure government effectiveness or strength of political leadership either in the West or elsewhere.

Table 2.6 compares the Index component scores for China, India, the United Kingdom and the United States using its three components, namely (1) rapid response, (2) risk environment and (3) health system,

Table 2.6 GHS Index scores and rankings by selected components and sub-components

GHS Index components	*United States*		*United Kingdom*		*China*		*India*	
	(2019)	*(2021)*	*(2019)*	*(2021)*	*(2019)*	*(2021)*	*(2019)*	*(2021)*
I. Rapid response	*72.8*	*65.7*	*68.1*	*64.8*	*48.8*	*38.8*	*42.1*	*30.3*
Emergency preparedness	83.3	83.3	50.0	50.0	50	50	41.7	41.7
Emergency response operation	66.7	66.7	66.7	66.7	33.3	33.3	33.3	33.3
Linking public health & security authorities	100	100	100	100	0	0	0	0
Risk communications	100	75	75	100	33.3	33.3	58.3	70.8
Access to communications infrastructure	84.4	84.8	85.2	87.0	75.0	77.8	48.6	41.2
II. *Risk environment*	*73.3*	*73.3*	*75*	*73*	*64.6*	*63.4*	*59.1*	*60.2*
Political & security risk	73.2	69.1	76.8	81.5	54.2	62.6	65.5	58.3
Socioeconomic resilience	73.1	73.1	85.6	85.5	66.7	66.5	71.5	71.9
Infrastructure adequacy	91.7	91.7	66.7	66.7	75	75	33.3	50.0
Public health vulnerabilities	76.3	75.9	83.2	82.7	60.1	60.8	59.9	61.0
III. Health System	*75.2*	*75.2*	*66.0*	*68.3*	*49.4*	*51.8*	*46.1*	*46.1*
Health capacity (clinics, hospitals)	70.6	70.5	48.9	65.1	22.7	44.5	37.1	36.9
Capacity to test & approve new countermeasures	100	100	100	100	75	75	50	50
Healthcare access	33.5	33.5	52.3	52.2	59.8	59.7	19.2	19.2
Infection control practices	100	100	100	100	100	100	100	100
Medical countermeasures & personnel deployment	50	50	50	50	0	0	0	0
Communications with healthcare workers	100	100	50	50	0	0	100	100

Source: Johns Hopkins University (2019, 2021)

which covers political and security risk and health vulnerabilities. Both China and India are given relatively low scores for rapid response, risk environment and capacity of the health system. Yet both these countries have performed much better. For example, the number of deaths per capita for China is the lowest and those of India at 375 are extremely favourable compared to 3105 for the United States and 3051 for the United Kingdom (Table 2.5). India's full vaccination rate of 68.5 is higher than that of the US rate of 66.8, and China's rate at nearly 91 is among the highest in the world (Table 2.4). How does one explain this paradox?

The United Kingdom and the United States receive the maximum score of 100 for "capacity to test," yet the United Kingdom had to send samples for testing to Italy and Cyprus. And in the United States, testing rate was low and poorly organized across the country. Testing and tracing were abandoned too quickly in both countries. Similarly, health capacity of clinics and hospitals is given a high score, but these institutions as well as care homes were too overstretched to cope during the peak of the pandemic.

The authors of the Index promised to include such variables as leadership and government effectiveness in future revisions of the index (Ravi et al., 2020), but Table 2.6 suggests that they were unable to do so in the 2021 iteration. Yet these issues are important as they determine how well any existing public health systems function (Mahajan, 2021).

The Index has received considerable attention and critical comments, which vary from its incompleteness (Ibid; Boyd et al., 2020), to "its limited value in assessing a country's capacity to respond to a global pandemic." (Ji et al., 2021, p. 293). Its value is limited partly because it is based entirely on existing publications, which may not be comprehensive. Many national governments or agencies may not have documented all their capacities. The Index is not based on hard facts about health capacity, and the mere *existence* of capacity does not guarantee its effective *utilization*. It is also very ambitious and heterogeneous in its scope and coverage. Yet the authors intend to add more indicators, questions and data to a long list, which may not necessarily improve the scores. As Mahajan (2021) argues, they have narrowly focused on technical issues relating to health security (e.g. pathology of laboratories and number of epidemiologists required) to the neglect of vital social and economic issues like health inequity, scientific infrastructure and human resources. Furthermore, such issues as overall risk are extremely difficult to define, much less quantify.

In its future iterations, the Index needs to concentrate on fewer components, a smaller number of questions and more in-depth factual investigation. In our framework developed in Chap. 3, the role of leadership is defined in terms of such functions as (a) design and formulation of a national strategy and plan of action for COVID-19, (b) preparedness and timely action and (c) regular communication and information dissemination. An efficient government calls for such actions as (a) plan implementation, (b) rule enforcement and (c) resource mobilization and deployment (see Bhalla & Fang, 2022). These roles may provide guidelines on what type of indicators to look for to measure the effectiveness of leaders and governments.

Admittedly, it is very hard to quantify the role of leaders, but so are risk environment and political and security risk, which the GHS Index has attempted. It may be feasible to consider such leadership indicators as the number of leaders who prepared national COVID plans of action and the number of speeches they gave on COVID-19. An index of leadership preparedness for future pandemics will also require some information on which countries/leaders prepared *anticipatory* policies and/or introduced institutional mechanisms (e.g. a National Security Council in the United States, which Trump disbanded).

Socioeconomic Fallout

Apart from the health outcomes discussed above, there were serious socioeconomic consequences of the pandemic which will continue to be felt. Severity of the economic fallout depends on several factors such as the length of lockdowns, the size, composition and resilience of different economic sectors and the size, duration and effectiveness of economic and fiscal stimulus packages offered by governments. Southern European countries like Greece, Spain and Italy were the most vulnerable because they depend on labour-intensive manufacturing, construction and tourism, which are more contact-intensive. These are also the activities along with retail and hospitality, which cannot be easily performed from home during lockdowns. On the other hand, financial services, information technology and banking are the best candidates for home work. Developing countries with large proportions of informal workers were particularly hard hit. As work is their only source of livelihood, their very survival depends on going out to work.

Economies with a larger proportion of small businesses suffered from a cash crunch and high unemployment which, in many cases, involved a massive increase in the loss of health insurance, which worsened workers' economic as well as health security and well-being.

Developing countries are at a particular economic disadvantage since their borrowing capacity is more constrained. Government debts are already very high, $20 trillion which represents about 25 per cent of the global debt. Their credit ratings have been downgraded, and FDI and exports have shrunk. Unless their debt repayments are rescheduled or written off, they would be very hard pressed to pay even interest on their loans. This situation is different from that during the 2008 economic and financial crisis when their main lenders were the multilateral institutions like the World Bank and the IMF as well as bilateral donor governments. Nowadays, private banks are big lenders which charge relatively high interest rates. Furthermore, financial support to developing countries through the IMF's SDRs may in fact not benefit the citizens of those countries. Instead, they may end up benefiting the creditors in the developed countries and banks' shareholders who keep receiving fat dividends. To prevent this happening requires that both the private sector and bilateral donors waive the developing-country debt repayments (Brown & Summers, 2020, April 14).

IMF growth projections for 2022 for different regions and countries were revised downwards in most cases following the relapse of COVID infections, imposition of prolonged lockdowns by China, supply-chain disruptions and war in Ukraine. At the end of October 2020, the IMF had raised the estimate of global economic loss from 3 to 4.4 per cent (IMF, 2020, October). It estimated the global economy to grow at over 6% in 2021 and only 3 per cent in 2022 (IMF, 2021, July). The growth forecast may turn out to be optimistic if the pandemic extends beyond 2023 and consumer and producers continue to shy away from consuming and investing. Indeed, the IMF has revised its forecasts of real GDP change downwards from 2022 to 2023 (see Table 2.7).

Economic recovery turned out to be better than expected with positive GDP annual change in 2020 in a number of countries. Krugman (2022, 14 January) argues that both the United States and France have done well, the latter particularly so especially in maintaining prime-age employment through subsidies to employers to keep workers on the payroll, which facilitated their return to work when vaccines became available. Yet forecast for both these countries for 2023 is very gloomy (see Table 2.7).

Table 2.7 Real GDP and unemployment (annual percentage change)

Region/country	*Real GDP*		*Projection*		*Unemployment*	*Projection*	
	2020	*2021*	*2022*	*2023*	*2019*	*2020*	*2021*
World	-3.0	6.0	3.2	2.7	–	–	–
Euro area	-6.1	5.2	3.1	0.5	7.6	8.9	9.1
Germany	-3.7	2.6	1.5	-0.3	3.1	4.3	4.2
France	-7.9	6.8	2.5	0.7	8.5	8.9	10.2
Italy	-9.0	6.6	3.2	-0.2	9.9	11.0	11.8
Spain	-10.8	5.1	4.3	1.2	14.1	16.8	16.8
Netherlands	-3.9	4.9	4.5	0.8	3.4	5.5	4.5
Austria	-6.7	4.6	4.7	1.0	4.5	5.8	5.5
Sweden	-2.2	5.1	2.6	-0.1	6.8	8.7	9.3
Denmark	-2.0	4.9	2.6	0.6	5.0	6.2	6.0
United Kingdom	-9.3	7.4	3.6	0.3	3.8	5.4	7.4
Switzerland	-2.5	4.2	2.2	0.8	2.3	3.2	3.6
Russia	-2.7	4.7	-3.4	-2.3	4.6	5.6	5.2
Poland	-2.2	5.9	3.8	0.5	3.3	3.8	5.1
Czech Republic	-5.5	3.5	1.9	1.5	2.0	3.1	3.4
Asia-Pacific	–	–	–		–	–	–
Japan	-4.6	1.7	1.7	1.6	2.4	3.3	2.8
South Korea	-0.7	4.0	2.6	2.0	3.8	4.1	4.1
Australia	-2.1	4.9	3.8	1.9	5.2	6.9	7.7
China	2.2	8.1	3.2	4.4	3.6	3.8	3.6
India	-6.6	8.7	6.8	6.1	–	–	–
Thailand	-6.2	1.5	2.8	3.7	1.0	1.0	1.0
Vietnam	2.9	2.6	7.0	6.2	2.2	3.3	2.7
North America	–		–		–	–	–
United States	-3.4.	6.0	5.2	1.0	3.7	8.9	7.3
Canada	-5.2	4.5	3.3	1.5	5.7	9.7	7.9
Latin America & the Caribbean	*-7.0*	*6.9*	*3.5*	*1.7*	–	–	–
Argentina	-9.9	10.4	4.0	2.0	9.8	11.0	10.1
Brazil	-3.9	4.6	2.8	1.0	11.9	13.4	14.1
Chile	-6.1	11.7	2.0	-1.0	7.2	11.4	10.2
Sub-Saharan Africa	*-1.7*	*4.5*	*3.8*	*3.7*	–	–	–
South Africa	-6.3	4.9	2.1	1.1	28.7	37.0	36.5
Nigeria	-1.8	3.6	3.2	3.0	–	–	–
Kenya	-0.3	7.5	5.3	5.1	–	–	–
Middle East & Central Asia	*-2.7*	*4.5*	*5.0*	*3.6*	–	–	–
Egypt	3.5	3.3	6.6	4.4	8.6	8.3	9.7
Jordan	-1.6	2.2	2.4	2.7	19.1	–	–
Saudi Arabia	-4.1	3.2	7.6	3.7	5.6	–	–
Morocco	-7.2	7.9	0.8	3.1	9.2	12.5	10.5

Sources: IMF (2020, 2021, 2022, October)

The high-income economies in North America and Europe were the worst hit in terms of output losses mainly as a result of prolonged lockdowns (Table 2.7). All economies in the group showed sharp contraction in output in 2020. According to the IMF, cumulative income per head at the end of 2022, will be 13 per cent below the pre-pandemic projections. In low-income countries excluding China, it will be between 18 and 22 per cent lower.[5] In terms of unemployment, the biggest losers amongst the high-income countries were Spain, followed by Italy, the United Kingdom and the United States. In South America, Argentina, Brazil and Chile were the worst hit, and in developing countries, South Africa.

Globally, ILO estimates suggest that working hour losses were much bigger than earlier estimated. In 2022, the total number of hours worked are forecast to be 2 per cent below the pre-pandemic level. The forecast for global unemployment, 207 million, exceeds the 2019 level by about 21 million (ILO, 2022).

Those in informal employment, especially women and ethnic minority workers, were disproportionately affected. Loss of jobs and income-earning opportunities of these vulnerable groups will worsen the pre-existing inequalities. Gains in poverty reduction achieved during the past decade may also be wiped out.

In general, employment has risen, but it remains below pre-pandemic levels. Several factors account for slow employment creation, namely continued rise in COVID cases due to the Omicron sub-variant BA.5 which is more infectious, workers' fear of health risks at the workplace without necessary public health precautions and employers' reluctance to hire in conditions of uncertainty and risk.

The above aggregate analysis conceals many types of economic and social—gender-based, community-based, spatial and ethnic and racial—inequalities. The pandemic has worsened the pre-existing disparities across regions and ethnic communities. Pre-existing and related conditions are inversely correlated with socioeconomic conditions and income poverty. Similar inequalities also occurred during the 1918 influenza and the 2009 H1NI pandemic. For example, the mortality and hospitalization rates for H1N1 were associated with deprived neighbourhoods of high deprivation and low educational attainment (Bibbins-Domingo, 2020). A study of Barcelona (Spain) on the impact of COVID-19 by income concludes that "districts with the lowest per capita income had the highest incidence of COVID-19 per 10,000 inhabitants." (Baena-Diez et al., 2020). Similar results were obtained for New York City boroughs (Bambra et al., 2020).

Deprived regions, which are generally inhabited by ethnic groups and minorities, have disproportionately higher COVID-19 infection and mortality rates. Few systematic studies on the effects of COVID-19 on different types of inequalities are available. Anecdotal evidence suggests that the adverse effects of the virus were significant. Locational inequalities are correlated with health and racial inequalities. Ethnic minorities tend to live in poor, polluted and depressed areas with limited or no access to healthcare. They are engaged in "essential" frontline activities in which social distancing is difficult to practise. Some social groups (e. g. the elderly, minorities and the poor) were worse hit by the pandemic given unequal access to healthcare, pre-existing conditions, crowded housing and densely populated living areas.

Gender-based inequalities exist as well. In general, women lost jobs more quickly than men, partly due to the need to educate children at home and care for families during lockdowns. Those engaged in service activities and healthcare were often forced to remain in employment to save lives and their own livelihoods. As a consequence, they suffered from higher rates of COVID infections due to exposure to patients and people in general.

In high-income countries with limited *informal* forms of childcare, women are obliged to stop working due to childcare demands at home. The ability of parents to continue working is influenced by such factors as education, whether they are single parents or couples and whether there is scope for remote working. Generally remote working is more common among highly educated parents.

Most high-income countries responded to the economic and social fallout of COVID-19 with *temporary* economic and social relief measures and direct transfer payments. Relief packages were intended to boost spending, save livelihoods, keep employees in jobs and keep corporations and small businesses afloat. Many countries allocated more resources for extra spending on healthcare, (2) temporary support of the unemployed, (3) deferred tax and rent payments and (4) support for small and medium enterprises to prevent business insolvency and lay-offs. Most of these temporary measures no longer exist, which has hit the poor hard in prevailing conditions of higher food and energy prices and inflation in general.

Table A2.1 Geographical distribution of Coronavirus deaths in Italian provinces

Region	*First Wave*				*Second Wave*		*Total*	
	March–May 2020		*June–September 2020*		*October–16 December 2020*			
	Number	*(%)*	*Number*	*(%)*	*Number*	*(%)*	*Number*	*(%)*
North								
Lombardy	16,359	47.6	607	33.0	7104	26.0	24,070	37.9
Val d'Aosta	143	0.4	6	0.3	206	0.8	355	0.6
Ligura	1516	4.4	138	7.5	974	3.6	2628	4.1
Emilia Romagna	4313	12.5	173	9.4	2232	8.2	6718	10.6
Piedmont	4091	11.9	126	6.9	1326	4.8	5543	8.7
Trentino A.A.	402	1.2	4	0.2	389	1.4	795	1.3
Veneto	1950	5.7	248	13.5	2884	10.5	5082	8.0
Friuli V.G.	346	1.0	21	1.1	632	2.3	999	1.6
Bolzano (Tyrol)	290	0.8	2	0.1	380	1.4	672	1.1
Centre								
Marche	981	2.0	7	0.4	223	0.8	1211	1.9
Tuscany	1045	3.0	96	5.2	1764	6.5	2905	4.6
Umbria	75	0.2	9	0.5	446	1.6	530	0.8
South								
Abruzzo	446	1.3	37	2.0	597	2.2	1080	1.7
Lazio	840	2.4	143	7.8	2099	7.7	3082	4.8
Apulia	524	1.5	75	4.1	1460	5.3	2059	3.2
Campagna	477	1.4	58	3.2	2102	7.7	2637	4.1
Molise	22	0.1	2	0.1	146	0.5	170	0.3
Sicily	300	0.9	57	3.1	1654	6.0	2011	3.2
Basilicata	29	0.1	2	0.1	143	0.5	174	0.3
Calabria	96	0.3	4	0.2	225	0.8	325	0.5
Sardinia	131	0.4	24	1.3	361	1.3	516	0.8
Total Italy	**34,376**	**100.0**	**1839**	**100.0**	**27,343**	**100.0**	**63,562**	**100.0**

Source: Institute of National Health (2020)

Table A2.2 Cross-country regression results

Dependent variable	*lndeath/mil.*
$\ln ageing_j$	0.255(1.03)
$\ln urb_j$	1.807(1.78)*
$\ln gov_j$	-0.622(-0.57)
$temp_j$	0.093(0.17)
$G5_j$	1.274(1.27)
EU_j	1.606(2.23)**
$D4_j$	1.066(1.09)
$ASIAN_j$	-0.681(-1.12)
CHN_j	-5.460(-3.00)***
Constant	-0.165(-0.03)
Obs.	50
R-squared	0.441

Notes: (1) t-statistics in parentheses. (2) $^{***}p < 0.01$; $^{**}p < 0.05$; $^{*}p < 0.1$. 3. The cut-off date of total deaths is 8 August 2021

Table A2.3 Coronavirus cases and deaths per capita and socioeconomic variables for selected Indian states

State	*Cases*	*Deaths*	*Population (2019) (million)*	*% of pop. 60 years & over 2021)*	*Cases per million*	*Deaths per million*	*Rate of urbanization*	*Per capita public exp. on health (Rs.)*
Maharashtra	1,726,926	45,435	122	12	14,155	372	47.4	824
Delhi	451,382	7143	20	9	22,797	361	99.0	1880
Karnataka	851,212	11,430	66	11	12,936	173	42.5	911
Tamil Nadu	748,225	11,387	76	14	9884	150	51.9	1121
Punjab	138,486	4358	29	12	4616	146	40.3	933
Andhra Pradesh	846,245	6814	52	12	16,211	131	34.1	1028
West Bengal	413,112	7403	97	11	4259	76	35.1	821
Haryana	187,777	1935	29	10	6475	67	39.7	933
Gujarat	182,557	3770	68	10	2688	55	46.7	1059
Kerala	495,712	1742	35	16.5	14,163	50	66.5	1363
Madhya Pradesh	179,068	3042	82	8.5	2184	37	28.5	673
Uttar Pradesh	501,311	7261	225	8	2228	32	23	613
Rajasthan	215,071	2008	77	8	2793	26	26	1015
Bihar	223,346	1156	119	8	1884	10	12	391
India	8,683,916	128,121	1333	10	6514	96	34.5	876

Sources: Population figures and urbanization rates are taken from GOI (2019).

Notes: (1) Figures are rounded; (2) Population projections are based on 2011 Census of India

Table A2.4 Observed and excess deaths in the American states

State	*Deaths (no.)*		*COVID-19 deaths*		*Population (million) * (2019)*	*COVID-19 deaths per million*	*Share of State pop. Above 65 years (%)*	*Share of State urban population (%)*
	Observed deaths	*Excess deaths*	*Reported deaths (no.)*	*Excess deaths (%)*				
States led by Democrat governors								
Illinois	54,014	10,601	7037	66	13	541	16	88
Kansas	11,545	653	394	60	3	131	16	74
Pennsylvania	63,070	9106	7595	83	13	584	18	79
Minnesota	20,530	1897	1635	86	4	272	16	73
Colorado	19,479	2864	1782	62	6	297	14	86
Rhode Island	5239	940	979	104	1	979	17	91
Virginia	32,582	4562	2394	52	8	299	15	75
Washington	25,803	2410	1505	62	8	188	15	84
Maine	6273	129	64	50	1	49	21	39
Delaware	4651	899	482	54	1	482	19	83
Kentucky	21,280	1593	815	51	4	204	16	58
New Jersey	48,048	18,004	14,043	78	9	1560	16	95
Oregon	16,217	1123	338	30	4	84	18	81
Louisiana	24,026	5052	3820	76	5	764	15	73
California	127,298	17,002	10,388	61	39	266	14	95
District of Columbia	3428	907	675	74	1	675	–	100
New Mexico	8771	1181	671	57	2	335	17	77
New York	103,811	40,863	31,996	78	19	1684	16	88
Hawaii	4828	-53	0	0	1	–		
Michigan	48,854	8797	5866	67	10	587	17	75

(*continued*)

Table A2.4 (continued)

State	*Deaths (no.)*		*COVID-19 deaths*		*Population (million) * (2019)*	*COVID-19 deaths per million*	*Share of State pop. Above 65 years (%)*	*Share of State urban population (%)*
	Observed deaths	*Excess deaths*	*Reported deaths (no.)*	*Excess deaths (%)*				
Wisconsin	23,991	1779	964	54	6	161	17	70
Montana	4379	82	26	32	1	26	19	56
Nevada	12,194	1395	888	64	3	296	16	94
States led by Republican governors								
Alaska	1851	28	0	0	0.7	–		
Vermont	2561	178	31	17	0.6	50	19	39
Massachusetts	32,562	8261	7886	95	7	1126	16	92
Maryland	26,091	5809	3859	66	6	643	15	87
Oklahoma	17,189	1741	639	37	4	160	16	66
Idaho	6377	558	178	32	2	89	16	71
Iowa	13,416	1006	922	92	3	307	17	64
Indiana	31,250	3809	2991	79	7	427	16	72
Mississippi	15,989	3104	1753	56	3	584	16	49
New Hampshire	5694	669	373	56	1	373	18	60
Georgia	41,107	5958	3830	64	11	348	14	75
Florida	101,389	14,250	8517	60	21	405	20	91
Alabama	25,172	3936	2071	53	5	414	17	59
South Carolina	24,488	4009	1877	47	5	375	18	66
Texas	100,951	17,772	10,026	56	29	346	13	85
Missouri	28,580	2171	1280	59	6	213	17	70
Utah	8818	953	311	33	3	104	11	91

Ohio	55,946	6455	3379	52	12	281	17	78
North Dakota	3144	155	60	39	0.7	60	15	60
South Dakota	3549	181	103	57	5	117	17	57
Arkansas	14,326	1221	585	48	3	195	17	56
Nebraska	7447	536	315	59	2	157	16	73
Tennessee	33,999	3189	1191	37	7	170	16	66
Arizona	32,780	7471	3933	53	7	562	17	90
West Virginia	9495	163	74	46	2	37	20	49
Wyoming	2079	160	0	0	0.6	–	16	65
United States	1,336,561	225,530	150,541	67				

Source: Wolf et al. (2020). Figures have been rounded

Notes: (1) Hawaii shows negative excess deaths because observed deaths were lower than would be predicted based on historical norms; (2) Data for Connecticut and North Carolina were omitted because of delays in reporting; (3) COVID-19 deaths include those deaths which were identified as COVID as the underlying cause among others

Table A2.5 Regression results for the American states

Dependent Variable	*ln(deaths/pop)*
ln$x$	0.997(0.85)
ln$y$	2.882(4.53)***
z	-0.095(-0.38)
Constant	-9.497(-1.83)*
Observations	45
R-squared	0.376

Note: (1) t-statistics in parentheses. (2) ***$p < 0.01$; **$p < 0.05$; *$p < 0.1$

Table A2.6 Coronavirus cases and deaths in care homes in the American states

State	*Cases (no.)*	*Cases per million*	*Deaths (no.)*	*Share of State deaths (%)*	*Deaths per million*	*Care homes per million*
I. *States led by Democrat governors*						
Illinois	17,098	216	2744	39	216	40
Kansas	722	249	190	71	65	11
Pennsylvania	18,759	1465	4564	69	356	13
Connecticut	9428	2619	2754	64	765	
Minnesota	2954	527	876	61	156	64
Colorado	4958	870	849	51	149	28
Rhode Island	2605	2605	550	59	550	62
Virginia	5183	610	821	48	97	28
Washington	3534	465	624	48	82	39
Maine	379	291	46	45	35	13
Delaware	690	711	228	45	235	30
Kentucky	1975	439	252	44	56	31
North Carolina	4131	393	565	43	54	
New Jersey	33,626	3821	6131	41	697	61
Oregon	547	130	85	42	20	11
Louisiana	7359	1600	1243	39	270	78
California	17,597	445	1963	33	50	22
Dist. of Columbia	860	1228	167	31	239	19
New Mexico	194	92	144	29	68	25
New York	10,527	543	6130	20	316	23
Michigan	7122	714	1666	27	167	24
Wisconsin	1031	178	75	10	13	36
Montana	34	34	6	27	6	1
Nevada	1039	335	127	26	41	24

(*continued*)

Table A2.6 (continued)

State	*Cases (no.)*	*Cases per million*	*Deaths (no.)*	*Share of State deaths (%)*	*Deaths per million*	*Care homes per million*
II. States led by Republican governors						
Vermont	172	287	32	57	52	10
Massachusetts	21,608	3131	4382	55	635	73
Maryland	10,137	1689	1469	47	245	44
Oklahoma	1379	353	174	46	45	24
Idaho	179	99	36	40	20	9
Iowa	1816	586	284	40	92	15
Indiana	4357	650	1149	44	171	35
Mississippi	1993	671	406	40	137	46
North Dakota	491	646	50	57	66	90
New Hampshire	1249	961	178	49	137	25
Georgia	8544	806	1040	38	98	40
Florida	9540	444	1230	37	57	40
Alabama	2786	568	301	33	61	1
South Carolina	2082	408	228	33	45	28
Texas	4482	154	790	33	27	19
Missouri	986	164	311	31	51	20
Utah	531	161	51	31	15	45
Ohio	8298	709	834	30	71	45
South Dakota	151	171	25	28	28	153
Arkansas	670	223	67	27	22	1
Nebraska	419	220	67	25	35	26
Tennessee	1220	179	138	24	20	10
Arizona	2351	322	352	23	48	29
Wyoming	52	87	4	1	7	7

Sources: *New York Times* database. See Yourish et al. (2020, May 11). US Census Bureau for population data

Notes

1. The study was prepared by the Institute for Health Metrics and Evaluation, Seattle. A large number of COVID-19 National Preparedness Collaborators participated in it.
2. This section first appeared in Bhalla, Ajit and Fang, Jing (2022). Leaders, institutions and people during COVID-19: Secret of Asian success, *Journal of Chinese Economic and Business Studies*, 20 (3), © The Chinese Economic Association-UK, reprinted by permission of Taylor & Francis Ltd., http://www.tandfonline.com on behalf of the Chinese Economic Association - UK.

3. A study of two Indian states, Andhra Pradesh and Tamil Nadu, which enjoy good primary healthcare facilities at the grassroots, also shows low incidence of mortality among the elderly population. The reasons for this peculiar result include stringent stay-at-home orders, regular contact with community health workers and possible underestimation of the incidence of mortality among lower-age groups due to poor surveillance systems (see Laxminarayan et al., 2020).
4. Based on the *New York Times* database. For details, see Yourish et al. (2020, May 11). One-third of the US coronavirus deaths are nursing home residents or workers.
5. Cited in Brown, Gordon (2021, p. 78).

References

Abassi, K. (2020, November 13). Covid-19: politicization, 'corruption', and suppression of science. *British Medical Journal.*

Adamaecz-Völgyi, A., & Szabo-Morvai, A. (2021). *Confidence in public institutions is critical in containing the COVID-19 pandemic.* Global Labor Organization (GLO) Discussion Paper no. 861, Essen 8.

Agus, D., et al. (2021, May). *Technical solutions for global genomic sequencing and surveillance.* Tony Blair Institute for Global Change/Lawrence J. Ellison Institute for Transformative Medicine of USC.

Akovali U., & Yilmaz, K. (2020). *Polarized politics of pandemic response and the Covid-19 connectedness across the U.S. states.* Koc University—Tüsiad Economic Research Forum Working Paper Series no. 2019.

Baena-Diez, J. M., Barrosso, M., Cordeiro-Coelho, S. I., Diaz, J. L., & Grau, M. (2020). Impact of Covid-19 outbreak by income: hitting hardest the most deprived. *Journal of Public Health, 42*(4).

Balmford, B., Annan, J. D., Hatgtraves, J. C., Altoè, M., & Bateman, I. J. (2020). Cross-country comparisons of Covid-19: Policy, politics and the price of life. *Environmental and Resource Economics.*

Balsari, S., Sange, M., & Udwadia, Z. (2020). Covid-19 care in India. *The Lancet.*

Bambra, C., Riordan, R., Ford, J., & Matthews, F. (2020). Covid-19 pandemic and health inequalities. *Journal of Epidemiol Community Health, 74.*

Bargain, O., & Aminjonov, U. (2020). Trust and compliance to public health policies in times of COVID-19. *Journal of Public Economics, 192.*

Belmin, J., Donaldo, C., Magri, M., Nghiem, Q. D., Oquendo, B., Pariel, S., & Lafuente-Lafuente, C. (2020). Coronavirus disease 2019 outcomes in French nursing homes that implemented staff confinement with residents. *JAMA Network Open, 3*(8).

Bhalla, A. S. (2021). *Leadership challenges and the COVID-19 pandemic.* Observer Research Foundation (ORF) Occasional Paper, Issue no. 299.

Bhalla, A. S. (1992). *Uneven Development in the Third World*. Macmillan.
Bhalla, A. S. (1995). *Uneven Development in the Third World*. Macmillan.
Bhalla, A., & Fang, J. (2022). Leaders, institutions and people during Covid-19: Secret of Asian success. *Journal of Chinese Economic and Business Studies, 20*(3). (Published online in October 2021).
Bibbins-Domingo, K. (2020). *This time must be different: Disparities during the Covid-19 pandemic*. Annals of Internal Medicine.
Blundell, R., Dias, M. C., Joyce, R., & Xu, X. (2020). COVID-19 and inequalities. *Fiscal Studies, 41*(2).
Booth, R. (2020, June 28). Risk of death in UK care homes 13 times higher than in Germany. *Guardian*.
Boyd, M. J., Wilson, N., & Nelson, C. (2020). Validation analysis of Global health Security Index (GHSI) scores 2019. *BMJ Global Health, 5*.
Brown, G., & Summers, L. H. (2020, April 14). The economic danger of doing too little too late. *Washington Post*.
Brown, G. (2021). *Seven ways to change the world*. Simon & Schuster.
Camakli, C., Demiralp, S., Kalemli-Özcan, Ṣ., Yeşiltaş, S., & Yıldırım, M.A. (2021, January). *The economic case for global vaccinations: An epidemiological model with international production networks*. Center for International Development (CID) Working Paper no. 390.
Cash, R., & Patel, V. (2020). Has COVID-19 subverted global health? *The Lancet, 395*.
Chathukalam, J., & Tharamangalam, J. (2021). *The Kerala model in the time of Covid-19: Rethinking state, society and democracy*. World Development.
Comas-Herrera, A., & Hernandez, J.-L. (2020, May 17). Estimates of number of deaths of care home residents linked to COVID-19 pandemic in England, Department of Health Policy. *London School of Economics*.
Crayne, M. P., & Medeiros, K. E. (2020, August 10). Making sense of crisis: Charismatic, ideological and pragmatic leadership in response to COVID-19. *American Psychologist*.
Government of India. (GOI). (2019). *Census of India, population projections for India and states*.
Gunter, J., & Pandey, V. (2020, December 11). Waldemar Haffkine: The vaccine pioneer the world forgot. *BBC News*.
Hanushek, E. A., & Woesmann, L. (2020). *The economic effects of learning losses*. OECD Education Working Paper 225.
Holt, A., & Butcher, B. (2020, May 15). Coronavirus deaths: How big is the epidemic in care homes? *BBC News*.
IHME (Institute for Health Metrics and Evaluation). (2022). *Modelling database*. Washington University.
ILO (International Labour Office). (2022, January). *World Employment and Social Outlook*.

IMF (International Monetary Fund). (2020). *World Economic Outlook.* Washington DC.

IMF (International Monetary Fund). (2021). *World Economic Outlook.* Washington DC.

IMF (International Monetary Fund). (2022). *World Economic Outlook.* Washington DC.

Institute of National Health. (2020, December). *Characteristics of SARS-CoV-2 patients dying in Italy: Report based on available data on 16th December.*

Ji, Y., Shao, J., Tao, B., Song, H., Li, Z., & Wang, J. (2021). Are we ready to deal with a global COVID-19 pandemic? Rethinking countries' capacity based on the Global Health Security Index. *International Journal of Infectious Diseases, 106*, 289–294.

Johns Hopkins University, Bloomberg School of Public Health. (2019, October). *Global Health Security Index: Building collective action and accountability.*

Johns Hopkins University, Bloomberg School of Public Health and Nuclear Threat Initiative. (2021). *Global Health Security Index: Building collective action and accountability amid global crisis.*

Jonathan, K. (2020, April 4). A German exception? Why the country's coronavirus relative death rate is low. *New York Times.*

Kottasova, I. (2021, March 1). How the Czech Republic slipped into a covid disaster, one misstep at a time. *Cable News Network (CNN).*

Krugman, P. (2022, January 14). Wonking out: France's economy is having a good pandemic. *New York Times.*

Ladhani, S. N., Chow, J. Y., Janarthanan, R., Fok, J., Crawley-Boevey, E., Vusirikala, A., Fernandez, E., Perez, M. S., Tang, S., Dun-Campbell, K., & Wynne-Evans, E. (2020). Investigation of SARS-CoV-2 outbreaks in six care homes in London. *EClinical Medicine, 26.*

Lahariya, C., Kang, G., & Guleriaa, R. (2020). *Till We Win: India's fight against the Covid-19 pandemic.* Penguin Books.

Laxminarayan, R., Wahl, B., Dudala, S. R., Gopal, K., Mohan, B. C., Neelima, S., Jawahar Reddy, K. S., Radhakrishnan, J., & Lewnard, J. A. (2020). Epidemiology and transmission dynamics of Covid-19 in two Indian states. *Science, 370.*

Lenton, T. M., Boulton, C. A., & Scheffer, M. (2022). Resilience of countries to COVID-19 correlated with trust. *Nature Portfolio Scientific Reports.*

Liu, M., Maxwell, C. J., Armstrong, P., Schwandt, M., Moser, A., McGregor, M. J., Bronskill, S. E., & Dhalla, I. A. (2020). COVID-19 in long-term care homes in Ontario and British Columbia. *Canadian Medical Association Journal (CMAJ), 192*(47).

Madeiros, K. E., Crayne, M. P., Griffith, J. A., Hardy, J. H., III, & Damadzic, A. (2022). Leader sensemaking style in response to crisis: Consequences and insights from the COVID-19 pandemic. *Personality and Individual Differences, 187.*

Mahajan, M. (2021). Casualties of preparedness: the Global Health Security Index and Covid-19. *International Journal of Law in Context, 17.*

Malani, A., Mohanan, M., Kumar, C., Kramer, J., & Tandel, V. (2020, June 28). *Prevalence of SARS-CoV-2 among workers returning to Bihar gives snapshot of COVID across India (draft).*

Masih, N. (2020, July 31). How a packed slum in Mumbai beat back the Coronavirus, as India's cases continue to soar. *Washington Post.*

McCormack, J. (2020, May 29). Coronavirus: Care home residents account for more than half of NI (Northern Ireland) deaths, BBC News.

Office of National Statistics. (2020a, July 3). *Deaths involving Covid-19 in the care sector, England and Wales: deaths occurring up to 20 June 2020* (provisional).

Office of National Statistics. (2020b, August 5) *Deaths involving coronavirus (Covid-19) in Scotland.*

Oldenberg, C. E., Pinsky, B. A., Brogden, J., Pinsky, B. A., Brogdon, J., Chen, C., Ruder, K., Zhong, L., Nyatigo, F., Cook, C. A., Hinterwirth, A., Lebas, E., & Redd, T. (2021). Effect of oral Azithromycin vs. placebo on COVID-19 symptoms in outpatients with SARS-CoV-2 infection: A randomized clinical trial. *Journal of American Medical Association (JAMA).*

Patterson, S., Jr. (2022). The politics of pandemic: The effect of stay-at-home orders on COVID-19 mitigation. *State Politics & Policy Quarterly, 22*(1).

Ravi, S. J., Warmbrod, K. L., Mullen, L., Meyer, D., Cameron, E., Bell, J., Bapat, P., Paterra, M., Machalaba, C., Nath, I., & Gostin, L. O. (2020). *The value proposition of the Global Health Security Index.* BMJ Global Health.

Stevis-Gridneff, M. Apuffo, M., & Pronczuk, M. (2020, August 8). When covid-19 hit, many elderly were left to die. *New York Times.*

Stiglitz, J. (2019). *People, power and profits.* New York: W.W. Norton & Co.

Tharoor, S. (2020, May 11). The Kerala model. *Project Syndicate.*

The Economist. (2020a, May 9). Vietnam and the Indian state of Kerala curbed Covid-19 on the cheap.

The Economist. (2020b, August 10). Coronavirus in Sweden: The odd one out.

The Economist. (2021a, March 13). India seems to have suffered surprisingly few deaths from Covid-19.

The Economist (2021b, March 27). Covid-19 in Brazil. Variants on a theme of disaster.

The Lancet. (2020, April 25). India under COVID-19 lockdown.

The Lancet. (2022, February 1). Pandemic preparedness and COVID-19: an exploratory analysis of infection and fatality rates, and contextual factors associated with preparedness in 177 countries, from January 1, 2020, to September 30, 2021.

Tourish, D. (2020). Introduction to the special issue: Why the coronavirus crisis is also a crisis of leadership. *Leadership.* Special Issue on *Leadership and the Coronavirus Crisis, 16*(3).

UNDP (United Nations Development Programme). (2021). *Human Development. Report.* UNDP.

WHO (*World Health Organization*). (2020, July 2). *Responding to Covid-19: Learnings from Kerala.*

Wolf, S. H. Chapman, D.A. Sabo, R.T. Weinberger, Hill L, D. M., & Taylor, D. D. H. (2020, March–July and October 20). Excess deaths from COVID-19 and other causes. *Journal of American Medical Association (JAMA).*

World Metereological Organization. (WMO). (2021, March 18). Review of metereological and air quality factors affecting the COVID-19 pandemic. *First Report of the WMO CoVID-19 Task Team.*

Yourish, K. R. Lai, K. K., Ivory, D., & Smith, M. (2020, May 11). One-third of all U.S. Coronavirus deaths are nursing home residents or workers. *New York Times.*

PART II

Leaders, Institutions, and People

CHAPTER 3

Understanding Leadership Challenges: A Framework

Political power is that power which every man having in the state of nature has given up into the hands of the society and therein to the governors and whom the society hath had set over itself, with this express or tacit trust, that it shall be employed for their good.
—John Locke, *Two Treatises of Government*

Different approaches have been adopted in the literature to understand leadership roles and behaviour. Most common among these is the traits-based approach, which views the nature and performance of leadership in terms of a leader's character and characteristics. There is no dearth of studies on leadership in governments and organizations. But despite the existence of a growing literature, there is as yet no generally accepted definition of what leadership is, how to study it and whether a suitable concept and strategy can be formulated to develop and exercise it.

Of the available studies, most deal mainly with the exercise of leadership in high-income countries. There are few which systematically examine leadership capacity in developing countries and how important it is for good governance and crisis management.

Difficulties in formulating a theory of leadership is due to an inherent complexity of conceptualization. Then there is the issue of devising measurable indicators of the impact of leadership capacity on the attainment of well-defined goals and objectives during crisis. What is *quality* leadership?

A. S. Bhalla, *National and Global Responses to the COVID-19 Pandemic*, https://doi.org/10.1007/978-3-031-29521-8_3

Is the same type of leadership suitable for both normal times, wars and other crises such as a pandemic? Finally, can the impact of a leader in crisis management be really isolated from other determinant factors such as the public institutions and the demands of citizens, besides the internal and external environment. Our aim is to show that it is a combination of leadership, public and private institutions and the public and communities at large that determine the outcomes in terms of such personal issues as health pandemics.

Different Approaches to Leadership

Traits-Based Approach

Most common among political scientists is a framework in which traits or characteristics and personality and style of a leader are dominant features, which explains his/her behaviour, actions and performance.

"Strongman" Leader

There are strong leaders and weak leaders, democratic as well as autocratic and authoritarian ones, whose performance may vary according to how they manage crises. A strong leader has been defined as one who amasses too much power in himself /herself. While this act may facilitate decisive and quick action, it can also lead to disastrous consequences (Brown, 2014). Cases of democratic leaders becoming autocratic and authoritarian, amassing unchallenged absolute power are not hard to find.

Self-centred leadership, almost a cult of personality, is often associated with power and authority, whereas a more collegiate and consensual leadership is viewed as a sign of weakness. But the advantages of the latter type of leadership are often overlooked. Yet as discussed in Chap. 4, this type has been far more successful in the management of the COVID-19 crisis (e.g. in Germany and New Zealand).

A strong leader can be described in different ways. A leader's strength is often equated with power and authority. Nye (2008, pp. 21-25) observes that "leadership involves power, but not all power relationships are instances of leadership." A mixture of hard and soft power skills, what he calls "smart power," is needed for a leader to be effective. There are also other interpretations. A strong leader may be one who can enforce laws and bring about order. But the strength of a leader may in the first place be a result of order and harmony, which may be derived not so much from strong leadership as from robust formal institutions and informal non-state capacity of community and civil-society groups. The quality and effectiveness of a leader may depend more on the strength of a country's institutions and the nature of its laws, than purely on his/her own traits.

With a recent surge of populism and nationalism, the strongman leadership has taken on a new meaning. Initially, popularly elected leaders like Trump, Johnson, Erdogan and Modi were considered (mistakenly) strong liberal reformers when actually the tide was turning against the neoliberal order (Rachman, 2022). These populist leaders rode on the wave of anti-immigrant, anti-elitist, anti-establishment and anti-globalization sentiments. They benefit from digital technology to communicate directly with the public bypassing established institutions. And electors seemed to be easily charmed by their savvy handling of the social media. Their savviness in exploiting social media is often misunderstood as sincere intent and capacity to introduce meaningful reforms. Instead, what we are seeing today is hunger for absolute power, growing cult of personality and a wilful intent to bend or even break the rule of law for personal and political objectives. The populist and autocratic leaders tend to exercise control and increase their powers by monitoring public behaviour.

Collegiate Leader
A collegiate leader represents a collective style of leadership, which contrasts sharply with the strongman leadership under which all power is concentrated in one individual. Regular consultations are held with cabinet colleagues to reach a consensus on major decisions. It is a feature of coalition governments common in Western Europe. It implies sharing of power with cabinet colleagues in charge of their departments. Power of a collegiate leader is also shared with the governing party on behalf of people who elected it. A single leader, howsoever qualified and competent, cannot be expected to have answers to all the serious social, economic and political issues. But having tasted power, even some collegiate elected leaders can become autocratic and dictatorial over time, for example, Nehru and his daughter Indira Gandhi. Their charisma and personalities enabled them to exercise power without consulting cabinet colleagues who were equally competent and who also enjoyed political support.

In totalitarian regimes, usually governed by single parties, a political leader has a choice to exercize power either through collective leadership or strongman leadership under an individual. The experience of China shows that both types of approaches were adopted since the Revolution in

1949. There were strong leaders like Mao, Deng and Xi, who were able to take bold decisions on their own. For example, Xi has assumed absolute powers. His astute anti-corruption campaign managed to kill several birds with one stone. It facilitated the centralization of power. Controlling rampant corruption by putting several senior party leaders in jail may have helped him to gain popularity with the public. The campaign also helped him eliminate most of his political rivals. But the lesser mortals like Hu and Zemin were forced to govern through collective leadership style (Lampton, 2014). In 2002, a Senior Chinese diplomat remarked that "Mao and Deng could decide but Jiang and the current leaders must consult."[1]

The dictatorial leaders do not have to be accountable to the population as do popularly-elected leaders. But they also need political legitimacy, which in China was provided by the leaders through remarkable and rapid poverty reduction and significant improvements in people's living standards and quality of life in the post-Mao period. In an implicit social contract, people are perhaps prepared to accept dictators in exchange for better life. On the other hand, public accountablity of democratic leaders seems exaggerated, particularly in the age of rising populism and a decline of democracy in Western liberal societies. While the electors can reject democratic leaders periodically at the time of general elections, they cannot do much in the period between elections. Of course, there are exceptions like the downfall of Thatcher and Johnson. But they were removed from office by their own party, not by the electors.

Charismatic and Transformational Leaders

The most relevant attributes in a leader would be his/her capacity to *inspire* and *persuade followers to change behaviour* or *comply* with required public health rules. Archie Brown (2014, p. 5) describes these traits in terms of *redefining* and *transformational* categories, which "aim to change people's thinking on what is feasible or desirable." Are strength and charisma preconditions for an inspiring and persuasive leadership for crisis management? Charisma may be bestowed on a leader by followers. Charismatic leaders can do good as well as harm. Similarly, strength of a leader may lead to quick and decisive action required in a crisis, but it may equally lead to disasters especially if he/she acquires too much power.

The ingredients necessary for strong/good leadership may include legitimacy, accountability and political commitment. They may also include personal traits or attributes such as charisma, popularity, experience and communication skills, which can help a leader generate "soft power" to win followers.

The traits approach is associated with different time phases, namely the first with the *traits* of a leader, the second with *styles* (autocratic or democratic, personalized or collegiate) of leadership, the third with a "*contingency*" approach which distinguishes between people-oriented and task-oriented leaders and finally, with *charismatic* and *transformational* leadership (Nye, 2008).

Leaders' Traits and COVID-19

A recent example of this last variant of trait-based approach is a study of *charismatic* (Trudeau), *ideological* (Bolsonaro and Trump) and *pragmatic* (Merkel) leadership in the context of COVID-19 (Crayne & Medeiros, 2020). A leader's response to COVID-19 need not be fixed. An uninformed leader may change/adapt his response when more information and experience are gained about the pandemic to take account of the external environment as well as followers' changing behaviour. Medeiros et al. (2022) argue that leadership style and sensemaking would vary as the COVID-19 progresses. Pragmatic leaders would respond as the crisis becomes more complex over time, whereas ideological and obstinate ones might not.

A charismatic leader is defined by such traits as a vision for the future, a willingness to reform and an ideology based on a set of predetermined values and nationalistic ideas of greatness (e.g. Make America Great Again) and a focus on reason, problem-solving and willingness to adapt to changing circumstances.

During the COVID-19 pandemic, when information about the virus was scarce, neither the public nor the leaders (with few exceptions) had any clear understanding or expertise. Under the circumstances, clarity of communications from leadership was critical. But as discussed in Chap. 4, few leaders provided such clarity through social media or direct contact with the public. Social media often exploited the vacuum by distorting facts and spreading conspiracy theories. An assessment of the responses of 16 leaders to the pandemic suggests that their traits alone do not explain the differences in their responses (see Chap. 4). Different leaders interpreted the pandemic differently and responded (or not) depending on their perception of the severity of the crisis and its impact on public health and the economy, as well as their experiences in the past with viruses. The nature of the administrative organization (centralized or decentralized) and people's behaviour also affected leaders' response.

Successful management of COVID-19 by many female political leaders has recently made popular a *gender-based* leadership debate (see Chap. 4). It is argued that women leaders tend to perform better than men in situations in which *empathy, collaboration, participation* and honest communications are the key. However, this gender-based approach is inadequate by itself because it does not attach enough importance to the role of institutions, organizations and agents as well as followers. Yet these two key players' contribution to political leaders' success, whether they are male or female, also depends on these actors' behaviour and performance, which has not received much attention in the above conventional approaches.

While the above traits and characteristics are relevant and *necessary*, they are not *sufficient* to determine outcomes. The impact of a leader may depend far more on the interventions and response of government agents, civil service as well as local administration and followers, not to speak of external environment on which a leader may have no control.

Nevertheless, a central political leader has both the power and authority to provide incentives and disincentives to encourage agents and followers to work in unison. Social order, harmony and success in the containment and control of the COVID-19 virus may be derived from both formal institutions and non-state informal capacity which is enshrined in community and civil-society groups.

The criteria for assessing a leader's success or failure can be input-oriented, output-oriented or both. The former discussed above relate to traits, style of leadership, charisma and popularity. Besides these, a leader's performance needs to be judged in terms of outcomes of his/her policy actions and responses to the pandemic. For example, these outcomes may be related to health indicators such as rates of infections, hospitalizations and deaths and economic and social disruptions. Economic indicators would relate to loss of growth, economic output, jobs and income and social inequalities besides loss of freedom, mobility, mental stress which may result from strict COVID measures (e.g. prolonged lockdowns and quarantine) and guidelines (e.g. physical distancing, wearing of mask mask).[2] As discussed in Chap. 4, different leaders do not assign equal weight to different objectives. In the context of the pandemic, leaders who downplayed it at least at the beginning attached much higher importance to growth and generation of incomes than to issues of public health and security. However, this is not to suggest that achievement of any of these objectives can be attributed almost entirely to smart leadership. Many causal factors, such as the external environment that is beyond a leader's control, may explain the outcomes.

A War Analogy

Another approach to leadership during the pandemic is that of a war analogy, which was invoked by many world leaders, notably, those from China, France, India, the United Kingdom and the United States, besides the UN Secretary-General. They have likened the health crisis to fighting a war, a clarion call which raises three pertinent questions, namely:

1. Are war leaders different from peace-time leaders and if so, in what ways?
2. Are there any parallels between actions required in a conventional war and those required for tackling the pandemic? and
3. Does the war analogy provide a suitable framework to assess leaders' responses to COVID-19 and their effectiveness in crisis management?

Political leaders in the past have often invoked war analogy. For example, Nixon declared a war on cancer, Lyndon Johnson pronounced a war on poverty in America and George Bush on terror. In the United Kingdom, Churchill, a wartime leader, became famous for his wartime audacity, but as a US army general observes, "over time the legacy of his bold successes would eclipse his audacious failures (e.g. in his Gallipoli campaign) …"(McChrystal et al., 2018, p. 370). Churchill's dominance during the war years, his inspiring oratory and his power of persuasion over Roosevelt to join the war are undeniable, but his impact on domestic policy may have been less significant (Brown, 2014, p.89). The qualities required to win a war may not be enough for a peace-time leader to successfully manage a domestic crisis. Chapter 1 noted that Woodrow Wilson, the American president, kept quiet about the 1918 influenza pandemic during World War I in order not to cause panic among the public, which might adversely affect the goal of victory. More than 100 years later, another American president, Donald Trump, lied and misled the public about COVID-19, not for any national goal but for personal and political reasons.

There are parallels between the war and the current pandemic. Both require advance planning and preparedness, the development of an early warning system, quick mobilization of manpower, equipment and other supplies and production and redeployment to areas of shortages from those of abundance. Other parallels include central and coordinated command, logistics, minimization of collateral damage, enforcement of discipline and boosting of morale and public support. These parallels and corresponding actions under the pandemic can be broadly grouped into:

1. *Preparedness* for emergency, testing and contact tracing, for enforcing isolation and quarantine of infected patients and for surveillance.
2. *Resource mobilization and (re) deployment* of manpower and medical equipment, for example.
3. *National solidarity and economic resilience* (e.g. through spread of known information, mass communications and economic packages).
4. *Discipline, morale and public trust* through transparency and good governance, for example.

Strong war leaders possess such qualities as boldness, audacity and courage since a lot is at stake in terms of loss of human lives, civilians as well as soldiers, not to speak of the possibility of defeat in the event of any missteps or miscalculations. They need to unify the country and win public's trust and cooperation to accept *temporary* restrictions on civil liberties and freedom of movement besides rationing of food and other scarce supplies. Citizens need to be united by war-time leaders in the same way as they need to do to ensure full compliance with public health measures (isolation, stay at home, social distancing and quarantine or strict lockdown).

Clear objectives and end goals need to be defined, and resources mobilized and deployed to defeat the virus. In fact, the personal protective equipment (PPE) used by the medical profession in the current pandemic is a war acronym (In a conventional shooting war, soldiers in the past have also complained about lack of PPEs).

In wars, dependence on external sources of supply could be suicidal. So is the case of the current pandemic as most countries have found out. Germany, China and South Korea are a few sources of essential supplies (e.g. masks, testing kits and ventilators), which most Western countries do not produce, presumably because it is not very profitable to do so.

It is generally easier for a political leader to unite the nation against a common external enemy during war time than behind any other domestic issue during peace. Such qualities of leaders as rhetoric, mass appeal and inspirational character are important to make all citizens fall in line during a war but not necessarily during peace times (see Chap. 4).

Finally, an arbitrary use of state power to curb civil liberties and freedom of movement is seen to be common not only to a war but also to the current pandemic. During war times, people willingly accept *temporary* loss of these liberties and freedoms but object to similar restrictions during a pandemic in peace times.

An Institutional/Behavioural Approach

A third approach to leadership during a pandemic is based on North's theory of institutions. North (1990), a Nobel laureate in Economics, incorporates institutional analysis into economics and demonstrates how institutions and agencies work. He distinguishes between *institutions* and *organizations* and between *rules and players* in developing the theory. Institutions need to be created to monitor the enforcement of rules and regulate human interactions to provide a suitable response to the coronavirus pandemic.

An institution is intended to reduce uncertainty by offering a stable structure to interaction between agents and followers and by reducing cost of transactions. But these institutions can be both good and bad or efficient and dysfunctional as well as bureaucratic and informal. As discussed in the following chapters, many public health and other agencies turned out to be slow, inefficient and dysfunctional during the pandemic.

There are both formal and informal constraints to *certainty* and *stability* of institutions. Formal constraints include laws, rules and regulations. They may also relate to political pressures and interference for narrow partisan ends, which may conflict with such goals as minimizing infections and deaths, keeping social disruptions in check and maintaining people's livelihoods. Partisan and political pressures can take several forms, for example, tampering with the conclusions of scientific agents, political appointments to technical departments and cutting of funds for opponents.

This situation arises because of the existence of a diversity of interest groups and their varying bargaining strengths. Rules and regulations require to be enforced, which will involve costs to administer compliance and establish enforcement machinery/agents to identify violators and to apprehend them. Violation of formal rules carries punishment in the form of fines and jail terms, for example.

There may also be informal societal constraints based on culture, codes of conduct and social mores. Although not necessarily punishable by law, violation of informal conventions is often met with social ostracism and public naming and shaming. Customs and traditions cannot be changed overnight through financial or physical incentives or disincentives. On the other hand, formal constraints can be changed more quickly.

In theory, widespread competition can weed out inefficient firms, agents or institutions and reward efficient ones with proven record of problem-solving and working for the common good (Alchian, 1950). But in practice, competition is rarely ubiquitous, and neither competition nor market/price incentives can correct distortions. As a result, both efficient and dysfunctional agents and institutions will continue to coexist. Such a consequence derives directly from a conflict between political leaders and governmental and non-governmental agents and followers.

The above mismatches may result from a difference between institutions and organizations. Interaction between the two determines the shape of institutional change. Organizations evolve as a result of the incentive structure created by institutions. Inefficiencies occur when both political and economic markets function poorly. Formal and informal rules and constraints are responsible not only for poor economic performance but also for creating/raising uncertainty and instability. Imperfect information and knowledge not only raise transaction costs but also uncertainty and risk, issues which apply equally well to the virus, its new variants and vaccines the impacts of which are not yet fully known (see Chap. 1). Many countries introduced strict and mandatory lockdowns violating which carried punishment. Some countries introduced only *partial* lockdowns whose observance was left to *voluntary* discretion of individual actors.

North's emphasis on human choices, which are guided by imperfect knowledge and customs and beliefs transmitted over generations, is also highly relevant to the people's behaviour and choices during the health crisis. As discussed below, in matters of personal health, individual's risk perception of the disease, inter alia, will determine attitudes and behaviour as well as intention to comply with public health guidelines. Those countries which relied on *voluntary* compliance to wear masks, keep physical distance and get vaccinated faced public defiance, poor enforcement and, as a consequence, large number of cases and deaths. This may have been partly because a top-down approach was adopted by many governments. A bottom-up approach involving local leaders and communities may be more successful in ensuring people's trust and compliance (Baum, 2007; Shet et al., 2021).

Distortions in the enforcement of rules are equally relevant to the control of the pandemic. Even in the most advanced countries, political bodies (political leaders and enforcement agents) often violate contracts, guided as they are by their narrow self-interest, which makes enforcement costly (see below and Chap. 4). The state and its agents enjoy coercive force which they can use to protect their own interests at the expense of those of people and society (North, 1990, pp. 58–59).

The above institutional framework is summarized in a matrix in Table 3.1.

An Integrated Framework

Different approaches to leadership discussed above are not mutually exclusive. Any leader's behaviour and performance will be influenced by his own *traits* and *style* of leadership, by the context and environment in

Table 3.1 A matrix of an institutional framework

Roles and outcomes	*Success*	*Partial success*	*Failure*
Leaders			
Planning & preparedness	Excellent	Moderate	Poor
Strategy design and formulation	Good	Reasonable	Non-existent
Communications, information	Excellent	Moderate	Poor
Agents			
Implementation, rule enforcement	Excellent	Good	Poor
Resource mobilization	Excellent	Good	Poor or nil
Followers	Excellent	Good	Poor
Trust and confidence in leaders/agents	High	Medium	Low
Discipline	High	Medium	Low
Social solidarity	Good	Moderate	Low
Relations between the three actors	Cooperation	Competition	Confrontation
COVID-19 outcomes			
Deaths per capita	Low	Moderate	High
Cases per capita	Low	Moderate	High
Loss of output	Low	Moderate	High
Loss of incomes and jobs	Low	Moderate	High

Source: Bhalla (2021)

which he/she has to operate and by interactions with public and private agents (e.g. public health departments, centres for disease control, pharmaceutical and vaccine producers) as well as with citizens, local communities and the public. The parallels of war and the pandemic, namely advance planning and preparation, mobilization of resources, enforcement of discipline and public's confidence and trust, are also useful indicators of an individual leader's performance in coping with COVID-19. The relations between the following three critical players and their behaviour will determine the nature of outcomes of policy responses to COVID-19.

Role of Leaders

A number of practical questions arise from the above discussion. How should a leader make sure that the agent acts for the common good and in the interest of the leader and not in his/her self-interest? What kind of incentives and disincentives should a leader use to make sure common interests are followed? In a perfect world, the interests of different parties may converge but not in the real world. The experience of four years of the Trump administration in the United States discussed in Chap. 4 demonstrates how the political and economic markets can be distorted by a political leader for his narrow personal goal of re-election. A leader's decisions may be based on a desire to downplay the seriousness of the virus, to avoid lockdowns so that the stock market does not suffer. How does a leader reconcile different social, economic and humanitarian objectives which may be in conflict, especially in the short run?

Strong leadership is needed to take decisions quickly because *timing* is critical in pandemics. COVID-19 crops up in different places and time phases and waves without any advance warning. It has to be fought within a country's own territory as well as globally. The situation has been likened to a forest fire, which can be put out in some places but not in others where it may keep burning as long as there is wood (read, human beings susceptible to COVID infection).

A political leader's main objective is to control the pandemic through advance planning, preparation, central design and strategy for necessary action. It also requires him to play a coordinating role for crisis management. Mobilization of medical and health manpower and other resources would not be timely or optimal unless leaders at state and local levels received clear overall guidelines from the centre. Therefore, it is important to define a clear objective from which a strategy and course of action will emerge. This is particularly important when a health policy is in conflict with economic policy. A leader needs to make sure that too much weight is not given to only one objective at the cost of another.

Change in consumption patterns during COVID-19 to avoid infections resulted in a decline in demand in many sectors. Some countries introduced such health measures as testing and tracing to suppress the virus from spreading. Others (e.g. the United Kingdom) also used fiscal policy to stimulate demand and minimize the economic fallout of COVID-19 which may contradict a government's COVID health policy. A recent UK study shows that a fiscal response to subsidize eating out (Eat-Out-to Help-Out Scheme) by up to 50% in August 2020 cost £850 million and "may have been responsible for between 8% to 17% in all newly detected COVID-19 infections ...." (Fetzer, 2022, p. 1216). Such unintended situations can be avoided through full cooperation between a political leader (a prime minister) and a leader in charge of health policy (a health minister). A leader's other tasks will include offer of other incentives and disincentives to agents and followers so that all are guided by the common objective of controlling the virus.

The leaders also need to formulate common rules and develop suitable institutional structures and machinery for the implementation of policy actions and people's compliance. These rules are not developed in a vacuum: they are the result of bargaining between different parties (trade unions, private sector lobbyists, contractors), with the result that many rules would not be efficient. They might reflect vested interests of special groups which are designed to restrict entry, curb competition and raise transaction costs. Because markets are imperfect, rules and institutions that reflect these interests turn out to be a mixed bag containing some which lower transaction costs, as well as others which raise these costs.

Political leaders are guided by political cultures, their party ideology and affiliation and the experience of their predecessors. Over time, in democratic societies, membership of the party has declined which may suggest that leader is less beholden to the party for his power.[3]

But political leadership is only one of many types of leadership, which is required to fight a pandemic. COVID-19 also requires enlightened and dedicated leaders in public health departments, medical professionals in hospitals, scientific leaders in research laboratories and industry leaders in pharmaceutical and other strategic industries. They need to be guided by the national goal of killing the virus. While the political, health and medical leaders may be driven by this goal, industry leaders are invariably in pursuit of profits and market power. Thus, leaders' behavioural response (like that of agents and followers discussed below) to COVID-19 and multiple objectives is neither uniform nor static. Their behaviour may change over time as they begin to be informed about the nature of the virus and its devastating impact as well as change in agents' and followers' behaviour.

Role of Agents

Different agents may be in conflict. Some agents may pursue their own gains, whereas others may aim at social/public good. It is the job of a committed leader to reconcile conflicting objectives and to persuade agents and followers to fall in line. As discussed in Chap. 4, very few current political leaders have powers of persuasion or charisma, moral stature and commitment to effectively achieve the declared objectives. Other leaders may turn out to be spoilers themselves. In some circumstances, agents may be strong or smart enough to ignore their leaders and continue to pursue their narrow selfish interests.

Governments across the world diverged in their policy choices and actions, which can be traced to political culture and partisanship and the nature of a political system, whether it is democratic or authoritarian and presidential or parliamentary. However, this dichotomy is oversimplified, considering that there are different shades of democracy and authoritarian regimes, and that powerful parliamentary leaders can also be presidential in their behaviour and actions. It is generally believed that an authoritarian regime can more easily impose restrictions (e.g. public health guidelines) than a democratic one because it is not answerable to either people or a parliament. However, actual experiences of responses to COVID-19 discussed in Chap. 4 show that the above assumption is not necessarily valid. Secondly, it is often assumed that authoritarian regimes are opaque and spread misinformation. But we show that democracies have also been at fault in spreading lies and conspiracy theories about COVID-19.

Partisanship between governing and opposition parties is another facet of COVID politics. Some studies show that extreme right-wing political leaders and their parties in Europe supported open economy in preference to the containment of COVID-19 at least in its first wave. On the other hand, left-wing parties favoured the containment and strict enforcement of public health guidelines (Rovny et al., 2022). Policy responses of governments may be based either on science or cultural ideology and value system.[4] Differences in political cultures of Europe and Southeast Asia throw these issues into sharp relief (see Chap. 4).[5]

Several other factors were at work such as public agents' behaviour (e.g. overconfidence and hubris, suspicions about local agents or citizens and the community) and quick fixes without any sound scientific basis. These *internal* factors need to be distinguished from such *external* factors as the existence of a unitary or federal constitution and a centralized or decentralized system of governance in which agents have to operate. As discussed in Chap. 4, the persistence of government failures in coping with crises and pandemics over long periods is more likely to be the consequence of political culture and structure of governance (Gaskell et al., 2020; Jennings et al., 2018).

Ever since North's 1990 seminal work on the role of institutions, scholars in other disciplines, in particular, political scientists, have pursued the same subject in several directions, notably, to answer the question about why governments often fail (Aoki, 2001; Foucault, 2008; Ostrom, 2005). One such direction is centralization under a unitary system of governance. Another is a decentralized structure under a federal system.

A number of scenarios are possible in which both centralized and decentralized systems of government can succeed or fail. Centralization within government may involve an increase in the power of an executive head and his staff at the expense of health and other ministries. Often the federal government may share responsibility for health and other social sectors with lower levels of government (Greer et al., 2022; Steytler, 2022). The federal system may suffer from lack of coordination and slow and ineffective responses to epidemics. But the issues of coordination, collaboration and harmony among different levels of government or between different departments of a given ministry also bedevil unitary systems of government. In a presidential system (e.g. in Brazil or the United States), authoritarian actions may be easier than under parliamentary systems. The latter tends to be slowed down by time-consuming coalition politics or collegial leadership.

Although health departments and centres for disease control are the most relevant public agents during a health crisis, other government departments (e.g. economy and finance) are also critical to determine which economic and social measures would be suitable for relief to suffering businesses and individuals under prolonged lockdowns, for example. Healthy collaboration between economic, finance and health departments of the government is required, but is often missing.

In principle, there is nothing wrong with centralized or decentralized systems per se. In practice, there has been a tendency for leaders and public agents to defend centralization as a tool for good COVID management. Equally, some governments may use decentralization of responsibility as a means of avoiding blame for failure. A precondition of success is central direction and supervision combined with effective coordination and collaboration among different players. In addition, administrative capacity (embodied in qualified, skilled and competent personnel) at different levels of government would be a necessary prerequisite for the enforcement of rules and the implementation of strategies and programmes (Chap. 4 describes many country cases of successes and failures under both centralized and federal systems of governance). Table 3.2 presents a stylized picture of outcomes under different situations of centralized and decentralized systems.

The *size* of a country may matter in addition to the *structure* of government. The issues of central direction, control and supervision would be minimal if there were only a small number of agents. Effective coordination would be a mammoth task in a federal structure with a large number of agents at the centre, state (provincial) and local levels. It would be simpler to minimize transaction costs in the political market if the agents at different levels were from the same political party. Quick and timely response would be more difficult when different parties are in power at the centre and the states. Opposition parties are in competition, whereas the agents of the same party have a common interest to cooperate.

Table 3.2 COVID-19 outcomes under centralized and decentralized systems

Structure of government	*Outcomes*		
	Failure	*Success*	*Indeterminate outcome*
Unitary government/centralized system			
– With central direction, control and coordination of public agents		x	
– Without central direction of public agents	x		
Federal government/decentralized system (sharing of responsibility)			
– Central direction/coordination		x	
– Autonomy to promote local community		x	
Combination of centralized direction and decentralized implementation		x	x

Other political science studies explore what constitutes good governance, the role of the state and markets and the art and technique of government (Deakin & Meng, 2020; Jennings et al., 2018; Lemke, 2007). Governance is defined as "the process through which, in a given entity or polity, resources are allocated, decisions made and policies implemented with a view to ensuring its continued effectiveness." The techniques of government include mechanisms which are used by governments to induce citizens' compliance of rules and regulations.

The literature on regime types (e.g. democratic and authoritarian) deals with their patterns and impacts on economic and social policy decisions. Authoritarian regimes characterized by centralized power and control may be quicker to act than the democratic ones, which require consultations and negotiations between different agents. But they are not effective in maintaining information flows. In the absence of a free press and media, these regimes fail to obtain feedback from their populations about public opinion.

But China and Cuba, two authoritarian regimes, have been far more successful in controlling COVID-19 than many Western democracies despite these limitations. Reasons for this unexpected result are not yet fully understood. A combination of contributory factors may explain the favourable outcome. A democratic government may fail because constitutional or legal norms are ignored or are poorly enforced. Or popularly elected leaders become autocratic and attempt to destroy formal institutions or bypass them. Examples of autocratic leaders in Western democracies have been growing during the past few years. Both these factors tend to damage the flow of accurate information and promote conspiracy theories and fake news.

Political institutions can influence a government's response to COVID-19 (Greer et al., 2018, 2021). Some initiatives may function better under some political systems but not in others. Some may require participation of government as well as private businesses and civil society for their success, especially when they relate to public health. Bekker et al. (2018) compare two voluntary collaborative public health agreements in the United Kingdom and the Netherlands. The former, *Public Health Responsibility Deal* (RD), was initiated in 2011 as an example of public-private partnership between government, business and NGOs. The Dutch programme, *All About Health* (AaH), started in 2012 as a national prevention programme, was intended "to connect small-scale, fragmented and ad hoc health initiatives in society." The British programme was quietly wound down in 2015, while the Dutch was extended.

The two programmes were similar in rationale (i.e. voluntary agreements are more suited for participation of business and civil society than government regulation), aims and objectives (public health improvements through popular participation) as well as content (voluntary public health agreements). But they were also different in important respects, namely the political regimes, nature of organization and system of governance. The RD was a top-down central government initiative, whereas the AaH was a bottom-up NGO initiative.

Bekker et al. (2018, p. 24) explored why the British programme failed while the Dutch survived. Their evaluation shows that the consensual coalition politics in the Netherlands in health matters had greater resilience and acceptance than the more centralized and autocratic British model characterized by "adversarial public-private relations." The authors conclude that the British civil-society organizations either refused to engage or withdrew on the grounds that it was based on a fundamental conflict of interest between business and public health imperatives.

The above examples pre-date the COVID-19 pandemic during which successful examples of local community-based initiatives are few and far between. The dynamics of state-civil society interactions to control COVID-19 show mixed results (see Chap. 4). Investment in local governance and leadership can go a long way in strengthening civil-society groups and grassroots NGOs.

Role of Followers

The followers' behaviour is influenced by several factors (e.g. selfishness or consideration for others' well-being, blind faith in traditions, religious and political orientation and trust (or lack of it) in government and institutions). Above all, it depends on the existence of social capital and social cohesion. Social obligations provide security and insurance against risk and uncertainty which the COVID-19 pandemic has created. Trust and social networks play an important part in the formation of social capital.[6] In societies suffering from social exclusion, *individual* behaviour may be less conducive to *public* health than in cohesive societies.

On an issue such as *personal* and *public* health, people and local communities are at the heart of public and private decisions during the pandemic. The dynamics of people's behavioural responses, their perceptions of risk and uncertainty and fear or lack of information about the consequences of the virus, reasons for people's differential response to given public restrictions, their trust in leaders and government and the different determinants of public trust and confidence are important subjects for further research and analysis. For example, what are the effects of top-down and bottom-up approaches to COVID-19?

Helplessness, which occurs in the face of major threats, can cause a sense of loss of control and a search for others to blame for the disease. Christakis (2020, p. 144) notes that "sometimes, the lengths people go to displace fear, restore a sense of control, and assign blame can be quite baroque." Leaders and public agents need to acknowledge the existence of these negative emotions and sense of powerlessness and find constructive ways in which these feelings can be channelled (Taylor, 2020).

Followers' confidence and trust (or lack of it) in their leaders and public and private agents will determine the outcome of public perceptions about the risk of COVID-19. A good deal of literature exists on risk perception and behavioural response of risk mitigation which is relevant to public's behaviour during the pandemic (Ibuka et al., 2010; Slovic, 1987; Shao & Hao, 2020). Human beings make decisions in the face of perceived risk of COVID-19 health hazard, a lack of information, misinformation, outright lies and conspiracy theories. Their response would be based on information at their disposal, which is generally obtained through the press and social media besides what the public agents, political leaders as well as scientists, public health officials and medical specialists convey. In the final analysis, individuals will rely on their own personal experiences especially in matters like health. Adoption of preventive public health measures (e.g. wearing of masks and social distancing) will depend on perceived levels of risk. The rate of adoption will tend to be higher if the level of perceived risk is higher, as suggested by the psychologists' theory of protection motivation (Rogers, 1975).

Risk perception is determined by socio-demographic factors (e.g. gender, age, ethnicity), education and experience, socioeconomic variables (e.g. income, jobs, economic inequalities) and political environment. For example, health risk perceptions will vary between professionals/experts and public at large which has a very limited experience of similar viruses.[7] Similarly, higher trust and confidence in leaders and governments will lower risk perception than low trust. In many countries, politics and partisanship have a lot to do with the failures to contain and control the virus.

Both democracies and autocratic/authoritarian regimes have managed to control COVID-19. Countries which have no tradition or reputation to achieve quick and positive results (e.g. Greece, Thailand and Vietnam) performed better in controlling the pandemic than many Western European countries with rich economies and robust and well-equipped public health systems (e.g. the United Kingdom and the United States). How should one explain this paradoxical outcome? An answer to this question is discussed below in terms of individual and collective behaviour of leaders, agents and followers.

The followers' risk mitigation behaviour will vary depending on how much value they attach to various determinant factors. Some individuals will enjoy greater foresight and show empathy for others. Others will be motivated and guided by the past and current best practices. Still others may act on the basis of instinct or by trial and error or imitation. As a consequence, individual and collective behaviour will not always converge, but a desired aim of controlling the disease requires such convergence (see below).

Some protective behaviour may be influenced by factors independent of the severity of risk. For example, public worry (an emotional response) about catching the virus may lead to a greater adoption of protective health measures (Khusravi, 2020). It may be reinforced by anxiety of family and friends or by the social context. Low-income groups would fear lack of access to and fair distribution of healthcare much more than the rich ones.

Above all, the followers' behaviour will be influenced by how well or badly government agents (and media) disseminate accurate information and consistent messages about the virus. Previous studies on 2009 H1NI pandemic show how governments, public agents and the media enhanced acceptance by providing timely and accurate information about the virus. In the Netherlands, telephone surveys during the 2009 H1N1 pandemic showed that public decisions to accept protective measures were influenced by the perception of government's sincerity in conveying accurate information. Initial high trust in the government gradually declined as the public started receiving conflicting/mixed messages from different sources (van der Weerd et al., 2011).

COVID-19 has impacted on public trust in different countries differently as discussed in Chap. 4. Cross-sectional studies show that trust varies according to people's risk perception and on the quality of leadership and government. Fukuyama (2020) observes that the success in controlling

COVID-19 depends on whether citizens trust their leaders, and whether those leaders preside over a competent and effective state.

The level of followers' trust in government and public institutions varies over time depending on the capacity and performance of agents. It would rise with good performance and fall with poor performance or failure of government to control the pandemic.

Young people in their impressionable years (18–25 years) tend to display less trust and confidence in leaders and governments than middle-aged and older people. Less educated people trust leaders and public institutions much less than the more educated ones (Boda & Medve-Balint, 2014). Urban residents tend to be more negative than rural residents. Women tend to display less trust than men (Aksoy et al., 2020; Oksanen et al., 2020; Rowe & Calnan, 2006). An empirical study of 750,000 respondents based on Gallup World Polls for 142 countries shows that the heterogeneity of impacts is more marked in low-income countries in which the public considers their governments more untrustworthy and unreliable regarding the pandemic (Aksoy et al., 2020). But similar impact is also observed in many high-income countries. The negative impact is shown to be larger in democratic than in autocratic countries.

Individual and collective human behaviour as well as traditions and failure to change can have both positive and negative outcomes. A high premium on individual/civil liberty and freedom of choice in going to pubs (the United Kingdom) or a failure to wear a mask (the United States), for example, have led to *negative* outcomes. On the other hand, long traditions such as wearing masks (Japan, South Korea) and trust in governmental authority (Japan, Singapore and South Korea) have resulted in *positive* outcomes (see Chap. 4).

Relations Between the Key Stakeholders

The stakeholders can be bound by a common goal, or they may be in conflict. In principle, public bodies are designed to achieve common good, whereas private agents may be guided more by self-interest and profit-maximization. But in the real world, vested interests, strong bargaining power of lobbyists and the elite, besides political partisanship, create imperfections that prevent the realization of the objectives of health protection and human welfare.

An analogy of interaction between a doctor and his/her patient can make this point clearer. A sick patient (a follower) with high fever is advised by his doctor (he/she may be a public or private agent) to take sick leave and stay at home for a few days. He/she has a choice to ignore advice and prolong illness or to listen and accept temporary restriction of freedom to move around as a small price to pay to get well soon. An enlightened patient would invariably heed medical advice in order to get well quickly.

In a wartime situation, leaders, agents, followers act jointly to fight a common enemy, which has not happened in the fight against the pandemic (see Chap. 4). Several factors explain why a leader may fail to provide sufficient incentives to agents and followers to fall in line. He/she may be guided by narrow self-interest, may be incompetent or blinded by hubris to grasp the gravity of the situation. A good leader will find resources to take timely action against the pandemic and provide economic relief to compensate those who are adversely affected.

Good leadership requires legitimacy, commitment and accountability. It may also require such personal attributes as charisma, experience, longevity and communication skills, collegiate style as well as moral stature to command respect and agents' and followers' trust and confidence.

The following are essential prerequisites for achieving success on COVID-19.

1. Consensus and cooperation between leaders, agents and followers.
2. Accurate and timely dissemination of complete information on the nature and severity of the virus.
3. Collaboration between agents and followers to ensure rules enforcement.

Different options are available to a leader when he/she is in conflict with agents and followers. For example, he/she may punish the dissidents and rule by dividing agents against each other. Alternatively, financial incentives may be offered to them. On the other hand, if the agents are more powerful, they may bypass the leader to mobilize followers for a common cause to fight the pandemic when the leaders fail to take responsibility.

Several scenarios of interactions between the three players are possible, which determine the nature of outcomes:

1. There is *full consensus and cooperation among the three players*, a precondition for an optimal outcome of success.

2. *Two out of three players may be in sync but not the third*. There may be competition between them. In this case, the outcome would be indeterminate and ambiguous. This may be a case of partial success or failure.
3. Finally, *if all three players are in conflict*, in which case a negative outcome in terms of high infections and deaths per capita (public health indicators of outcome) or loss of output and jobs (economic indicator) would be a consequence.

The above three situations present a stylized integrated framework, which shows that success and failure to control the pandemic do not lie in the enlightened leadership alone. A coordinated and coherent response of leaders, agents and followers working in unison is required. While leaders' charisma, pragmatism and commitment are important in leading the way, actions of public and private agents to plan and prepare, mobilize and deploy medical and health resources and enforce rules and compliance are equally important.

Enforcement of Rules

The enforcement of rules and guidelines on public healthcare are an essential prerequisite for the control of the pandemic. Invariably, the state and its public agencies are charged with enforcing the rules. But the situation becomes problematic when the state itself is led by political leaders who are either corrupt or promote their own narrow objectives. This raises the transaction costs of enforcement. The followers who have to comply with those rules weigh the costs and benefits of doing so. They may find that the costs far outweigh the benefits when the state and its agents do not work for *collective* welfare but their own. On the other hand, benefits will outweigh the costs when leaders are committed and do not manipulate the system to their advantage at the expense of opposition parties and the followers. In this situation, the followers will respond positively to incentives to ensure compliance. They might even be prepared to accept some coercion and temporary restrictions on their freedom of choice and movement in exchange for protection of their health and well-being.

A second option for enforcement is to select a third party, for example, civil-society groups. They may reduce transaction costs and raise benefits of contracts between the agents and followers only if they are free from temptation of greed and vested interests (North, 1990, pp. 58–59).

The civil-society groups may also be guided by vested interests in the same way as some states are. Therefore, the third-party option need not be superior. The above-mentioned groups may not be independent of the state even in democracies. In that case, a question arises: how to ensure that the state allows them to behave in an impartial manner to enforce the rules. The state enjoys authority over voluntary civil-society groups since many receive public funds to survive, which raises the state's bargaining power. It is possible that the third-party may become subservient to the state with the latter simply banning it from performing such functions as challenging government decisions or mobilizing people to oversee the state's performance so that it does not become Hobbes' *Leviathan*.

The above discussion involves serious policy implications about ***voluntary*** compliance of public health guidelines, which have been tried in a large number of countries with rather poor results.

Outcomes vary between countries and regions because actions and behaviour of the three key players vary. Some leaders are more competent, decisive and committed than others. Similarly, agents' and followers' behaviours are also different.

The different players make different policy choices and take actions depending on their external environment (e.g. institutional arrangements) and their behavioural characteristics. Furthermore, some players may enjoy only imperfect knowledge, especially the followers and agents who may be denied full information about the leaders' intended objectives and policy choices. For example, if a leader's objective is to enrich himself or get re-elected or to help his family and friends to get rich, he would exercise his unlimited power and authority to create unnecessary constraints, which raise transaction costs and render inefficient many hitherto effective organizations. These distortions may increase difficulties of coordination between the key players, and reduce chances of success in the fight against the pandemic.

Some government leaders and agents may base their responses to COVID-19 on science, whereas others may rely more on instinct or conspiracy theories. The issue of the merits of scientific knowledge and its dissemination and those of high technology to control the pandemic are briefly discussed below.

Scientific Knowledge, Information and Technology

The importance of scientific knowledge and technology and their proper use are preconditions for an effective policy for COVID-19. High concentration of science and scientists has led to important breakthroughs including the development of vaccines to cure the virus. Their development in a record time is a tribute to modern science and technology. Yet many populist leaders have condemned science and scientists, which is ironical.

The speed with which the vaccines have been produced has its downside as well. It has sown doubts about their safety in the minds of the public and potential users, leading to mistrust of the vaccines and a perception of a risk of side effects. For example, controversy surrounding AstraZeneca when some patients developed blood clots has had an adverse effect. Many European countries temporarily halted its use, and the US FDA, its approval.

Advanced technology has enabled the application of different types of devices and apps to test and trace COVID-19 patients. Testing enhances a government's capacity to identify the virus carriers. The government needs information to distinguish between those infected with the virus and others who are healthy, which mass testing can provide. In the absence of such information, it may be obliged to resort to indiscriminate quarantines or lockdowns. Testing and tracing can be both complements and substitutes of these more aggressive policy measures (Piguillem & Shi, 2022).

As discussed in Chap. 4, different national strategies and policies have been adopted in response to COVID-19, namely (1) containment, (2) suppression (or zero-COVID), (3) mitigation and (4) non-intervention (or laissez faire). Outcomes varied depending on which policy response was adopted. In the initial phases, leaders and policymakers, who downplayed the existence of the virus, were in the non-intervention mode. They believed in the rational behaviour of individuals to self-isolate and wear masks in public gatherings. As the virus spread, many believed at least initially that containment would be sufficient especially following the development of COVID vaccines. But subsequent exponential spikes of the virus shattered these beliefs. Many countries with limited public health capacity and infrastructure decided to introduce strict lockdowns to buy time to strengthen domestic capacity to cope with the pandemic. They may have also learnt from the success of the 2002 SARS. Other considerations that guided the choice of one strategy or another may include short-term trade-offs between lives and foregoing output, the high cost and limited reliability of testing, and the coercive nature of apps technology and people's negative response to its use in a free society.

The links between scientific knowledge and institutional structures and how pure knowledge is translated into applied knowledge are not always clearly understood. The existing institutional structures influence how pure knowledge is applied, besides the importance of pure science itself. This factor alone may explain variations across countries in the development and application of science and in the acquisition of scientific knowledge. It further highlights the importance of science and technology institutions.

It is a myth to believe that science offers only one clear answer to a problem. A research inquiry may raise more questions than it answers. It may point towards different avenues of research and hypotheses to test. As discussed in Chap. 1, there are many unanswered questions about COVID-19. It may take time and sizeable amount of resources before scientists and medical experts find definitive answers to all of them.

The technology underlying the Pfizer and Moderna vaccine (mRNA) was never used to develop a coronavirus vaccine although it has been used in cancer-related applications. Technological breakthrough for developing the coronavirus vaccine was achieved through public-private partnership and research collaboration across national boundaries: Pfizer, an American company collaborated with the German BioNTech owned by a Turkish immigrant couple.

Despite the above caveats, science-based policy prescriptions are much more likely to succeed in curing COVID-19 than those based on conspiracy theories or ignorance. The latter may be very dangerous.

It is no coincidence that political leaders who followed scientific principles and listened to scientists (e.g. Merkel of Germany, Mitsotakis of Greece and Ardern of New Zealand) were more successful than populist leaders and showmen like Bolsonaro in Brazil, Johnson in the United Kingdom and Trump in the United States (see Chap. 4).

Without political or other biases, an individual would most likely seek accurate information and scientific knowledge on health issues through such sources as (1) official, (2) mainstream media and (3) personal experiences. As noted above, official information is often biased, incomplete or vague. Three types of official government information have been described: (1) *information*, that is, factual statements about COVID-19 which are consistent with the best available evidence; (2) *disinformation*, which is incorrect information but provided in good faith without any intention to deceive; and (3) *misinformation*, which is meant to deceive the public (Newton, 2020). Inaccurate, vague and untimely information offered to the public may lower trust and confidence in government, resulting in adverse effects on compliance.

Non-governmental information is obtained through the mainstream media and the digital social media (e.g. Facebook, Google and Twitter). It would be useful if the media exposed official government misinformation. However, in actual practice, mainstream media is often politically biased and supports or opposes the government.

Finally, people can rely on their own personal experiences about healthcare in the absence of accurate and unbiased official government or media information. Invariably on matters of personal health, judgements are more likely to be made on the basis of personal experiences or those of family members and friends. Agents and organizations as well as political leaders also need to acquire knowledge and coordination skills through different means.

Demand for knowledge acquisition is a function of the level of income, age as well as innate ability and the level of education. Individuals vary in their capacity or ability to acquire and process knowledge. The task of public agents to enforce public health guidelines and lockdowns would become all the more difficult in the absence of reliable information and its dissemination (see Chap. 4).

As many political leaders have likened the fight against coronavirus pandemic to a war situation, it is logical to ask which leaders have been true to their word to behave and act like war leaders? How did other leaders who did not liken themselves to war presidents or prime ministers perform in comparison? These questions need to be answered by assessing their performance in the high-income countries (North America, Europe and Australia and New Zealand) as well as middle-income, low-income and very poor countries in Africa, Asia, Latin America and the Caribbean and the Middle East. These issues of leadership are discussed in Chap. 4 by assessing the actual performance of national leaders, agents and followers.

Notes

1. Interviewed by David Lampton in Beijing on August 16, 2002.
2. For a detailed discussion of the input-and output-oriented criteria and the leadership question in general, see Bhalla (2019).

3. Rovny et al. (2022) discuss the results of a survey of the political parties in the European Union member states plus Norway, Switzerland, Turkey and the UK, which was conducted in June–July 2020.
4. Gelfand et al. (2021) have estimated that countries with 'loose' culture (e.g. Italy, Spain, the UK and the US) have nearly nine times the number of deaths in 'tight' societies. The latter (e.g. Japan and South Korea) cooperate against collective threats more quickly and enjoy higher survival rates.
5. For a discussion of democratic and authoritarian leadership and the issues of party membership and election outcomes, see Archie Brown (2014).
6. For a fuller discussion of such concepts as social capital, social exclusion and solidarity, see Bhalla and Lapeyre (2004).
7. For a review of risk perception studies in relation to COVID-19, see Shao, and Hao (2020, July 25). Confidence in political leaders can slant risk perception of COVID-19 in a highly polarized environment.

References

Aksoy, C. G., Eichengreen, B., & Saka, O. (2020, June). The political scar of epidemics. *National Bureau of Economic Research (NBER) Working Paper* no 27401.

Alchian, A. A. (1950). Uncertainty, evolution and economic theory. *Journal of Political Economy, 58*(3).

Aoki, M. (2001). *Toward a comparative institutional analysis.* MIT Press.

Baum, F. (2007). Cracking the nut of health equity: Top-down and bottom-up pressure for action on the social determinants of health. *Promotion & Education, 14*(2).

Bekker, M. P. M., Mays, N., Helderman, J. K., Petticrew, M., Jansen, M. W. J., Knai, C., & Ruwaard, D. (2018). Comparative institutional analysis for public health: Governing voluntary collaborative agreements for public health in England and The Netherlands. *European Journal of Public Health, 28*(Supplement), 3.

Bhalla, A. S. (2019). *Asia's trouble spots: The leadership question in conflict resolution.* Rowman and Littlefield International.

Bhalla, A. S. (2021, February). *Leadership challenges and the Covid-19 pandemic.* Observer Research Foundation (ORF) Occasional Paper no. 299.

Bhalla, A. S., & Lapeyre, F. (2004). *Poverty and exclusion in a global world.* Palgrave Macmillan.

Boda, Z., & Medve-Balint, G. (2014). Does institutional trust in eastern Central Europe differ from Western Europe? *European Quarterly of Political Attitudes and Mentalities, 3*(17).

Brown, A. (2014). *The myth of the strong leader: Political leadership in the modern age.* Vintage Books.

Christakis, N. (2020). *Apollo's arrow: The profound and enduring impact of coronavirus on the way we live*. Little, Brown, Spark.
Crayne, M. P., & Medeiros, K. E. (2020, August 10). *Making sense of crisis: Charismatic, ideological and pragmatic leadership in response to COVID-19*.
Deakin, S., & Meng, G. (2020). The governance of Covid-19: An anthropogenic risk, evolutionary learning and the future of the social state. *Industrial Law Journal, 49*(4).
Fetzer, T. (2022). Subsidising the spread of Covid-19: Evidence from the UK's eat-out-to-help-out scheme. *Economic Journal, 132*(643).
Foucault, M. (2008). *The birth of biopolitics: Lectures at the College of France 1978–79* (G. Burchell, Trans.). Palgrave Macmillan.
Fukuyama, F. (2020). *The pandemic and political order: It takes a state*. Foreign Affairs.
Gaskell, J., Stoker, G., Jennings, W., & Devine, D. (2020). Covid-19 and the blunders of our governments: Long-run system failings aggravated by political choices. *The Political Quarterly, 91*(3).
Gelfand, M. J., Jackson, J. C., Pan, X., Nau, D., Pieper, D., Denison, E., Dagher, M., Van Lange, P. A. M., Chin, C.-Y., & Wang, M. (2021). The relationship between cultural tightness-looseness and COVID-19 cases and deaths: A global analysis. *Lancet Planet Health, 5*(3).
Greer, S. L., Bekker, M. P. M., Azzopardi-Muscat, N., & Mckee, M. (2018). Political analysis in public health: Middle-range concepts to make sense of the politics of health. *European Journal of Public Health, 28*(Supplement), 3.
Greer, S. L., King, E. J., Massard da Fonseca, E., & Peralta-Santos, A. (Eds.). (2021). *Coronavirus politics: The comparative politics and policy of COVID-19*. University of Michigan Press.
Greer, S. L., Rozenblum, S., Falkenbach, M., Löblova, O., Jarman, H., Williams, N., & Wismar, M. (2022). Centralizing and decentralizing governance in the COVID-19 pandemic: The politics of credit and blame. *Health Policy, 126*.
Ibuka, Y., Chapman, G. B., Meyers, L. A., Li, M., & Galvani, A. P. (2010). The dynamics of risk perceptions and precautionary behavior in response to 2009 (H1N1) pandemic influenza. *BMC Infectious Diseases, 10*(296).
Jennings, W., Lodge, M., & Ryan, M. (2018). Comparing blunders in government. *European Journal of Political Research, 57*(1).
Khusravi, M. (2020). Perceived risk of COVID-19 pandemic: The role of public worry and trust. *Electronic Journal of General Medicine, 17*(4).
Lampton, D. M. (2014). *Following the leader: Ruling China, from Deng Xiapoing to xi Jinping*. California University Press.
Lemke, T. (2007). An indigestible meal? Foucault, governmentality and state theory. *Distinktion. Journal of Social Theory, 8*(2).
Locke, J. (1824). *Two treatises of government*.

McChrystal, G. S., Eggers, J., & Mangone, J. (2018). *LEADERS: Myth and reality*. Penguin Random House.
Medeiros, K. E., Crayne, M. P., Griffith, J. H., & Hard, J. H., II. (2022). Leader sense-making style in response to crisis: Consequences and insights from the COVID-19 pandemic. *Personality and Individual Differences, 187.*
Newton, K. (2020). Government communications, political trust and compliant behaviour: The politics of Covid-19 in Britain. *The Political Quarterly, 91*(3).
North, D. C. (1990). *Institutions, institutional change and economic performance.* Cambridge University Press.
Nye, J. S. (2008). *The powers to lead.* Oxford University Press.
Oksanen, A., Kaakinen, M., Latikka, R., Savolainen, L., Savela, N., & Koivula, A. (2020). Regulation and trust: 3-month follow-up study on Covid-19 mortality in 25 European countries. *JMIR Public Health and Surveillance, 6*(2).
Ostrom, E. (2005). *Understanding institutional diversity.* Princeton University Press.
Piguillem, F., & Shi, L. (2022). *Optimal Covid-19 quarantine and testing policies.* Economic Journal.
Rachman, G. (2022). *The age of the strong-man: How the cult of the leader threatens democracy around the world.* Bodley Head.
Rogers, R. W. (1975). A protection motivation theory of fear appeals and attitude changes. *Journal of Psychology, 91*(1).
Rovny, J., Bakker, R., Hooghe, L., Jolly, S., Marks, G., Polk, J., Steenbergen, M., & Vachudova, M. A. (2022). Contesting covid: The ideological bases of partisan responses to the Covid-19. *European Journal of Political Research.*
Rowe, R., & Calnan, M. (2006). Trust relations in health care—The new agenda. *European Journal of Public Health, 16*(1).
Shao, W., & Hao, F. (2020). *Confidence in political leaders can slant risk perception of COVID-19 in a highly polarized environment.* Social Science and Medicine.
Shet, A., Dhaliwal, B. K., & Bloom, D. (2021, January 8). *We have built them, and people will come: A 'bottom-up' approach for COVID-19 vaccines.* CEPR (Center for Economic Policy Research) and VOX (CEPR's Policy Portal).
Slovic, P. (1987). Perception of risk. *Science, 236.*
Steytler, N. (Ed.). (2022). *Comparative federalism and Covid-19: Combating the pandemic.* Routledge.
Taylor, S. (2020). *The psychology of pandemics.* Cambridge Scholars Publications.
van der Weerd, W., Timmermans, D. R., Beaujean, D. J., Oudhoff, J., & van Steenbergen, J. E. (2011). Monitoring the level of government trust, risk perception and intention of the general public to adopt protective measures during the influenza a pandemic (H1N1) in The Netherlands. *BMC Public Health, 11*(1).

CHAPTER 4

Leaders, Agents and Followers: An Assessment

The initial response to the outbreak of a pandemic has always been denial. National and local governments have always been late to respond and have distorted facts and manipulated figures, to deny the existence of the outbreak.
—Orhan Pamuk, *Nobel laureate in Literature*

The excerpts from speeches below on COVID-19 by political leaders reveal their traits such as commitment and seriousness of purpose besides style of leadership. In an hour of crisis, many leaders were in denial, at times even arrogant and overconfident. Many others were pragmatic and modest, alert and quick to act and serious in their resolve. Still others were an admirable symbol of empathy and honesty towards their people.

> We have it totally under control. It is one person coming from China … It's going to be just fine" (January 22, 2020) …." The Democrat policy of open borders had brought the virus" (end February, 2020); "I did not know people die from flu (March 6, 2020)." "The federal government is not supposed to be out there buying vast amounts of items and shipping, you know we are not a shipping clerk. (March 12, 2020). (*Donald Trump*)

> Britain would soon send coronavirus packing … an option is not to close schools or sporting events but to take it on the chin, take it all in one go and

A. S. Bhalla, *National and Global Responses to the COVID-19 Pandemic*, https://doi.org/10.1007/978-3-031-29521-8_4

> allow the disease as it were, to move through the population, without taking as many draconian measures. (5 March 5, 2020). (*Boris Johnson*)

> We fight neither against an army nor against another nation, but the enemy is there, invisible, elusive and advancing. (March 12, 2020). (*Emmanuel Macron*)

> We are a community in which every life and every person counts. For someone like me, for whom freedom of movement was a hard-won right, such restrictions as are imposed can only be justified as an absolute necessity, which at the moment are indispensable to save human lives. (March 19, 2020) (*Angela Merkel*)

> We intend to go hard, and go early in our response … (March 14, 2020). (*Jacinda Ardern*)

> Frankly, it is not possible to conquer this fight with only the government's power. We are aware that we are causing trouble for the Japanese people, but we also humbly ask for cooperation of each and every person. (February 20, 2020). (*Shinzo Abe*)

> I ask all government organizations to transition into emergency situation rooms that operate around the clock … (March 3, 2020) …. The time is never right for complacency, yet preemptive and transparent quarantine measures combined with the public's voluntary and democratic participation in such efforts are bringing gradual stability. (March 26, 2020). (*Moon Jae-in*)

> This crisis is so big and global that all Indians need to combat the situation with resolve. … Saving ourselves from Covid-19 needs to be the primary priority in our lives. (March 19, 2020). (*Narendra Modi*)

In this chapter, we test the leadership framework developed in Chap. 3 with actual experiences of countries and their leaders, agents and followers. The choice of these key stakeholders is guided by a number of factors: geographical representation, successes and failures as well as government systems (democracies and autocracies) and structures (federal and unitary and centralized and decentralized), severity of transmissions (cases and deaths) and the effectiveness (or lack thereof) with which response measures were introduced.

Selected Political Leaders

The performance of 16 national leaders is assessed below in the light of three main criteria, namely (1) leaders' traits and styles, (2) preparedness and public trust and confidence in leaders and their governments and (3) their relationship with agents and followers.

Donald Trump (United States)

Former President Trump declared himself a wartime president but failed to unite the country against the enemy. He divided states, governors and citizens (Abutaleb & Paletta, 2021; Beschloss, 2018, 2020; Yong, 2020); minimized the risk of the virus; spread misinformation; criticized experts and failed to prepare any plan of action.

He encouraged his supporters to protest against such public health measures as stay-at-home orders. He even raised the issue of the second amendment, which gives the US citizens right to bear arms. His own campaign rallies, where hardly anyone kept physical distance or wore masks, may have caused thousands of infections. In a speech in Tulsa (Oklahoma), he told health officials to slow down testing so that the growing number of cases would be hidden (Wright, 2021, p. 243). He deflected all blame by declaring that "I take no responsibility at all." (Oprysko, 2020). According to two public health scholars, "Trump's astounding incompetence was a political determinant of the US covid-19 epidemic." (Yamey & Gonsalves, 2020).

Trump manipulated scientific/technical bodies such as the Centers for Disease Control (CDC) and Food and Drug Administration (FDA) for political and personal gains. The CDC was sidelined from the White House Task Force on COVID-19. Its scientific contribution was either ignored or contradicted. FDA was forced to grant emergency approval of unproven malaria drug (hydroxychloroquine), which had to be rescinded following widespread condemnation by scientists and the discovery of its lethal side effects on patients.

He disbanded the National Security Council office which was designed to provide early warning. Funding and staff of CDC were also cut. Trump's disdain for public health measures (testing, social distancing and wearing masks) and failure to shut down the economy (by introducing any lockdowns) were politically motivated. He saw major economic disruption spoiling his chances of re-election, which led him to give priority to the economy and the stock market (Béland et al., 2021). Yet, as discussed in Chap. 1, these public health measures recommended by experts were indispensable in the absence of any curative medicine or a vaccine.[1]

Although Trump set up a central Task Force on COVID-19, he did not attend its meetings for several months. He frequently changed its chairmanship. First, the Health Secretary was put in charge. Then he took the centre stage himself, later vice-president Pence and Kushner, his son-in-law, were appointed. These frequent changes did not provide any continuity in decision making, which is essential for a well-planned action. Trump reluctantly invoked a Korean war-time Defence Production Act but refused to implement it, insisting that the private sector would respond. The failure of his leadership led individual governors and the Federal Emergency Management Agency (FEMA) to compete for limited world medical supplies from a few suppliers.

Trump's autocratic behaviour and arbitrary hiring and firing of senior staff out of revenge, failure to admit responsibility for mismanagement of the pandemic and refusal to concede defeat to president-elect Biden and to allow a smooth transition of the new administration had some serious consequences.

To conclude, Trump's performance resembles more a reality TV series on the pandemic crisis than good governance. Biden's victory as the new US president raised hope of correcting Trump administration's failures. However, as discussed below, his early success in controlling COVID-19 gradually started fading in the face of continued resistance, inter alia, by anti-vaxxers and political opponents (most being Trump supporters).

Justin Trudeau (Canada)

Prime Minister of the Liberal Party, Trudeau was a political novice (a school teacher at the time of election) although he belongs to a well-known political family (He is the son of Pierre Trudeau, Canada's former Prime Minister). But to his credit, he surrounded himself with competent Cabinet colleagues and advisers.

Trudeau's early success in managing the pandemic showed leadership. His charismatic appeal and youthfulness stood him in good stead despite his political inexperience. Trudeau explained why government measures, based on scientific and expert advice, were needed. He called upon Canadians to remain calm and united to fight a common enemy. He won the support and confidence of the opposition parties and Canadian public through transparent communications and effective crisis management. A study based on Twitter accounts of Canadian MPs concludes that all the three political parties behaved responsibly and in unison to fight the pandemic (Merkley et al., 2020). Trudeau showed courage to condemn Trump's decision to ban the export of N95 masks to Canada and other countries (Martin, 2020).

Canada's central command structure for COVID-19 consisted of the prime minister, his cabinet, scientific experts and the centralized health system to oversee the work of provinces. The prime minister and his team managed the pandemic well through strict enforcement of public health guidelines.

His close cooperation with provincial governors and the public helped bring about a positive public response to government measures. A survey showed that two-thirds (86 per cent) of Canadians supported government measures as compared to only 62 per cent in the United States. The above favourable opinion remained fairly consistent till the end of 2020 (*Press Conference*, 2020, April 22).

Trudeau regarded people (followers) as the focus of crisis management, which encouraged the public to move in step at least initially (Crayne & Madeiros, 2020). He presented a hopeful vision of Canada, calling for "a better, more equal society." However, critics pointed to the "costly unpreparedness," and lack of transparency in conveying to Canadians the cost of COVID-19 actions and the likely benefits. Trudeau became unpopular over time when the public as well as some members of his own liberal party protested against prolonged lockdowns, besides other coercive measures like vaccine passports and travel restrictions.

One example of Trudeau's participatory leadership is his public recognition of the positive contribution of immigrants to the Canadian health and long-term care systems. He has been described as a transformational leader who motivated people to obey public health guidelines and enhanced their awareness of COVID-19 through regular communications (Farhan, 2021).

His globalist credentials were on display at the second Summit on COVID-19 (Washington DC, May 2022) when Trudeau made a generous financial pledge to Access to COVID-19 Tools-Accelerator (ACT) (see Chap. 6) for the fair and global distribution of vaccines to poor developing countries.

Boris Johnson (United Kingdom)

Like Trump, Johnson undermined experts and bureaucrats. When other leaders were strictly observing "social" distancing, Johnson was busy shaking hands with everyone and holding parties at Downing Street. Nobody can question Johnson's communicative skills, but he did not utilize them to prepare for a crisis. When other European leaders were shutting down non-essential businesses, schools and universities, he carried on with business as usual. He has been likened to Henry V (the wartime king) on stage who does not know how to play the part (Russell, 2020). Zakaria (2020, pp. 80-81) provides an unusual explanation for Johnson's "delayed and botched-up" response, noting that as mayor of London, he panicked at Neil Ferguson's (government epidemiologist's) exaggerated warning about the 2009 swine flu, which may account for his slowness now.

Johnson and his advisers adopted a strategy of "herd immunity," which meant letting the virus spread. A vaccination rate of 60 to 80 per cent of the population is required for the strategy to work, a target hard to achieve in the short run. A Parliamentary inquiry (UK, 2021 October 12) made a scathing attack on the choice of the strategy. Scientists recommended strict lockdown in early December 2020, which Johnson ignored. He allowed large gatherings over Christmas in parts of England, which led to further spike in cases and deaths (Mueller, 2021). But widespread criticism by the scientific community, health services and the public at large forced him to implement the same liberty-curbing lockdown measures as were introduced across the continent.

Johnson may have listened to a narrow group of epidemiologists and scientific "insiders" whose advice was not shared by outsiders. The views of one "outsider," Professor Costello, a public health expert at University College London, make clear the point about the neglect of wider group of public health experts and behavioural scientists in favour of modellers. Many scientists, notably, Sir Paul Nurse, Nobel laureate and former president of the Royal Society, slammed the "shroud of secrecy" about COVID decisions introduced to escape scrutiny (Ford, 2020). Lack of transparency meant that Johnson failed to command the trust of many agents and followers despite his communicative skills.

Despite Johnson's claim that science and politics were kept separate over the virus, scientific inputs and data were manipulated to suit the government's option. In her statement to the House of Commons (November, 2020), Theresa May, the former prime minister, remarked that "figures are chosen to support policy on coronavirus rather than the policy being based on figures." Johnson withheld information from both the public and the parliament.

On several occasions, Johnson defied scientists' call for caution. He declared 19 July 2021 as Freedom Day' in England and lifted all restrictions despite a surge of infections and hospitalizations while the three other nations maintained them. With the rapidly spreading new variant, Omicron, towards the end of 2021, Johnson was forced to reintroduce such restrictions as wearing of masks (but not in schools in England), COVID pass, and working from home.

To his credit, Johnson organized a successful campaign for the development and delivery of a COVID vaccine, AstraZeneca, which reduced hospitalizations and deaths. But as demonstrated in Chap. 2, this success was perhaps too little too late. The death rate in the United Kingdom remained much higher than that of other high-income countries during the course of the pandemic (see Table 2.4).

Frequent U-turns ruined his credibility, which suffered a real blow with the revelations that he and his staff organized Christmas parties at 10 Downing Street in violation of COVID restrictions. Johnson's feeble response to this charge was that "he thought he was attending a work event." When his closest adviser (Cummings) defied public health guidelines with impunity, Johnson defended him. Public anger was an inevitable consequence of his double standards and hypocrisy (Fancourt et al., 2020; Sample, 2022). For the violation, Johnson was fined by the Metropolitan Police, which along with other lapses, finally led to his final downfall and replacement in September 2022.

For his leadership failure, Johnson has been widely criticized by the press, by distinguished scientists and by two parliamentary inquiries. He missed five meetings of the Scientific Advisory Group for Emergencies (SAGE) and was nicknamed a "part-time prime minister" who was "missing in action." His approval rating for handling the crisis had a free fall, from 40 per cent in May 2020 to -6 per cent in July (Newton, 2020, p. 506).

Angela Merkel (Germany)

The German chancellor did not crave for the limelight unlike many other leaders. In an address to the nation (19 March 2020), her mood was sombre and her message one of empathy, solidarity and community spirit.

Modesty and effectiveness were the hallmarks of her crisis management of the pandemic.

She is a scientist who could handle numbers and facts and who did not believe in wild conspiracies. The head of the Institute of Virology at the Charité Hospital in Berlin observed that her sound leadership "comes down to her character—her thoughtfulness and ability to reassure …." (Spinney, 2020). Unlike many other leaders, Merkel did not mix politics and science. She stayed away from partisanship.

Despite falling infection rates in March 2020, Merkel warned that it was too soon to loosen strict public health measures. Her rational, measured and honest statements stand in striking contrast to the hollow rhetoric of populist leaders like Trump and Johnson who simply wished away the virus. Merkel also understood early on that "the more we endure at the beginning of the pandemic and thus push the infection down, the more we serve not only human health but economic and social life." This simple truth eluded many other political leaders.

Merkel's address to the nation announcing restrictive measures met with little political opposition. The measures recommended by her received massive support (Oltermann, 2020; Stafford, 2020). The Chancellor and the Federal Health Ministry closely collaborated with the state and local governments and the Robert Koch Institute, which provides scientific advice. Merkel took the lockdown and related restrictive measures after full consultations with country's leading scientists as well as with all the stake holders at provincial and local levels. However, the second-wave lockdown was delayed due to lack of political unity and the public's growing "corona fatigue."

Her self-discipline, sincerity and selflessness made her popular. Merkel referred to "joint solidarity" in her address to the nation, implying a leader's responsibility and commitment as well as that of the citizens. In an opinion survey about Merkel's performance, a vast majority of Germans believed that she was doing a very good job and could be relied upon in a time of crisis. Her approval rating was 82 per cent and her Christian Democratic Union party, formerly in doldrums, soared in the polls (Marcus, 2020; Ehni, 2020; Sauerbrey, 2020).

But Merkel was not without critics who blamed her for a very narrow epidemiological approach, which underestimated economic issues as well as psychological and social burdens (Feldenkirchen, 2021). Critics attacked her for a slow vaccination rollout on which she did not have much control.

The vaccination plan was decided upon and implemented on an EU-wide basis to ensure equitable distribution of vaccines.

Merkel stepped down in September 2021 after 16 years in power. Her above failings need to be weighed against her strong performance as a scientist politician. A *Nature* editorial (2021, September 16) noted that her "support for science and rigour in policymaking has been transformative—except in climate change," and "scientist Angela Merkel will be a hard act to follow." (Mintrom et al., 2021; *Nature Editorial*, 2021).

Emmanuel Macron (France)

Macron demonstrated global leadership qualities by quickly contacting Trump as the chair of G7 to call for a video conference to prepare a coordinated G7 response, which sadly did not occur. He appealed to the rich EU leaders to join forces to assist worst-hit member states. He called upon G20 to declare a moratorium on African debt. But on the domestic front, like most Western leaders, he failed to take timely action to procure required medical supplies (e.g. testing kits and masks), which exposed the patients as well as medical professionals, nurses and health workers to unnecessary risk of virus infection (Hassenteufel, 2020). He was criticized for a slow rollout of COVID vaccine (Greer et al., 2022).

Macron made a clarion call to arms in March 2020, announcing that nurseries, schools and colleges would be shut down. But the public did not heed the call. With growing "corona fatigue" among the French, Macron had to strike a delicate balance between individual liberties and public health restrictions. With only a year to go before presidential elections, he could not afford to alienate an exasperated public and face an open revolt.

He responded to COVID-19 reasonably well through a centralization of crisis governance and close cooperation with public agents and trusted advisers. He imposed a lockdown and a generous but temporary economic relief package was introduced for businesses and individuals. Millions of workers received at least 80 per cent of normal wages from the state. Between March and October 2020, Macron gave six addresses to the nation to make these announcements and to communicate with the nation. Unlike Trump and Johnson, he was transparent and clear in his communications with the public: he did not spread misinformation.

Despite the above measures, Macron's popularity remained low. How does one explain this paradox? (Sadoum-Kerber & Wahnich, 2022). First and foremost, it may be the French national character. The French public rarely trusts any political leader or government. Second, Macron was somewhat of an outsider in French politics who did not enjoy any unquestioned political support from the right or left. Third, his "superior" attitude and aloofness may have partly explained an adverse public sentiment. His failure to lead by example and strictly observe public health restrictions may also explain public and media hostility. Although he often wore a mask, Macron was also seen shaking hands with supporters and attending large dinners.

During the second wave of the pandemic (end of 2020), Macron announced that the worst of the second wave was over since the infection and hospitalization rates were finally declining. To avoid another lockdown, he eased public health restrictions but not the strict lockdown in force.

During the third wave linked to Delta variant, in July 2021, he took a bold decision to overcome people's vaccine hesitancy and introduced incentives/disincentives (even some coercion) such as "health pass" to enter cafes and restaurants and other public places (*The Economist*, 2021d, September 18). The gamble worked: the health passes became popular with the public and millions of French signed up for vaccination despite some protests against the restrictive measures. This shows that an appropriate balance between a stick-and-carrot approach can enable leaders to change people's behaviour.

Giuseppe Conte (Italy)

Conte, the former Italian prime minister, was a university professor of Law till June 2018, when he became prime minister to head a coalition and technocratic/populist government. His limited political experience may partly explain lack of urgency, seriousness of purpose and failure to quickly prepare a plan of action to control the pandemic. Delay in Italy's response to COVID-19 was caused mainly by Conte's failure to convince regional prime ministers and coalition partners of the need for a *uniform* strategy.

There were tensions between Conte and the provincial governors who consistently fought for greater autonomy. Renzi and his party, Italia Viva, (formed in September 2020) withdrew from the coalition, which led to a collapse of the government in January, 2021, at a time when the country needed a stable government to control COVID-19 and economic recession (Capano, 2020; Ferraresi, 2020; Rubinelli, 2020). Conte's average performance resulted partly from an environment of Italy's proverbial dysfunctional politics and governance. The country's federal structure further limited the constitutional authority of the central government since health care is the responsibility of provinces. North-south divide and inter-party rivalry further made *policy coordination* difficult.

Although Conte was himself partly responsible for underestimating the need for draconian measures, he shifted the responsibility to governors of Lombardy, Piedmont and Veneto, the three worst-hit northern regions. Regional governors were equally to blame for complacency, which is evidenced by the Lombardy Northern League governor's description of the virus as "a little more than a normal flu" in a typical Trumpian style. Two correlation surveys found political polarization between the far-right political parties and Conte's allies (Bull, 2021; Di Cicco & Sensales, 2021).

Failure to develop a coherent and transparent communications strategy also weakened Conte's management of the pandemic. His mixed messages to people and frequent leaks to the press of cabinet deliberations exposed him to criticism from his political opponents as well as the public (de Marino, 2020; Rello, 2021).

But Conte communicated directly with the public and used social media and digital platforms extensively to send reassuring messages. He managed to build a rapport with the followers and strengthened his credentials mainly by changing his leadership style. Within the government, he set up a crisis management team (a personal task force in his Office) to tackle the COVID crisis.

Apart from early lapses, Conte showed total control of the situation like a wartime leader, listened to experts regularly, and appealed to Italians for calm, unity and solidarity. He listened to scientists and experts. His call for discipline and collective solidarity was generally heeded. The Italian public believed that their prime minister was effective in handling the pandemic.

Pedro Sanchez (Spain)

Sanchez heads a coalition government of the Socialist party and the Far-left party (*Unidas Podemos*). He called the COVID-19 spread in Madrid and elsewhere in the country as "the most serious situation the country has faced since the civil war." On 9 March 2020, he confidently announced that "we have a shock plan that we are going to implement as soon as possible ... We have a robust health system." (Royo, 2020). This up-beat statement seriously overestimated the capacity of the health system (which suffered serious financial and staff cuts following the 2008–2009 financial crisis) as well as his own political capital to fight against COVID-19.

He failed to reach out to the opposition for several weeks, which led to serious political infighting between rival parties. He preferred to take unilateral actions, presumably to avoid delays in decision making, being cognizant of the deep political divisions. There was no agreement within coalition partners on the best policy choices: when to impose a state of emergency or a lockdown, for example. Unlike political unity in neighbouring Portugal, which has a socialist minority government, Spain witnessed fragmentation of policy response and the failure of the different parties to agree on a *common* centralized action. Different regions introduced conflicting policies/actions in the absence of any central strategy or plan of action.

Sanchez delegated responsibility for COVID-19 in the post-emergency period largely to regional authorities, having failed to formulate a *national* plan acceptable to different political parties and regional governments.

Sanchez relied too much on a *partial* lockdown (factories, farms and construction work remained open) to the neglect of other public health measures, which failed to contain COVID-19. Eventually, he was forced to impose a national emergency and a *nationwide* lockdown, which had to be extended several times in the face of regular spikes in cases and deaths. To his credit, Sanchez managed to exploit the national emergency to centralize policing and health services which are normally provincial subjects.

He established an inter-ministerial committee to deal with the pandemic. Although the institutional and coordination machinery for action at the federal and provincial levels was in place, he failed to provide any central direction and coordination.

The Spanish citizens trusted Sanchez for engaging them through regular communications. In a poll undertaken in the separatist Catalan region, paradoxically, the respondents gave higher marks to Sanchez and his central government than to the regional one which had handled the pandemic rather badly (*The Economist*, 2020c).

To conclude, Sanchez failed to manage the COVID-19 crisis on three counts: *efficiency* and competence, *transparency* of information and messaging and *public participation* in decision making. Community involvement in public health matters is crucial, but it was completely ignored by both Sanchez and regional governors.

Vladimir Putin (Russia)

Putin's behaviour in dealing with the health crisis was out of character since he preferred not to assume additional powers to oversee the pandemic. In view of his sagging popularity in opinion polls, he may have adopted a risk-averse strategy to put others in charge to avoid any blame for the worsening situation. But in a vast country such as Russia, the only way to effectively implement measures to control the pandemic is to delegate the responsibility to regional governors.

Putin set up special machinery to handle the health crisis, entrusting key role to the health ministry. But it took him full one month to put Moscow's mayor in charge of coordinating the national response to COVID-19. But the role of Russian oligarchs in managing response to COVID-19 was more significant. They took proactive measures such as urging regional governors (including oligarchs) to lockdown cities and regions in which their production is concentrated. They own business empires of steel, fertilizers and other major industries. They have the resources and often own regional airports and other logistical infrastructure, which are crucial for the distribution of medical personnel and supplies. Putin is in holy alliance with these oligarchs (Troianovski, 2020).

At the beginning, Putin downplayed the severity of the pandemic. Only piecemeal measures were adopted such as sealing the border with China (end January 2020), banning of entry to foreigners (mid-March, 2020), and large gatherings. Some regions closed schools. While stay-at-home measure was proposed by Putin himself, he allowed the economy to remain open. When the number of infections dramatically increased, it was Moscow's mayor, not Putin who announced lockdown and quarantine measures. To be fair, on 13 April, Putin warned that the coronavirus situation in Russia was becoming worse (*Moscow Times*, 2020, April 13; Stronski, 2021). He also announced some economic relief measures for those suffering from the impact of COVID-19. But to the frustration of government officials, in an effort to slow the spread of the virus, Putin granted a week-long paid holiday to workers, a measure which backfired. Many Russians went on vacation instead of staying at home, thus spreading infections. Putin introduced other measures as well, namely, more and faster testing and tracing of the infected and their stricter isolation, reducing the number of hours for restaurants and other public amenities to remain open.

It is puzzling that Putin would send medical kits to Italy and the United States in military planes when his own country was so desperately short of medical equipment to cope with the pandemic. One wonders whether it was a public relations exercise or a delusion of a great power. Like Trump, Putin made no national plan to combat the pandemic. This job was left to the mayor of Moscow and other local and regional leaders.

Jacinda Ardern (New Zealand)

New Zealand's young female leader showed remarkable qualities of decisive, collaborative and consensual leadership. These traits were combined with quick action, empathy and respect for scientists and experts.

Adern's initial zero strategy was to be implemented through self-isolation measures, which were soon followed by a strict lockdown (Jamieson, 2020; Mazey & Richardson, 2020; Wilson, 2020). Tourists were shut out, a highly costly decision for a country which depends so heavily on them. An alert system was introduced to regulate the relaxation of restrictions and to decide when and how much to relax.

Ardern appointed an Epidemic Response Committee to monitor and evaluate progress and to adapt to changing circumstances if and when necessary. It also played a coordinating role to provide oversight on participating agents in the COVID response.

She ordered a 20 per cent cut in her salary for six months as well as that of her Cabinet colleagues. Clarity of message, setting of a personal example, empathy with the public and a recognition of their sacrifices won her full support for restrictive measures and almost full compliance by followers. Collective community effort was successfully mobilized through regular sharing of information at daily press conferences and through an official website, posters and Facebook, among other social media.

When infections rose towards the end of 2021 and early 2022 due to Omicron, Ardern reintroduced strict measures while keeping the economy open. But as a pragmatist, she abandoned the zero strategy which is unattainable. With the easing of the COVID situation, she decided to abolish vaccine passes and other coercive measures. She gave high priority to vaccination, an action which achieved a very high rate of success (over 80%).

Ardern's success is attributed to the promotion of national unity, an effective public communication system, regular contact with the public, full enforcement of public health guidelines, healthy cooperation between public and private sectors, and quick adaptation to changing circumstances. She may have also been helped by the remoteness and smallness of her country and a low density of its population.

Shinzo Abe (Japan)

Abe, Japan's former prime minister, presents somewhat of a contrast to other political leaders. He managed COVID-19 poorly although he did take some positive steps such as passing of the state-of-emergency laws and a stimulus package including some relief measures. More than half the public disapproved of his handling of the virus. Governors of Osaka and Tokyo were more popular than Abe for regular TV appearances in which they urged Japanese people to take precautions and adhere to public health guidelines (*The Economist*, 2020a). Abe's declining popularity was partly related to several political scandals at the time.

He did not provide any central direction and coordination. His government was slow and complacent in handling the pandemic. Each prefecture adopted its own strategy at the local level without any central input. Abe insisted on hosting the Olympic Games when two-thirds of the Japanese preferred postponing them for fear of spreading the virus. He pretended normalcy in the hope that the games would go ahead according to schedule (Kato & Yoshimato, 2020).

Although Abe set up a central scientific task force and an expert panel for COVID-19, he did not provide for any mass testing of the population. Only patients with very clear symptoms or those in contact with the cruise ship were tested, which raised the risk of spreading the virus infection through the wider population. Mobilization of medical resources was also poor. Abe's scheme to send each household two masks backfired since many turned out to be either defective or too small.

According to opinion polls, more than half of the Japanese population thought that Abe had mishandled the response to COVID-19. An opposition member of parliament believed that "citizens and the private sector were far ahead of the government." (*The Economist*, 2020b, 2020d).

Unexpectedly, Japan brought infections under control during the first phase in spite of Abe's poor leadership. Much of the credit for this success goes to the public institutions and Japan's citizens (see below).

Moon Jae-in (South Korea)

Moon mobilized the entire government, the nationalized health system and the private sector on a war footing. He was rewarded with a landslide victory of his party in the elections for his success in controlling the virus.

He showed political commitment and made full use of scientists and experienced doctors to undertake advance planning and to prepare a strategy and action plan to control the pandemic. The source of infection (a church congregation) was quickly identified, and appropriate health measures were introduced almost immediately.

A central command unit was established under the prime minister, that is, a Central Disaster and Safety Countermeasures Headquarters with two deputies, the health minister supported by the centre for disease control and the minister of interior and safety, whose task, inter alia, was to coordinate central and local governments.

His crisis management was facilitated by the country's experiences of the earlier outbreaks (SARS and MERS) and the availability of tool kits for mass contact tracing. Moon signed several presidential decrees to fast-track mass testing and expand the production of medical supplies. He learnt lessons from the failed experience of his predecessor (Ms Park) to control MERS in 2015 and avoided her mistakes. He recognized the need for speedy action based on scientific advice and good communication. Nearly half of Moon's presidential addresses (30 January to 8 May, 2020) were devoted to COVID-19 (Lee et al., 2020).

Moon frequently emphasized the need for popular participation, transparency and timely communications with the public, which ensured the full enforcement of public health instructions and guidelines (Fisher & Sang-Hun, 2020; Moon, 2020; Park & Chung, 2021).

Xi Jinping (China)

Xi Jinping provided centralized control and direction to provinces and local institutions (e.g. resident committees property management companies and homeowners' associations), as soon as he learnt about the coronavirus in Wuhan through whistleblowers.[2] Two Yale scholars observed that the initial response of local authorities was "prompt albeit not without error …" (Roach & Shan, 2020).[3]

He stressed the need for prevention and control and for "putting people's safety and health" at the centre of all efforts (*People's Daily*, 2020a,

January 21). He also “demanded better communications with the World Health Organization, related countries, as well as Hong Kong, Macao, and Taiwan to join efforts to curb the spread of the virus.” (*People’s Daily*, 2020c, September 8).

Despite initial protests and anger in China, Xi emerged stronger by controlling the virus quickly as well as restoring economic growth. An American academic (who lived in China during the outbreak) noted that “surprisingly Xi was poised to politically profit from the deadly outbreak both at home and abroad.” (Reilly, 2020).

Sensing a global political vacuum, Xi decided to sell desperately needed personal protective equipment (PPEs) to France, Germany, Italy and Spain and donated it to all the poor African countries. China also donated ventilators and masks to New York city. Critics of China may be cynical enough to say that it is a public relations gimmick (in which all countries indulge regardless of political system), but the fact remains that China is the only country which can meet a real demand at a short notice, being the world’s largest manufacturer.

Xi decided not to change his zero-COVID policy (unlike Australia and New Zealand which have abandoned it) despite high economic and social costs. Xi believed that China is engaged in a war against COVID-19, which can be won through perseverance, science and party spirit. As few Chinese have natural immunity, abandonment of the above policy and associated control measures may carry greater risks (see Epilogue).

His heavy handedness in implementing zero-COVID policy triggered protests in the country. Regardless, Xi’s position remains unchallenged as witnessed by an unprecedented third term for him approved by the Party Congress in October 2022.

Xi has been a steadfast spokesperson for global cooperation on COVID-19, a position he reiterated at the UN General Assembly in his address in late September 2020. However, public pronouncements may be somewhat misleading. Rivalry between the United States and China has led Xi to become more nationalistic and less globalist in the midst of growing geopolitical tensions.

Nguyen Phuc (Vietnam)

President Phuc (earlier prime minister) was one of the first to act quickly against COVID-19. He recognized that *timing* was critical since Vietnam shares a border with China where the virus started. He appealed to the population to fight the pandemic like an enemy. He committed his government to sacrifice short-term economic benefits for the protection of public health. He issued a decree (27 March, 2020) declaring that saving human lives would be the top priority of his government. In his address to the nation, he urged that "every business, every citizen, every residential area must be a fortress to prevent the epidemic." Well aware of the weak health care system and limited resources, he sent out soldiers, teachers, students and business people to support health care workers (Ha et al., 2020; Nguyen et al., 2021; Trevisan et al., 2020).

He mobilized a successful people-driven and community-driven campaign which helped raise people's trust and confidence in their leader and the government. He strictly enforced two strategies: (1) "three in advance," that is, identify, proactively prevent and plan and (2) "four on the spot," that is, onsite resources, leadership, facilities as well as logistics.

Phuc gave high priority to the development of a vaccine despite resource constraint and technology limitations. He directed the ministry of health to identify research partners, the types of vaccines to be imported and the priority groups for vaccinations as a matter of urgency.[4] However, initially he underestimated the importance of launching a vaccination campaign, which led to an outbreak of COVID-19 in Ho Chi Minh city in late 2021. It was his successor, the new prime minister, Pham Minh Chinh, who launched a successful vaccination campaign by importing adequate quantities of vaccines. The campaign enabled Vietnam to attain the second highest vaccine rate (92%) in the world (see Chap. 2, Table 2.4).

Phuc and the former vice-premier are rumoured to have been embroiled in the COVID-19 test-kit scandal (involving Viet A Technologies Company) in which party officials were bribed to supply overpriced test kits to hospitals (Strangio, 2022, June 7).

He set up a task force to coordinate his government's response to COVID-19. Several ministries, press, media and TV were represented in it. Phuc himself appeared daily on TV to give updates on the COVID-19 situation and to explain the rationale behind the restrictive measures. He set up a National Steering Committee chaired by the Vice-prime minister besides a committee in each ministry and province to ensure quick dissemination of information and full compliance with public health guidelines.

Narendra Modi (India)

Another populist leader in the mould of Trump, Johnson and Bolsonaro, Modi initially downplayed the seriousness of the health crisis. But under pressure from the WHO and seemingly out of panic when the cases grew exponentially during the first wave, he abruptly decided to lock down the country, which was a monumental decision for any political leader, but more so for a poor country which could ill afford a high economic cost. But a hard choice had to be made between health of the people and that of the economy, given the poor or non-existent local health infrastructure and primary health care facilities.

An unintended consequence of the strict lockdown was a significant loss of jobs and livelihoods and subsequent mass movements of migrant workers (Roy, 2020). Modi and his government failed to foresee and prepare for serious dislocations and hardships of poor migrant workers. This unfortunate situation could have been avoided through careful planning.

Modi launched the Prime Minister CARES Fund for Citizen Assistance and Relief in Emergency Situations, which attracted substantial donations from industrialists, philanthropists, religious organizations and even ordinary citizens. He ordered a cut in his own salary and that of his Cabinet colleagues for six months to show solidarity with the suffering population. Setting of a personal example may have enhanced his popularity.

He set up a central command consisting of the health minister and the All India Institute of Medical Research (AIIMR), which provides expert advice. However, policy measures such as the prescription of unproven (and even dangerous) drugs such as hydroxychloroquine were not based on scientific advice.

Modi regularly communicated with the public about COVID-19 and made it a society-wide *people-driven* attack on the virus (Sambaraju, 2022; Trivedi, 2020). In his communications with the people over TV and radio broadcasts, he developed personalized relations with his audiences. He provided information and instructions about their compliance. The government's decision to extend the lockdown by two additional weeks was taken following close consultations with all state chief ministers who showed political maturity by relegating partisanship. Even those states which are run by opposition parties supported the extension.

Modi and his government were applauded for a massive vaccination drive. But with a new wave of shockingly fast infections in April 2021, these efforts seemed too little too late. The vaccine drive had to be slowed down in the face of shortage of vaccine supplies. His complacency and permission to hold a large Hindu religious festival without any precautions, besides holding massive political rallies for state assembly elections, were failures of judgement, a sense of overconfidence and a lack of foresight to anticipate the new wave. Modi lost popularity for failing to take timely action to prevent or at least contain the new wave. But his fortunes improved once again when his administration managed to vaccinate a remarkable number (one billion) out of 1.3 billion people.

Jair Bolsonaro (Brazil)

Bolsonaro, dubbed as "Trump of the Tropics," downplayed the pandemic and questioned its very existence when he stated: "It's just a little dose of flu … we are going to face the virus like a man, dammit, not like a little boy." An ideologue full of hubris, his Macho instinct and right-wing political credentials undermined the efforts of his own government's fight against the pandemic. Twice he threatened to fire his health minister, who was far more popular for the management of the health crisis. Two resigned in quick succession for disagreeing with the president over the right strategy to control the pandemic.

He clashed with provincial governors over reopening of the economy. His call for reopening churches contradicted scientists' recommendations. He also mounted a legal challenge to governors' quarantine orders (Blasberg, 2021).

Bolsonaro opposed vaccination and sowed doubts about it in people's minds (*The Economist*, 2021c). His indifference to the gravity of the pandemic in the face of new variants (e.g. Gamma which originated in Brazil), lack of empathy and disdain for public health restrictions are strikingly similar to that of Trump. His messaging and communications were also mixed and contradictory (Melo, 2020; *The Economist*, 2021a, March 27). He attended mass rallies of his supporters despite having been tested positive of the virus. His words and speeches influenced his followers' behaviour in defying the public health restrictions. A study (using a social distancing index at the municipal level) shows that Bolsonaro strongly influenced his supporters in many localities against compliance with social distancing measures (Ajzenman et al., 2020).

Bolsonaro's popularity plummeted following continued mishandling of COVID-19, supreme investigations of corruption and calls for his impeachment. In October 2021, a Brazilian Senate committee charged him for crimes against humanity for mishandling COVID-19, for causing more than 300,000 deaths through opposition to public health measures such as vaccination and mask wearing and for promoting ineffective drugs like hydroxychloroquine. According to polls by the Datafolha Institute, in July 2021, his disapproval rating rose to 51 per cent ahead of the 2022 elections, which he lost (*The Economist*, 2021b, October 23).

Cyril Ramaphosa (South Africa)

Ramaphosa declared "a national disaster" within two weeks of detection of the virus. He was decisive and bold in announcing a nationwide lockdown. He acted quickly and listened to expert advice. He may have learnt from the failures of his predecessor (Mr. Mbeki) to control HIV/AIDS. His message to the nation was one of the most detailed and well thought-out among world leaders. It described the lockdown measures which were backed by the utilization of the army and police to ensure enforcement. He elaborated on stay-at-home, self-isolation and hand-washing measures and why they were required.

He promptly closed the country's borders and imposed lockdown, which bought time to expand health capacity, increase care beds and build field hospitals. He outlined a national COVID strategy and plan of action, which consisted of five alert levels depending on the differences in the extent of virus spread and the capacity and readiness of the health sector. It was based on preparations, primary prevention, lockdown and primary surveillance. Ramaphosa was forced to announce a partial lockdown in June 2021 following a new wave of infections (Sekyere et al., 2020).

His timely action and efficient management of COVID-19 and regular communication with the public were widely praised. He ensured that each minister and department was involved in the government response to COVID-19. WHO delegation to South Africa lauded its response structure as effective and successful (Ramadan & Talisana, 2021).

Ramaphosa established a central structure to coordinate the national response: An Inter-ministerial Coordinating Committee, an Emergency Operations Centre and the National Coronavirus Command Council. The last coordinated action plans for the nation, provinces, districts and metropolitan cities. He also established a Ministerial Advisory Committee to advise him and the health minister.

He introduced very generous economic support and social relief measures (amounting to about 10% of GDP), which provided temporary relief to the poor who willingly cut down spending to minimize economic hardships. The package of support included R20 billion for cash-strapped municipalities, which significantly contributed to the pandemic management (Republic of South Africa, 2021, p. 46). This timely relief made compliance with lockdown measure much easier. It may have also restored people's trust and confidence in the president and his government.

A Typology of Leaders

The above sample of 16 world leaders is admittedly too small to permit any generalizations or draw any firm conclusions. Yet, the performance of these leaders allows at least a rough classification into the following categories:

1. *Populist showmen* (Trump, Johnson, Putin, Modi, Bolsonaro) whose divisiveness and self-promotion may be at the cost of greater good.
2. *Selfless, modest and pragmatic leaders* (Merkel, Moon) whose lives are governed by a sense of discipline, duty and selflessness. Their individual interests are likely to converge with the national interest.
3. *Bold democratic leaders* (Ardern, Macron and Ramaphosa) who are courageous, sometimes hasty and are prepared to take risks.
4. *Inexperienced leaders* (Conte, Sanchez and Trudeau) who can rise to the occasion in an hour of crisis.
5. *Dictatorial leaders under planned systems* (Phuc, Xi) who are not afraid to take drastic actions during crisis. Though not popularly elected, they also need political legitimacy and acceptance by their populations.

The above categories are not watertight. A given leader can belong to more than one group. For example, a modest leader like Merkel may also be quietly inspiring although less charismatic and bold than Macron. Personality traits vary among leaders. Some are more dynamic, responsible, driven and politically committed than others. Some are ideological and politically to the extreme right whereas others are less so.

There are different ways in which a typology can be presented. Leaders can also be grouped as those who were pandemic prepared, took action through early detection, and others who were totally unprepared and downplayed the pandemic, failed to mobilize medical resources and mass testing and tracing. They may also be classified as *globalists* who seek multilateral cooperation to fight COVID-19 (e.g. Macron, Merkel and Xi) and *nationalists/populists* (e.g. Bolsonaro, Johnson, Modi and Trump) who are antiglobalization, protectionist and inward looking.

Public and Private Agents

Agents' role in a pandemic is to enforce public health rules and restrictions, mobilize and deploy medical and health resources and to provide adequate, regular and transparent channels of communication to the public. Both government and non-governmental agencies played their part in national and local responses to the pandemic. But their role was not sizeable enough to make up for leadership and government failures.

Public Agents

A few country examples of public agents are assessed below.

In the *United States*, different government departments failed to mobilize medical/health manpower and other resources in time. State governors and mayors had to compete with FEMA for scarce but critical medical supplies. Centers for Disease Control (CDC) failed to trace passengers returning from China due to an outdated data reporting system and technology. It made early mistakes in testing and tracing. Its other lapses include failure to communicate regularly with the public; breakdown of its communications with the states; combining of data from antibody tests with that on diagnostic tests, which is a breach of standard practice; and yielding to political pressures and unscientific theories to withdraw public health guidelines on testing, wearing of masks and social distancing. A litany of complaints about CDC included encouraging the use of unvalidated treatments under political pressures, technical blunders, use of old technology and contradictory messages to the public (Guharoy & Krenzelok, 2021). In a blistering letter, a former CDC director wrote to the then-Director, Robert Redfield, that the "CDC had been a colossal failure in its Covid-19 response" and that "the agency had gone from gold to tarnished brass." (*Science*, 2022). The development of a national strategy and plan of action was complicated by the existence of thousands of state, local and tribal health departments, each guarding its turf. Party politics at different levels of government affected COVID-19 response (Patterson Jr., 2022).

Although the US administration and private vaccine developers (Operation Warp Speed) succeeded in quickly developing vaccines, the government failed to invest adequately in storage, transportation and staff training, crucial requirements for their distribution and delivery. Consequently, logistical difficulties resulted in an initial slow rate of vaccination. The American vaccination rate is slightly lower than the Indian. Vaccine hesitancy persists: the unvaccinated are largely responsible for a rise in cases of infections and hospitalizations.

The COVID situation improved under Biden, but vaccine and mask resistance remained the key obstacles. For example, Biden's vaccination mandate was suspended by a federal judge. Persuasion failed to change people's minds: the administration was reluctant to use coercion in the face of widespread opposition. Slow rate of booster shots and shortage of testing facilities made matters worse when more infectious Omicron spread (*The Economist*, 2021b). Former members of Biden's Covid Advisory Board mention other missed opportunities: lack of a comprehensive reporting system for at-home tests, lack of improvement in indoor air quality, failure of the Congress to appropriate federal funds for COVID-19, limited capacity for data collection and analysis to track new variants and poor response to long COVID (Emmanuel et al., 2022, October 19).

The *United Kingdom* did not set up a new central command structure for COVID-19, which may be partly because the prime minister, the health secretary and the chief medical officer were tested corona-positive soon after the lockdown measures were introduced. Cabinet takes decisions through COBRA, which discusses national emergency issues. A highly centralized National Health Service (NHS) failed to provide clear central guidance or adequate number of PPEs to health care staff, or training health care workers. The Institute of Public Policy Research believed that the NHS was too fragmented to cope with such pandemics (Thomas, 2020).

Under attack for slow testing, the government gave overinflated estimates of testing kits and failed to communicate the difficulties—reflecting a tendency to hide bad news, which also occurs in democracies. It demolishes the generally held view that only authoritarian and poor developing countries hide ugly facts. Testing and tracing were discarded too quickly during the early phase of the pandemic. The government missed several opportunities to participate in a European Union bulk-buying scheme.

The laissez faire policy of sending English children back to school without any mask or vaccine requirements and lifting of all restrictions to keep the economy open significantly raised virus infections. But cases in Scotland among school children have been falling because when a child tests positive for COVID, all the siblings must stay at home, not just the tested child as is the case in England. Children have to wear masks in schools unlike in England. Excessive reliance on high rate of vaccination did not help in the absence of public health measures, partly because early injections in the United Kingdom were those of AstraZeneca, which is less effective against the Delta and Omicron variants.

The above two examples of public agents clarify what can go wrong if leaders and health institutions fail to cooperate. In the United Kingdom, relations between these key players were *conflictual* partly for lack of proper consultations with the four nations and local governments (Majeed et al., 2020).

Germany started preparations early and introduced persistent testing and tracing as well as isolation and quarantine. Measures were promptly undertaken to procure protective equipment through imports and domestic production for which a new division was created in the Economy Ministry. The federal government provided central direction and coordinated regional and local health care bodies across the 16 states. However, during the second wave hospitals and health clinics were under stress and suffered from shortages of protective gear and ICU beds. Public agents (e.g. regional governments, health agencies and district administrators) failed to provide an app to trace infected people, expand testing labs/kits and supply adequate number of medical masks. Too much reliance was placed on lockdowns to the neglect of other public health measures.

Politics was partly responsible for the failure to provide a more robust response. Political and electoral calculations and regional and local interests during the election year of 2021 came to the fore partly as a result of "pandemic fatigue." (Gaskell et al., 2020, p. 530; Schumacher, 2020). Germany's vaccination rate (especially of booster shots) remained quite low, and the government faced stiff opposition to strict measures by a coalition of strange bedfellows.

In *France*, medical resources could not be rapidly mobilized due to frequent lockdowns and disruption of global supply chains, which prevented the procurement of spare parts. But retooling of industry was undertaken ingeniously, especially in older textile centres in northern and western France, as was the use of re-equipped high-speed trains to move sick patients to remote areas. Army's Military Medical Service and all its departments were involved in the fight against COVID-19 (Pasquier et al., 2020). France launched "Operation Resilience," which consisted of such actions as massive new investments in the health sector. Despite high vaccine hesitancy and initial slow vaccine rollout, France has achieved one of the highest vaccination rates, the credit for which goes to the president's decision to introduce a vaccine pass and public agents' competence.

In *Italy*, as in the United Kingdom, there were insider "experts" to advise the government and "outsiders" who often disagreed on the course of action to control the pandemic. At the beginning, the central government was totally unprepared: national lockdown was imposed on 11 March 2020, four weeks after the first case was detected. Competition between a coalition government in Rome and regional governors, and a blame game played by different political parties were the major reasons for slow crisis response. In Italy, the regional presidents are elected following a presidential system unlike the national parliamentary system, an asymmetry which may favour regional presidents (who enjoy popular legitimacy) to act autonomously (Capano, 2020; Vicentini & Galanti, 2021). But the Italian Health Ministry played a positive role in checking misinformation and conspiracy theories about COVID-19 (Lavari, 2020). Italy was the first European country to introduce a Green Pass for all workers. It made vaccination mandatory for those over 50 following a sharp rise in infections at the end of 2021.

Spain's weak coalition government wasted time in internal infighting at the onset of COVID-19. Despite the mounting cases of infections, public gatherings were allowed, the state of emergency was declared too late and the lockdown was largely ineffective since the government made too many exceptions. The shortage of testing kits did not allow timely mass testing and tracing. The medical department in Madrid underestimated the magnitude of infections, which led to long delays in working out a coping strategy. Government agents were complacent and relied heavily on a very high rate of vaccination. Despite a spike in Omicron cases, new restrictions (e.g. a COVID pass) were not introduced during the holiday season.

The *Russian* federal government's response remained slow despite rapid spread of the virus infection. The inadequate health care services and hospital capacity led regional governors and rich oligarchs to step in to finance the building of new hospitals, the expansion of bed capacity, and purchase of CT scanners, ventilators and PPEs for hospitals. Fewer than half the number of regions had introduced any COVID-19 restrictive measures. The government also failed to overcome high vaccine hesitancy (over 40%), which partly reflected mistrust of the government and Sputnik V vaccine which was hastily and secretively approved (Hopkins, 2021).

The governments of *Australia* and *New Zealand* controlled COVID-19 through strict lockdowns, isolation and travel bans. New Zealand set up an Epidemic Response Committee to monitor and evaluate progress and to oversee agents participating in the COVID-19 response. Army was deployed to help manage the quarantine and shut out foreign tourists. An alert system was introduced to decide when and how much to relax restrictions. But quarantine for international passengers and security of quarantine hotels were poorly enforced, which may partly explain the spike in infections. New restrictions were imposed to check Omicron cases at the end of 2021.

Australia restricted travel and enforced isolation until vaccines were widely available. It gave priority to elderly people for vaccination before lifting public health restrictions and reopening of the country. Both governments were forced to abandon its erstwhile "zeroCOVID" strategy as it was no longer enforceable with Omicron and its sub-variants reinfecting already fully vaccinated people. A recent review (Shergold et al., 2022, October 20) stressed a lack of transparency in decision making, an imbalance between health and economic outcomes as major government lapses.

Japan managed the pandemic well thanks to an efficient and well-funded healthcare system and compliant public. Japan enjoys health care readiness and government efficiency. The Health Department urged people to avoid crowded places and close human contact as well as dinner parties serving alcohol. Notwithstanding, the government made several mistakes. For example, citizens were allowed to return home without quarantine, a state of emergency was declared late and was prematurely lifted, economic activity was reopened too quickly, and domestic tourism was subsidized to boost the economy.

In general, the record of most Western governments in the management of the COVID-19 pandemic is poor. Most failed to coordinate policy interventions. Generally, the Nordic countries except Sweden performed much better, thanks to close collaboration between different levels of governance and decentralized decision making combined with *consensual* central leadership (Christensen & Laegreid, 2020). Sweden's response was less successful due partly to lack of central direction and coordination, low governance capacity at the regional and local levels, poorly trained staff, limited communication between different agents and delegation of total control to experts (Pierre, 2020). Unlike other Nordic countries, Sweden (and a few other countries as well) adopted a more liberal policy to maintain economic normalcy at the cost of a much larger number of infections and deaths. Its policymakers valued economy more than people's health and human lives, which involves normative value judgements. According to the IMF data, Denmark's real GDP decline in 2022 was identical to that of Sweden, but its mortality rate was much lower. In 2021, the growth rate for the two countries was almost identical, whereas Denmark's mortality rate was one-third of Sweden's (Chap. 2, Tables 2.5 and 2.7). One wonders whether the followers ever forgave government leaders for choosing economic over human health and ignoring the social contract, which involved enormous loss of human life.

On the other hand, a large number of countries were prepared to forego economic benefits in order to protect human lives. Using data for early waves of COVID-19, Balmford et al. (2020, p. 525) estimate "price of life" which varies enormously, "ranging from as low as $100,000 (the US, UK and Italy) to in excess of $1 million (e.g. Denmark, Germany, New Zealand, and Korea)." The enormous differences may be due to a host of factors such the underreporting of cases, poor testing and tracing and the timing of covid restrictions and their poor enforcement.

In Eastern and Central Europe also, most countries recorded some of the highest death rates in the world despite low infections and death rates in the early waves (see Chap. 2). Reasons for such poor results are manifold, in particular, lax rules of public health guidelines and their poor enforcement, large campaign rallies during regional elections, failure of the leaders to listen to scientists and experts and low vaccination rates (Kottasova, 2021, March 1).

On the other hand, governments in Asia and the Pacific generally performed much better by adopting different approaches to the control of COVID-19. *China* took draconian measures as did *South Korea*, though to a lesser extent, but *Japan* was very late in introducing social distancing and self-isolation. *India* imposed a strict lockdown and tried to enforce it given all the difficulties which were not foreseen (e.g. mass movement of migrant workers). *Hong Kong*, *Singapore* and *Taiwan*, which are much smaller, adopted travel restrictions, isolation and quarantine. They were quick to act very early because of their past experience of SARS and their proximity and close links to China. *Taiwan* rationed the distribution of surgical masks and regulated their price.

China, South Korea and Vietnam were particularly successful in controlling the virus until the Omicron wave at the end of 2021. In *China*, a large network of local institutions, resident committees (or neighbourhood-level government bureaucracy), property management companies and homeowners' associations were mobilized. Homeowners' associations and government employees were put in charge of tracing the infected persons, enforcing the wearing of masks and taking the temperatures of residents entering and leaving compounds (Ren, 2020). However, the ferocity of Delta and Omicron sub-variants (BA.4 and BA.5) and subsequent spike in cases has ruined any chances of eliminating the virus, a policy adopted by the Australian and Chinese leaders (which has now been abandoned; see Epilogue) as well as those of New Zealand and Singapore. But Asia caught up on rates of vaccination after a slow start. Asians generally believe in the vaccines as the only real cure for COVID.

The Chinese zero-COVID policy has been criticized in the West. But it was very successful in keeping infections and deaths low (see Epilogue). A Chinese scholar based at Columbia University (Wei, 2022, December 6) has made a rough estimate of the costs and benefits of COVID restrictions. He concludes that China's containment policies may have saved at least a million lives with a statistical value of $1 trillion, which is far more than $384 billion in lost GDP assuming a decline in China's growth rate in 2022 by 2.2 per cent. Of course, the exact value of the cost will depend on the value policymakers assign to freedom lost as well as loss in terms of mental stress, decline in educational attainment and a possible increase in domestic violence.

In *South Korea*, although implementation was delegated to the local level, central and local authorities closely collaborated. The government purchased the bulk of the total supply of masks (Lee et al., 2020; Park, 2021). It mobilized the private sector to produce medical equipment and supplies. A coordinated network of public health centres at the district level, which regularly transmitted information to the centres for disease control and prevention; timely hiring of epidemiologists to do mass testing; the adoption of intrusive measures (e.g. the use of drones and app) and an effective communications system to inform the public about COVID-19 were among the other policy responses, which explain South Korea's success. In early 2022, the government was compelled to change course following a substantial rise in Omicron infections. It could no longer cope with looking after all patients. Those who had tested positive were sent home to look after themselves.

Vietnam, a communist/socialist government, was among the very successful countries to control COVID. It achieved excellent results despite being relatively poor with weak health care system. The Emergency Epidemic Prevention Centre was activated as soon as the first case of COVID-19 infection was identified. The government introduced several measures to check the spread of the virus, for example, land-border controls and airport screening of incoming passengers; quarantining infected patients; social distancing; school closures; cancelling festivals; and requisitioning military buildings, university halls and dormitories as quarantine camps. An official website was created for information campaigns. A mobile app was launched to trace high-risk cases. Declaration of health status and travel history of people through the app were made compulsory.

India classified the districts as red, yellow and green zones depending, inter alia, on the number of cases. Some states used local self-governments (*panchayats*) to conduct house-to-house screening. The public agents at the federal and state levels became complacent when the virus infections declined, probably through wearing of masks and strict enforcement of public health restrictions, police monitoring and fines (Frayer, 2021). Failure to cope with new Delta and Omicron variants can be attributed to initial shortages of vaccine supplies and very low rates of vaccination. Slowness in placing orders for vaccine purchases, inadequate investment in expanding manufacturing capacity and challenges of coordination in distributing vaccines from factory to vaccination sites were some of the major lapses. But by the end of 2022, India managed to significantly raise the vaccination rate, which is now comparable to that of other countries (see Chap. 2, Table 2.4).

South Africa imposed strict lockdowns, deployed army and police force, set up mobile COVID units and trained community health workers in case detection, testing and tracing (Stiegler & Bouchard, 2020). Lockdown and stay-at-home measures considerably reduced people's mobility, which played an important role in reducing the initial rate of new COVID infections (Carlitz & Makhura, 2021). Effective coordination between different levels of government and participation of local municipalities also played their part. But low rates of vaccination, shortages of PPEs, lack of testing facilities and variations in virus infections across provinces complicated government's response (Harris, 2021).

To conclude, both successful and failing countries suffered from new spikes of cases and deaths, which are attributed largely to the deadly Delta and Omicron variants, continued vaccine hesitancy and a large unvaccinated minority (especially in the US and Eastern Europe) and pandemic fatigue. Most Western governments reacted (perhaps overreacted out of panic) to Omicron by introducing ban on travellers mostly from South Africa (where it was discovered) and other African countries. In the absence of serious global efforts to accelerate vaccination in low-income countries, the ban would serve little purpose (since it was too late to prevent Omicron spread!) except to buy some time for political leaders to sort out their national responses. The ban may be politically expedient, but it is not based on scientific logic (Mallapaty, 2021).

Private Agents

Private agents such as the pharmaceutical industry (Big Pharma), NGOs, charity organizations, social networks and volunteers played an important role in the fight against the pandemic. These are discussed below.

The Big Pharma

The dominant position of large pharmaceutical corporations in basic and applied R and D and the world market for drugs and vaccines has continued unabated. The Big Pharma has precluded competition from generic drugs produced by developing countries. The race to develop a COVID vaccine quickly triggered an ugly competition for ownership of research results and making them available to those who invested in R&D or financed parts of it. Even in normal times, American pharmaceutical companies have kept generic firms at bay (by using intellectual property provisions of trade agreements) to maintain their profits and prices. Strong lobby of the Big Pharma prevented the US Congress and Senate from passing any legislation to introduce drug price reduction provision in the emergency spending package. According to Stiglitz (2019, pp. 211-12), "America's private health insurance system is far more costly with far poorer results than the public programs in Europe." Obama's Affordable Health Care Act (Obamacare) provided public with more and wider access to health care, but it did not go far enough. The *public* option proposed in it was suppressed under pressure from *private* companies which feared competition.

Nevertheless, the confrontational behaviour of governments and the big pharma during COVID-19 may have also led to some cooperation among large companies, which should discourage rent seeking and make it easier to undertake trials for the manufacture of drugs and vaccines (Ledford, 2020). Indeed, traditional drug companies have already started working together (see Chap. 6).

Public and Private Partnerships
Apart from this inter-firm cooperation, close cooperation between the US government and big vaccine developers made possible the development of coronavirus vaccines in a remarkably short time. Although Pfizer developed the vaccine through its own resources without government funding, it received an indirect insurance against a high-risk venture through U$1.95 billion as an "advance purchase" agreement with the government. In 2020, Moderna received about $2–5 billion for research from the government's Operation Warp Speed programme (Buranyi, 2020). AstraZeneca accepted from the US government $1.2 billion for 300 million vaccines and $1 billion for basic research in vaccine development.

The development of Pfizer and Moderna vaccines in less than a year with a 95 per cent efficacy rate, a remarkable scientific feat would have been impossible without public funding, public–private partnerships, political commitment and research cooperation. Of course, there are other reasons explaining the rapid development of these vaccines. COVID-19 is a new type of virus which shares some features similar to those of SARS and MERS, perhaps its poor cousins. Furthermore, gene sequencing may have made the process quicker. In January 2020, Chinese laboratories from Wuhan shared the genetic sequence of COVID-19 for other countries to use in developing specific diagnostic kits. Moreover, synthetic versions of parts of viruses may be built without necessarily requiring complete samples of the pathogens. These shortcuts may have also helped reduce the time required to develop a COVID vaccine.

The Oxford-AstraZeneca vaccine was welcomed by developing countries for which it is more suited than either Pfizer-BioNTech or Moderna vaccine. It is easier and quicker to produce and it does not require extremely low temperatures for storage. It is also cheaper because the AstraZeneca (unlike others such as Pfizer and Moderna) offered to make it available to developing countries on a cost basis. But its trials did not include a large sample of persons over 65 years of age, which has led many countries not to recommend it for older people. AstraZeneca vaccine also seems less effective against the new variants like Delta and Omicron. A UK study suggests that two doses of vaccine are not as effective as three against Omicron (Madhi et al., 2022; Mallapaty et al., 2021; Nealon & Cowling, 2022). The rapid spread of new Omicron variants (BA.4 and BA.5) led Moderna and Pfizer to develop a new vaccine against the variants, which was approved by the Food and Development Administration (FDA) and the European Medical Agency (EMA) at the end of August 2022.

NGOs, Social Networks and Volunteers

Private agents in many countries supplemented public agents' efforts to manage the pandemic. For example, in the *United States*, several voluntary and independent agents such as universities and charity organizations mobilized people and networks to help the elderly and sick patients. Invisible Hands, a voluntary organization, was established to deliver groceries to elderly people (Christakis, 2020, p. 208). In the *United Kingdom*, nearly one million youth volunteered to work for the NHS to fight the coronavirus. Mutual good-neighbour organizations were set up to keep volunteers in contact through social media. Private efforts led to several start-ups to help overcome shortages of PPEs, for example, the development of low-cost ventilators to treat two patients at once, online doctor consultation and telemedicine platform powered by Artificial Intelligence (see Chap. 7). In *Russia,* Oleg Deripaska, the steel magnate, offered to spend $17 million to buy ventilators, PPEs and CT scanners for Russian hospitals besides supporting charities working on COVID-19 (Troianovski, 2020).

Many volunteers in *India* established vigilant groups to help the elderly with shopping and health care besides monitoring compliance and providing food and shelter to migrant workers (Kant, 2020; Lahariya et al., 2020). India's response to COVID-19 was *people-driven*, which led to a *Janata* curfew (people's voluntary curfew) to promote self-isolation.

Several NGOs set up community kitchens and shelters for the homeless. In *China,* commercial and tech companies donated funds and medical supplies for COVID-19 prevention and control (Fan, 2020a, January 31 and February 3). For example, Alibaba Foundation, a charitable organization, donated 100 million yuan ($142.9 million) for COVID-19 vaccines research and development (Ibid., February 5). It launched a global direct sourcing platform to purchase medical equipment and medicines from home and abroad and delivered to Hubei province (Fan, 2020b, February 5). In *Vietnam*, VinGroup donated four million doses of

COVID-19 vaccine to the Ministry of Health in addition to thousands of ventilators, as well as millions of US dollar for research on vaccine development. Vietcombank, Vietinbank, Bank for Investment and Development of Vietnam (BIDV) and Agribank donated nearly $7 million to finance the purchase of COVID-19 vaccines (*Saigon Online*, 2021, May 22).

A Typology of Agents

Responses to COVID-19 by the agents are grouped below according to the three criteria, discussed in Chap. 2, namely (a) preparedness, (b) mobilization and redeployment of resources and (c) public trust and national solidarity. Countries that were well *prepared* included China, Denmark, Finland, Germany, Singapore, South Korea, Vietnam among others. Countries such as Finland, Germany, Singapore and South Korea were particularly successful in mobilizing medical personnel and supplies. In such countries as Austria, Denmark, Finland Norway and most Southeast Asian countries, public trust and confidence in government and institutions was strong.

The successful public and private agents were those who took early action, made action plans, heeded scientific advice and WHO's call for early and mass testing, contact tracing and isolation as well as providing incentives for raising vaccination rates.

Followers

In principle, followers should be responsible for compliance with public health rules and guidelines, show a sense of discipline, social responsibility and trust in leaders and agents. In practice, very few countries met all these criteria. The followers' behaviour, besides policy responses of leaders and agents, also influences rates of COVID-19 vaccination, which helped control the epidemic (Chap. 2, Table 2.4; also see below).

A climate of *fear* (of new waves of variants and infections), *uncertainty* (about when the pandemic might end) and *difficulties* in maintaining distances (in some economic activities) affected human behaviour. In the *United States*, the followers' responses were made in a highly charged political environment besides social and economic divide. A study on health behaviour and attitudes towards the virus showed political bias (Barrios & Hochberg, 2020; Bentley, 2020). Prolonged lack of African Americans' access to health care has generated mistrust of the government and medical establishment. According to a Pew Research report, fewer African Americans (42 per cent) are willing to get vaccinated than Whites (49 per cent), Hispanics (61 per cent) and Asian Americans (48 per cent) (Gadarian et al., 2020). Two-thirds of the people believed that the development of a vaccine was rushed for political reasons (Tyson et al., 2020).

The *European* publics did not trust their leaders because they spread false information about the pandemic, or made sudden and frequent U-turns, or recommended unsafe drugs. It is unreasonable to expect self-discipline and sense of responsibility from citizens when their national leaders themselves cannot exercise it. Generally, progressive and liberal parties had greater trust and confidence than the populist parties. A sizeable proportion believed that scientists were involved in politics and were manipulated by governments. In the *United Kingdom*, followers were partly to blame for their failure to adhere to the public health guidelines when Johnson decided to do course correction and announced stay-at-home and social distancing measures. Few people decided to self-isolate, which may be explained partly by the failure of the government to compensate them for the negative financial and psychological impact of self-isolation. Countries such as Germany, which provided such incentives for two years, performed much better. Lack of proper health care precautions and adequate child-care facilities made many parents reluctant to send their children to school. Although the average rate of vaccine hesitancy was low (14%), it is exceptionally high among the Black, Asian, Minority Ethnic (BAME) people: Blacks (72%) and Pakistanis/Bangladeshis (42%) (Krastev & Leonard, 2020). A host of factors explain the lack of vaccine acceptance, ranging from conspiracy theories to mistrust of government, institutions and vaccines, fear of side effects and mixed messages. Johnson and his advisers were busy partying (Partygate) in 2021 when people were observing the rules, which eroded whatever trust the citizens had in the government. The government's failure to communicate led the people to rely more on news media and their own knowledge and personal experience (Newton, 2020; Robertson et al., 2021).

In *France*, the public is known for mistrust of leaders and governments. The French defied the president's call for observance of public health guidelines and continued to gather in bars and restaurants. Vaccine reluctance was also quite pronounced. In an online survey of over 5000 households conducted in April 2020 during the peak of the pandemic, about a quarter of respondents would not agree to be injected if a vaccine was available (Ward et al., 2020). Reasons given for vaccine hesitancy ranged from general reluctance to try any vaccination to rushed vaccine development, uselessness of COVID vaccine and a general lack of trust in politics, medicine, science and the pharmaceutical industry.

In *Germany*, a general acceptance of the lockdown and other restrictive measures in the early stages may be due to the government's "soft" approach of "nudging rather than that of 'direct enforcement' adopted by France, Italy and Spain. Government's quick response in the form of economic relief measures such as 'short-term work allowance'" (*Kurzarbeitergeld*) for temporary and regular workers and bailouts for all economic sectors may explain widespread compliance (Dostal, 2020). Over 80 per cent of the population believed that policy decisions concerning COVID-19 should be science based. More people trusted scientists than politicians (Dohle et al., 2020).

In *Italy,* as discussed above the public confidence in Prime Minister Conte and his government was partly due to his direct and regular communication on COVID-19. But disinformation and conspiracy theories circulated freely in an environment of political instability, partisanship and differences among experts. Italians are known to have much less confidence in the impact of technological and scientific innovations on their health (51%), in comparison with the other countries (76.5%). Neither do they trust scientists nor public institutions (Institute of National Health, 2020).

In *Spain*, public trust in the government and public institutions has been eroded over time. According to the opinion poll by the European Council on Foreign Relations, 58 per cent of Spanish voters believed in the poor performance of their government in fighting COVID-19 compared to 61 per cent in France. On the other hand, 60 per cent of voters in Denmark supported their government's performance (Krastev & Leonard, 2020). Nearly a year later, only 37 per cent of respondents were either fully or reasonably supportive of the government in France compared to 56 per cent in Germany, 48 per cent in the United Kingdom and 52 per cent in Italy (*Le Monde*, 2021, February 23).

Nearly half the *Russians* (March 2020) believed that the health system was unprepared for the health crisis. About a quarter questioned the accuracy of the official information on COVID-19 which was reported in the media (*Moscow Times*, 2020). Lack of trust was further reinforced by people's lack of confidence in the Sputnik V vaccine which was approved prematurely (Cohen, 2020). An Ipsos survey undertaken during summer of 2020 showed that Russians were more sceptical of the vaccine than the public in the 27 countries in which polling was done (Troianovski, 2020). Fifty-nine per cent of Russians did not want to be vaccinated even though it was free. In contrast, the acceptance rate among the Chinese was over 90 per cent (Lazarus et al., 2021; Sallam, 2021). Yet scientists found the Russian Sputnik V vaccine quite effective and safe (Jones and Roy, 2021).

In *New Zealand,* people trusted Ardern because she empathized with their hardships, set a personal example by taking a cut in her own salary. She dismissed the health minister who breached the rules unlike Johnson in the United Kingdom who defended his political advisers. It demonstrates how a consensual and collaborative leader can change public behaviour and obtain popular support.

The followers' behaviour can be more enlightened and responsible than that of leaders and agents. For example, when Australian Prime Minister Scott Morrison and his government lifted all restrictions in early 2022 mainly for political (it was an election year) and economic reasons (to revive the economy) despite a spike in cases and deaths, people continued to stay at home (Zhuang, 2022).

Japan has a long tradition of social solidarity and respect for central authority, which is also shared by other Southeast countries. Most Japanese heeded government's *voluntary* guidelines to stay at home as soon as any virus symptoms were noticed. Culture, discipline, mask wearing and peer pressure ensured very high rate of compliance. In spite of lapses by the government discussed above, Japan has one of the lowest mortality rates (see Chap. 2, Table 2.5) thanks to this factor besides willingness to vaccinate.

In *South Korea* as in Japan, people's sense of discipline, community spirit and confidence in the government helped control the coronavirus. The public as well as opposition parties rallied behind the government. Over 77 per cent of people (May, 2020) thought that president Moon handled the pandemic well (Lee et al., 2020; Moon, 2020). Popular participation and a sense of social responsibility ensured the enforcement of public health guidelines.

In *Vietnam*, public trust and confidence in the prime minister and his government was very high. Over 62 per cent of participants supported the government measures (Tran et al., 2020). Vietnamese people did not object to sharing of health data on an app and compulsory stay-at-home orders, which were considered necessary *emergency* action required for public safety. Cynics would say that people do not have a choice in socialist regimes like the Vietnamese. But similar measures were also accepted in democratic societies of Australia, Israel, Japan and South Korea. If frequent curfews are accepted during war, why not *temporary* restrictions on freedom during a war on the pandemic.

The *Chinese* people complied with public health guidelines and restrictions. The very protesters who were angry with Xi for initial slowness later praised him for effective crisis management! One wonders if this change of heart could be attributed to Confucian philosophy. According to the president of the Chinese Academy of Medical Sciences, the Chinese culture of social solidarity and respect for people's life and health was key to the containment of the pandemic (*People's Daily*, 2020b, May 21). But long and frequent lockdowns and stay-at-home orders in 2022 angered many people who protested against China's continued adherence to zero-COVID strategy.

In *India*, people, who are generally unruly and undisciplined, showed self-discipline (with few exceptions), sense of national purpose and community spirit during the first wave. Voluntary 'virus squads' enforced compliance of the lockdown. Vaccination of over 20 million people in one day at the end of 2021 restored some public confidence, which was lost for a lack of government preparedness for a new wave of infections. Followers' compliance (which was high at the beginning) seems to have declined over time. A longitudinal survey of their behaviour in adhering to mask wearing and social distancing, which was nearly 90 per cent, declined in subsequent waves (Schaner et al., 2022).

In *Brazil*, people failed to observe such measures as social distancing. A large number of informal workers in the labour force limited the efficacy of stay-at-home measures. Brazil is a highly polarized society riddled with violent crime, corruption and low public security in which people's trust in government and political parties has weakened over the years. Bolsonaro's supporters were less enthusiastic about complying with public health restrictions than his opponents. In this respect, Brazil's experience is very similar to the American.

In *South Africa*, despite national solidarity, people's attitudes are generally fatalistic, strict enforcement of such measures as social distancing would be most difficult if not impossible. It is remarkable that people in general trusted the president and his government. Compliance with lockdown measures was generally high judging from the drastic reductions in people's mobility especially in hard-hit areas. But prolonged lockdowns, curfews, limited gatherings at funerals and religious meetings, mandatory wearing of masks in public places and ban on the sale of alcohol have made Ramaphosa and his government unpopular.

The above discussion suggests that the followers' defiance of public health restrictions is in part a result of the following failures of leaders and public agents:

1. Mixed and conflicting messages.
2. Lack of transparency and accuracy of official information and failure to sensitize people through mass information campaigns.
3. Governments' failure to provide adequate and timely supply of PPEs and other medical goods.
4. Lack of clarity in government policies which were often based on political considerations instead of science and facts.
5. Piecemeal, fragmented and contradictory nature of policies and measures which led to public confusion.

It is hard to determine whether the above human behavioural response amounts to foolhardiness, lack of social cohesion/solidarity, low perception of risk, fight for individual liberties or the failure of governments to provide adequate incentives. There is no such thing as unlimited freedom to choose. With freedom of choice also comes a sense of social responsibility to others. It is puzzling that people are prepared to observe *permanent* traffic rules (speed limits, red lights and safety belts) but not *temporary* public health restrictions. There was much less resistance to previous immunization campaigns. Mildness of the early version of Omicron may have led followers to believe that adherence to strict rules was unnecessary. It also created a false sense of *complacency* on the part of leaders and governments who *prematurely* lifted all public health restrictions.

A Typology of Followers

The followers can be divided into the following three categories:

1. Those who ignored all public health guidelines and COVID vaccination because they did not trust their leaders and governments.
2. Those who refused testing, stay-at-home orders or use of WhatsApp or similar device for contact tracing because it tampered with their privacy and individual freedom.
3. Those who violated the rules because they perceived low risk or did not believe in the existence of the virus. They lacked sense of social responsibility and believed in conspiracy theories.

As noted above, there is a close connection between the actions of leaders, agencies and followers. All three need to move in step. Few countries have fulfilled the conditions for success discussed in Chap. 3. In many cases, all three key players turned out to be spoilers who were guided by self-interests. The most successful cases were invariably found in Southeast and East Asian countries, which are known for followers' trust and confidence in their leaders and governments.

Conclusion

We conclude that cooperation between the three stakeholders was crucial in the fight against the pandemic. Vaccination roll-out is a good example of how they interacted (or failed to do so) in practice. Generally, Western Europeans were more willing to be inoculated than Americans and Russians, for example. Despite initial issues of low vaccine supplies, Europe surpassed the United States in achieving generally high vaccination rates, but in Eastern & Central European countries like Bulgaria, Romania and Ukraine, immunization remains extremely low due to deep mistrust of state institutions and vaccine hesitancy.

It is surprising that the United States, a major vaccine-producing country, has been unable to raise the vaccination rate despite government efforts at persuasion. Failure to take any coercive action when persuasion did not work, combined with people's lack of trust in political leaders, government institutions and vaccines, partly explain this situation. The leadership failures corresponded to low American vaccination rates (67%) not only relative to those in Europe but also to those of such emerging and poor developing countries as Bangladesh (74%), Cambodia (87%), China (91%), Cuba (88%) and Vietnam (92%) (see Chap. 2, Table 2.4). Lack of emphasis on the organization of distribution and delivery of vaccines in the United States is a reflection of poor political leadership and management failures of public agents. That political and policy decisions to encourage people to get vaccinated can be successful is demonstrated by the mass increase in vaccinations in France following Macron's decision to prevent the unvaccinated from entering restaurants, cafes and other public places.

In the West, even well-funded and robust healthcare systems were ill prepared and inadequate to cope with the rapidly rising virus infections. Most failed to introduce mass testing and tracing and avoided high-tech devices such as app for tracing infected patients despite their proven success in democratic and authoritarian countries in Asia (Cha, 2020). Several other factors account for failure to fight the virus, namely (1) arrogance and hubris; (2) complacency; (3) exceptionalism; (4) excessive individualism and obsession with personal freedom without social responsibility; (5) deep and rising economic and social inequalities; (6) lack of social cohesion and community spirit; (7) Partisanship and polarization and (8) unwillingness to learn from others' successful experiences. Arrogance of power and hubris often lead to overconfidence, complacency, lack of urgency and unpreparedness (Bhalla & Fang, 2022).[5]

The political leaders in many Western countries publicly shamed agents or followers to deflect from their own failures (Lincoln, 2020). Trump blamed China and the WHO as well as Democrat governors and mayors; Johnson the NHS, and Italian mayors, joggers for not keeping social distance.

Culture of individualism prevented the adoption of such measures as self-isolation, social distancing, wearing of masks and testing and tracing (O'Rourke, 2020). As health services are largely private, health is treated as a commodity and a matter of personal choice as any other consumer good. In Europe, massive protests against public health restrictions and temporary lockdowns even in such countries as the Netherlands and Sweden, traditionally known for social cohesion, are symptomatic of growing individualism and loss of social solidarity.

The pandemic has worsened the pre-existing poverty and inequalities, which breeds resentment against the state, political leaders and agents. At the global level also, lack of access to new drugs and vaccines ('vaccine nationalism' discussed in Chap. 5) will worsen global inequalities in health care and economic well-being. The effects of weak leadership on inequalities and governance are not well understood or researched.

Deep and widening inequalities have resulted in loss of social cohesion, which can lead to a lack of confidence in political leaders and government agents. Many leaders politicized the pandemic and launched disinformation campaigns which further eroded public trust and confidence. Delays in imposing public health restrictions resulted directly from political polarization, lack of cooperation between the ruling and opposition parties and prolonged disconnect between people and their political masters. Krugman (2020, November 5), Nobel laureate in Economics, wondered whether the country (the United States) was already on the verge of a failed state, in which "government is no longer able to exert effective control."

On the other hand, in Southeast Asia, leaders' *preparedness* and *timely action* were critical besides *government's competence* in medical resource mobilization and *enforcement* of rules and *public compliance*, *social solidarity* and people's *trust in leaders/governments*. Cooperation between the three stakeholders was backed by the willingness to learn from the past experiences and current best practices. Asians have been more willing to accept smart phones for digital tracing, considering it as a civic duty (Cha, 2020). As noted in Chap. 3, cultural tightness of society also has had some impact on COVID-19 cases and deaths.

Countries' performance on COVID-19 needs to be examined in relation to the main objectives, for example, minimization of infections, hospitalizations and deaths, keeping economic losses low. We find that generally Western leaders scored low marks, whereas Nordic countries (especially Denmark, Finland and Norway) and those in Southeast Asia (China, Singapore, South Korea, Thailand and Vietnam) and the Pacific (Australia and New Zealand) performed much better. Some countries gave priority to economy over public health, others struck a better balance between the two, and the Southeast Asian countries made rapid economic recovery while keeping infections and deaths relatively low. Despite social disruptions due to COVID-19, China and India not only achieved low death rates but also high economic growth (over 8 per cent and nearly 9 per cent, respectively, in 2021 according to the IMF) (see Chap. 2, Table 2.7).

Limitations of Conventional Divides

The pandemic has shown the limitations of such divides as North and South, advanced and developing, and democratic and authoritarian in explaining the leadership pattern. It has attacked all countries rich and poor, small or large. The success and failure to fight the virus also cut across these divides. Although some poor countries such as Vietnam have shown remarkable success, invariably good performance is associated with rich Western countries which enjoy the benefits of well-equipped and well-funded health care systems and services. But the score card on COVID-19 has shown how false this assumption is.

Democracies are generally touted as success stories compared to authoritarian regimes. Yet China, Cuba and Vietnam, 'communistic' countries, controlled the virus exceptionally well and long before Western democracies. In particular, China and Cuba did so by using their own distinct strategies and locally made vaccines. Cuba has one of the highest vaccination rates in the world (see Chap. 2, Table 2.4). It is also known for global health cooperation by providing vaccines as well as doctors and health workers (Huish, 2020). So did Thailand under a government led by a military general. On the other hand, the United Kingdom and the United States, considered to be the beacons of democracy, have dismal records.

There is an unexpected pattern of greater success of *female* leaders (e.g. Ardern and Merkel discussed above) along with those of Denmark, Finland, Iceland, Norway and Taiwan in their fight against COVID-19 compared to their *male* counterparts (e.g. Bolsonaro, Johnson, Modi, Orban and Trump). A study of 194 countries pairs each of the female-headed countries with their nearest male-headed neighbour on the basis of population size, for example, Germany and the United Kingdom, New Zealand and Ireland, Bangladesh and Pakistan (Garikipati & Kambhampati, 2020). It finds that female-headed countries have lower cases and deaths, reasons for which are unclear, given the sample bias, differences in timing of lockdowns and a host of other factors. The female leaders' empathy, their openness to diversity of opinions, more democratic and participative leadership style and greater inclusiveness of institutions (agents), may explain their greater success.

Concluding Remarks

In this chapter, we have reviewed 16 political leaders, countries with diverse public and private agents, and followers in an attempt to test the leaders-agents-followers framework developed in Chap. 3. Our analysis has shown that generally political unity and healthy cooperation between all three led to success in the fight against COVID-19, whereas disunity and divisions caused large losses of human life and economic hardships.

The role of human behaviour (of both leaders and followers) in a health crisis is far more important than is often realized. Mixed or conflicting messages were responsible for people's anger and mistrust of political leaders and public institutions. COVID protests in the name of freedom in many countries are symptomatic of a more general discontentment with leaders and governments.

Local circumstances such as low/slow cooperation of communities, religious groups and citizens, varying capacities of the existing health systems and infrastructure and early or late start in fighting the virus affected the leaders' performance. In some cases, positive responses of a government agency (e.g. public health care), or private sector or civil-society groups made up for poor political leadership. However, smart and effective leadership remains crucial for central direction and preparation of well-designed, comprehensive and coordinated strategies and plans of action.

Surprisingly, leaders of countries least known for their "smart" leadership have demonstrated a rare capacity to manage the pandemic well. Their greater foresight, quick action and empathy won followers' confidence in their leadership. Their clear messages and regular communications inspired public trust.

Despite the above differences, there are several common elements in the leaders' and their governments' responses. Most failed the test of advance planning and preparedness and did not prepare *anticipatory* policies, which were perceived to be expensive and time-consuming. Neither were national action plans indicating priorities on who and which state should receive which health product and services. In many advanced western democracies, political leaders and their advisers as well as ministers failed to observe public health rules while expecting the followers to comply, thus raising serious doubts about accountability, rule of law and moral authority. Most governments and their leaders underinvested in their health sectors and in disaster preparedness.

A premature reopening of the economy following lockdowns when new infection cases were rising (especially without necessary precautionary measures) turned out to be shortsighted. It cost both more lives and bigger economic losses, which resulted from renewed lockdowns and new waves of infections. A war analogy may be relevant here. If the end of a war is declared early, and the troops are withdrawn from the frontlines, renewed fighting may involve bigger loss of life and higher costs of reconstruction and recovery.

Strict lockdowns became necessary in countries when infections became alarming and leaders were slow in taking early action. The only course of action left to contain the pandemic was to suddenly stop all economic activity. Prolonged and strict national lockdowns were not inevitable. Mass testing and enforcement of public health guidelines could have prevented the need for national closure of the economies (Piguillem & Shi, 2022). Targeted lockdowns and vaccinations are *necessary* but not *sufficient*. A *multi-pronged* public health strategy is needed which includes traditional public health measures as well.

Notes

1. A WHO-funded project which reviewed 172 studies from 16 countries underlined the usefulness of such measures in reducing COVID infections as wearing of masks, keeping physical distance and keeping eyes protected and providing proper indoor ventilation (Chu et al., 2020). A more recent study on the effect of stay-at-home orders on COVID(Patterson Jr., 2022) showed that compliance raised COVID case growth early in the pandemic.
2. Shih (2020, April 8) notes that Dr. Li Wenliang, who sounded the alarm on the coronavirus, was quickly declared a hero as soon as the Wuhan lockdown ended. The authorities laid the blame on local party officials.
3. Roach and Shan (2020, April 8) observe that Western media distorted Dr. Li's role in whistleblowing. He was not the first doctor who had raised the alarm; neither was he trained in respiratory diseases. It was Dr. (Ms.) Zhang Jixian, director of the respiratory and intensive care department at the Wuhan hospital, who sounded the alarm about an unknown disease.
4. Private communication with Dr. Nguyen van Quang, Vice Dean, Faculty of Economics, College of Economics, Technology and Fisheries, Bac Ninh Province, Vietnam.
5. These factors are discussed at length in Bhalla and Fang (2022) in a section entitled: "Why did Asia succeed while the West failed?"

References

Abutaleb, Y., & Paletta, D. (2021). *Nightmare scenario: Inside the Trump administration's response to the pandemic that changed history*. Harper.

Ajzenman, N., Cavalcanti, T., & Da Mata, D. (2020). More than words: Leaders' speech and risky behavior during a pandemic. *Social Science Research Network (SSRN), 3582908.*

Balmford, B., Annan, J. D., Hargreaves, J. C., & Altoé, M. (2020). Cross-country comparisons of Covid-19: Policy, politics, and the price of life. *Environmental and Resource Economics, 76.*

Barrios, Y. M., & Hochberg, Y. V. (2020, April). *Risk perceptions through the lens of politics in the time of Covid-19 pandemic.* National Bureau of Economic Research (NBER) Working Paper 27008.

Béland, D., Rocco, P., & Segatto, C. I. (2021). Trump, Bolsonaro, and the framing of the Covid-19 crisis: How political institutions shaped presidential strategies. *World Affairs, 184*(4).

Bentley, G. R. (2020). Do not blame the BAME: Ethnic and structural inequalities in susceptibilities to COVID-19. *American Journal of Human Biology, 32.*

Beschloss, M. (2018). *Presidents of war.* New York: Broadway Books.

Beschloss, M. (2020, April 1). What Trump can learn from real wartime presidents. *Washington Post*; *Presidents of war*. (2018). Doubleday Books.

Bhalla, A., & Fang, J. (2022). Leaders, institutions and people during Covid-19: Secret of Asian success. *Journal of Chinese Economic and Business Studies, 20*(3).

Blasberg, M. (2021, January 21). An entire country suffers as president sabotages immunization campaign. *Der Spiegel International Edition*.

Bull, M. (2021). Italian government response to Covid-19 and the making of a prime minister. *Contemporary Italian Politics, 13*(2).

Buranyi, S. (2020, December 17). Big Pharma is fooling us. *New York Times*.

Capano, G. (2020). Policy design and state capacity in the COVID-19 emergency in Italy: If you are not prepared for the (un)expected, you can only be what you already are. *Policy and Society, 39*(3).

Carlitz, R. D., & Makhura, M. N. (2021, January). Life under lockdown: Illustrating trade-offs in South Africa's response to COVID-19. *World Development*.

Cha, V. (2020). Asia's COVID-19 lessons for the west: Public goods, privacy, and social tagging. *Washington Quarterly, 43*(2).

Christakis, N. A. (2020). *Apollo's arrow*. Little, Brown Spark, Chapter 6 on Banding Together.

Christensen, T., & Laegreid, P. (2020). *Balancing governance capacity and legitimacy: How the Norwegian government handled the Covid-19 crisis as a high performer* (p. 2020). Public Administration Review.

Chu, D., Akl, E. A., Duda, S., Solo, K., Yaacoub, S., Schünemann, H. J., El-Harakeh, A., Bognanni, A., Lotfi, T., Loeb, M., & Hajizadeh, A. (2020, June 1). Physical distancing, face masks and eye protection to prevent person-to-person transmission of SARS-CoV-2 and Covid19: A systematic review and meta-analysis. *The Lancet*.

Cohen, J. (2020, November 11). Russia's claim of a successful Covid-19 doesn't pass the 'smell test' critics say. *Science*.

Crayne, M. P., & Madeiros, K. E. (2020, August 10). Making sense of crisis: Charismatic, ideological and pragmatic leadership in response to COVID-19.

de Marino, L. (2020). *The Italian style: Giuseppe Conte's 'half-populist' leadership during Covid-19*. LSE European Politics and Policy (EUROPP) Blog.

Di Cicco, G., & Sensales, G. (2021, November). *Survey on the representations of populism and pandemic among Italian citizens of different political orientations: First results on the attitudes towards Conte's effectiveness as a political leader*. Internal Report, Spienza University of Rome. (draft).

Dohle, S., Wingen, T., & Schreiber, M. (2020). Acceptance and adoption of protective measures during the COVID-19 pandemic: The role of trust in politics and trust in science. *Social Psychological Bulletin, 15*(4).

Dostal, J. M. (2020). Governing under pressure: German policymaking during the coronavirus crisis. *The Political Quarterly, 91*(3).

Ehni, E. (2020, April 2). Tendence en allemagne: Grande confiance dans Merkel & Co. *WDR (Westdeutscher Rundfunk.* A regional broadcasting station of North Rhine Westphalia).

Emmanuel, E. J., Michaels, D., Bright, R., & Ostersholm, M. T. (2022, October 19). We advised Biden on the pandemic: Much work remains to face the next crisis. *New York Times.*

Fan, F. (2020a, January 31; February 3). Tech companies donate funds, medical supplies and equipment. *China Daily.*

Fan, F. (2020b, February 5). Alibaba launches platform to better source medical material. *China Daily.*

Fancourt, D., Steptoe, A., & Wright, L. (2020, August 15). The Cummings effect: Politics, trust, and behaviour during the COVID-19 pandemic. *The Lancet.*

Farhan, B. (2021). A new strategic leadership model for surviving and coping: Lesson's from Canada's leadership approach to COVID-19. *Cogent Business and Management, 8*(1).

Feldenkirchen, M. (2021, February 18). Chancellor Merkel's failure in the coronavirus pandemic. *Der Spiegel International Edition.*

Ferraresi, M. (2020, March 9). "Italy's politicians are making the coronavirus crisis worse. *Foreign Policy.*

Fisher, M., & Sang-Hun, C. (2020, March 23). How South Korea flattened the curve. *New York Times.*

Ford, J. (2020, April 15). The battle at the heart of British science over coronavirus. *Financial Times.*

Frayer, L. (2021, February 1). The mystery of India's plummeting Covid-19 cases. *National Public Radio (NPR).*

Gadarian, S. K., Goodman, S. W., & Pepinsky, T. B. (2020). Partisanship, health behaviour and policy studies in the early stages of the Covid-19 pandemic. *PLOS ONE, Public Library of Science, 16*(4).

Garikipati, S., & Kambhampati, U. (2020, June 21). Women leaders are better at fighting the pandemic. *VOX, Centre for Economic Policy Research (CEPR) Policy Portal.*

Gaskell, J., Stoker, G., Jennings, W., & Devine, D. (2020). Covid-19 and blunders of our governments: Long-term system failings aggravated by political choices, 530.

Greer, S. L., Rozenblum, S., Falkenbach, M., Löblova, O., Jarman, H., Williams, N., & Wismar, M. (2022). Centralizing and decentralizing governance in the COVID-19 pandemic: The politics of credit and blame. *Health Policy, 126.*

Guharoy, R., & Krenzelok, E. P. (2021). Lessons from the mismanagement of the COVID-19 pandemic: A blueprint to reform CDC. *American Journal of Public Health, 78*(18).

Ha, B. T. T., Ngoc Quang, L., Mirzoev, T., Tai, N. T., Thai, P. Q., & Dinh, P. C. (2020). Combating the COVID-19 epidemic: Experiences from Vietnam. *International Journal of Environmental Research and Public Health, 17.*

Harris, J. (2021). Confronting legacies and charting a new course? The politics of coronavirus response in South Africa. In Greer et al. (Eds.), *Coronavirus politics: The comparative politics and policy of COVID-19.* University of Michigan Press.

Hassenteufel, P. (2020). Handling the COVID-19 crisis in France: Paradoxes of a centralized state-led health system. *EPA (European Policy Analysis), 6.*

Hopkins, V. (2021, October 19). Reluctance among Russians to get vaccinated has led to a surge in cases and deaths. *New York Times.*

Huish, R. (2020). Cuba. In N. Georgeou & C. Hawksley (Eds.), *State responses to Covid-19: A global snapshot at June 1, 2020.* Western Sydney University.

Institute of National Health, Italy. (2020). *Characteristics of SARS-CoV-2 patients dying in Italy.* Report based on available data on December 16.

Jamieson, T. (2020). "Go hard, go early": Preliminary lessons from New Zealand's response to Covid-19. *American Review of Public Administration, 50*(6–7).

Jones, I., & Roy, P. (2021, February 21). Sputnik V COVID-19 vaccine candidate appears safe and effective. *The Lancet, 397.*

Kant, A. (2020, May 25). Empowered groups have joined hands with government against Covid. *Indian Express.*

Kato, S., & Yoshimato, I. (2020). Why did Abe's popularity fall during the pandemic? *East Asia Forum Quarterly, 12*(3).

Kottasova, I. (2021, March 1). How the Czech Republic slipped into a covid disaster, one misstep at a time. *CNN.*

Krastev, I., & Leonard, M. (2020, June 24). Europe's pandemic politics: How the virus has changed the public's world view. *European Council on Foreign Relations.*

Krugman, P. (2020, November 5). Is America becoming a failed state? *New York Times.*

Lahariya, C., Kang, G., & Guleria, R. (2020). *Till we win: India's fight against the COVID-19 pandemic.* Penguin Books.

Lavari, A. (2020). Spread (dis) trust: Covid-19 misinformation and government intervention in Italy. *Media and Communication, 8*(2).

Lazarus, J. V., Ratzan, S. C., Palayew, A., Gostin, L. O., Larson, H. J., Rabin, K., Kimball, S., & El-Mohandes, A. (2021). A global survey of potential acceptance of covid-19 vaccine. *Nature Medicine, 27.*

Ledford, H. (2020, June 4). The coronavirus outbreak could make it quicker and easier to trial drugs. *Nature.*

Lee, S., Hwang, C., & Moon, M. J. (2020). Policy learning and crisis policy-making: Quadruple loop-learning and Covid-19 responses in South Korea. *Policy and Society, 39*(3).

Lincoln, M. (2020, September 15). Study the role of hubris in nation's COVID-19 response. *Nature, 585.*

Madhi, S. A., Ihekeweazu, C., Rees, H., & Pollard, A. J. (2022, February 18). Decoupling of omicron variant infections and severe COVID-19. *The Lancet.*

Majeed, A., Maile, E. J., & Bindman, A. B. (2020). The primary care response to COVID-19 in England's National Health Service. *Journal of the Royal Society of Medicine, 113*(6).

Mallapaty, S. (2021, December 2). Omicron-variant border bans ignore the evidence, say scientists. *Nature.*

Mallapaty, S., Callaway, E., Kozlov, M., Ledford, H., Pickrell, J., & Van Noorden, R. (2021, December 16). How Covid vaccines shaped 2021 in eight powerful charts. *Nature.*

Marcus, I. (2020, March 22). How good are Germany's top corona crisis managers. *The Berlin Spectator.*

Martin, L. (2020). Canada's handling of the pandemic so far is putting the US to shame. *Globe and Mail.*

Mazey, S., & Richardson, J. (2020). Lesson-drawing from New Zealand and Covid-19: The need for anticipatory policy making. *The Political Quarterly, 91*(3).

Melo, M. (2020, April 13). A sobrevida dos governadores. *Folha da Sao Paulo.* Cited in Greer, S. L., King, E. J., da Fonseca, E. M., & Peralta-Santos, A. (2020). The comparative politics of COVID-19: The need to understand government responses. *Global Public Health, 15*(9).

Merkley, E., Bridgman, A., Loewen, P. J., Owen, T., Ruths, D., & Zhilin, O. (2020). A rare moment of cross-partisan consensus: Elite and public response to the covid-19 pandemic, Canada. *Canadian Journal of Political Science, 53.*

Mintrom, M., Rublee, M. R., Nnotti, M., & Zech, S. T. (2021). Policy narratives and public justification: Responses to COVID-19. *Journal of European Public Policy.*

Moon, M. J. (2020). Fighting Covid-19 with agility, transparency, and participation: Wicked policy problems and new government challenges. *Public Administration Review.*

Moscow Times. (2020, April 13). Russia's coronavirus outbreak is 'changing for the worse,' Putin says.

Mueller, B. (2021, January 22). How British scientists found the more infectious coronavirus variant. *New York Times.*

Nature, Editorials. (2021, September 16). Scientist Angela Merkel will be a hard act to follow, 597.

Nealon, J., & Cowling, B. J. (2022, January 19). Omicron severity: Milder but not mild. *The Lancet.*

Newton, K. (2020). Government communications, political trust and compliant behaviour: The politics of Covid-19 in Britain. *The Political Quarterly, 91*(3).
Nguyen, Q. V., Cao, D. A., & Nghiem, S. H. (2021). Spread of Covid-19 and policy responses in Vietnam: An overview. *International Journal of Infectious Diseases, 103.*
O'Rourke, M. (2020, March 12). The shift Americans must make to fight the coronavirus. *The Atlantic.*
Oltermann, P. (2020, April 16). Angela Merkel draws on science background in covid-19 explainer. *Guardian.*
Oprysko, C. (2020, March 13). I don't take any responsibility at all. Trump deflects blame for coronavirus testing fumble. *Politico.*
Park, J. (2021). Institutions matter in fighting Covid-19: Public health, social policies, and the control tower in South Korea. In Greer et al. (Eds.), *Coronavirus politics: The comparative politics and policy of COVID-19.* University of Michigan Press.
Park, J., & Chung, E. (2021). Learning from past pandemic governance: Early response and public-private partnerships in testing of COVID-19 in South Korea. *World Development, 137.*
Pasquier, P., Luft, A., Gillard, J., Boutonnet, M., Vallet, C., Pontier, J. M., Duron-Martinaud, S., Dia, A., Puyeo, L., Debrus, F., & Prunet, B. (2020). How do we fight COVID-19? Military medical action in the war against the COVID-19 pandemic in France. *British Medical Journal.*
Patterson, S., Jr. (2022). The politics of pandemic: The effect of stay-at-home orders on COVID-19 mitigation. *State Politics & Policy Quarterly, 22*(1).
People's Daily. (2020a, January 21). Xi orders resolute efforts to curb virus spread.
People's Daily. (2020b, May 21). China's cultural, institutional strength vital to curbing Covid-19: Political adviser.
People's Daily. (2020c, September 8). Chronicle of Xi's leadership in China's war against coronavirus.
Pierre, J. (2020). Nudges against pandemic: Sweden's COVID-19 containment strategy in perspective. *Policy and Society, 39*(3).
Piguillem, F., & Shi, L. (2022). *Optimal covid-19 testing policies.* Economic Journal.
Press Conference. (2020, April 22). Justin Trudeau: Canada COVID-19 Ottawa.
Ramadan, O. P. C., & Talisana, A.O. (2021, January 26). *WHO Covid delegation to South Africa.* Interview for the South Africa COVID-19 Country Report (First Edition). Department of Planning, Monitoring and Evaluation, Republic of South Africa, Pretoria, June.
Reilly, T. (2020, March 19). Covid-19 and Xi Jinping: How the strongman got stronger. *The Diplomat.*
Rello, L. (2021). The COVID-19 pandemic and the personalization of government: .... *Italy. International Journal of Public Leadership, 17*(2).

Ren, X. (2020). Pandemic and lockdown: A territorial approach to COVID-19 in China, Italy and the United States. *Eurasian Geography and Economics, 61*(4–5).

Republic of South Africa. (2021, June). *South Africa COVID-19 country report.*

Roach, S., & Shan, W. (2020, May 18). The fable of the Chinese whistleblower. *Project Syndicate.*

Robertson, E., Reeve, K. S., Niedzwiedz, C. L., Moore, J., Blake, M., Green, M., Katikireddi, S. V., & Benzeval, M. J. (2021, January 2). Predictors of COVID-19 vaccine hesitancy in the UK household longitudinal study. *medRxiv preprint.*

Roy, A. (2020, April 3). Pandemic is a portal. *Financial Times.*

Royo, S. (2020). Responding to COVID-19: The case of Spain. *EPA (European Policy Analysis), 6.*

Rubinelli, L. (2020). The Italian state, its regions and the virus. *The Political Quarterly, 91*(3).

Russell, J. (2020, March 26). Boris Johnson is not cut out for this crisis: UK needs a real leader, not a joker. *New York Times.*

Sadoum-Kerber, K., & Wahnich, S. (2022). Emmanuel Macron face à la Covid-19: un Président en quete de réparation d'image. *Augmentation & Analyse du DISCOURS, Open Edition Journals*, 28.

Saigon Online. (2021, May 22). Health Ministry receives nearly US$7 billion, 4 million Covid-19 dose support.

Sallam, M. (2021, January 4). COVID-19 vaccine hesitancy worldwide: a systematic review of vaccine acceptance rates. *medRxiv preprint.*

Sambaraju, R. (2022). My countrymen have never disappointed me': Politics of service in Modi's speeches during Covid-19. *Discourse, Context and Media*, 47.

Sample, I. (2022, July 8). How will Boris Johnson's handling of the Covid crisis be remembered? *Guardian.*

Sauerbrey, A. (2020, July 7). How Germany fell back in love with Angela Merkel. *New York Times.*

Schaner, S., Theys, N., Angrisani, M., Banerjee, J., Khobragade, P. Y., Petrosyan, S., Agarwal, A., Chien, S., Weerman, B., Chakrawarty, A., & Chatterjee, P. (2022). Adherence to COVID-19 protective behaviours in India from may to December 2020: Evidence from a nationally representative longitudinal survey. *BMJ (British Medical Journal) Open, 12.*

Schumacher, E. (2020). *Germany's coronavirus response: Separating fact from fiction.* Deutsche Welle.

Science. (2022, August 26). It is an incredible place: CDC Director Rochelle Walensky on how she hopes to reform her battered agency. *An Interview.*

Sekyere, E., Bohler-Muller, N., Hongoro, C., & Makoae, M. (2020, April). *The impact of Covid-19 in South Africa.* Wilson Center Africa Program Occasional Paper.

Shergold, P., Broadbent, J., Marshall, I., & Verghese, P. (2022). *FAULT LINES: An independent review into Australia's response to COVID-19*. e61 Institute.

Shih, G. (2020, April 8). As Wuhan's lockdown ends, residents leave messages for the dead doctor who sounded the alarm on coronavirus. *Washington Post*.

Spinney, L. (2020, April 26). Germany's Covid-19 expert: For many I am the evil guy crippling the economy. *Guardian*.

Stafford, N. (2020). Covid-19: Why Germany's case fatality rate seems so low. *British Medical Journal, 369*.

Stiegler, N., & Bouchard, J.-P. (2020). South Africa: Challenges and success of the covid-19 lockdown. *Anales Médico-Psychologiques, 178*.

Stiglitz, J. (2019). *People, power and profits*. W.W. Norton & Co.

Strangio, S. (2022, June 7). Vietnam's Communist Party dumps officials over COVID-19 Test-kit scam. *The Diplomat*.

Stronski, P. (2021). *Russia's response to its spiralling COVID-19 crisis is too little, too late*. Carnegie Endowment for International Peace.

The Economist. (2020a, March 28). Covid-19 in Japan: Blowing out the flame.

The Economist. (2020b, March 28). Japanese politics: Unscathed but scathing.

The Economist. (2020c, March 28). Spain: The emergency room.

The Economist. (2020d, May 23). Japanese politics: Unscathed but scathing: Voters are unimpressed by the prime minister's handling of Covid-19.

The Economist. (2021a, March 27). Covid-19 in Brazil: Variants on a theme of disaster.

The Economist. (2021b, October 23). Brazil's woes: President anti-vaxxer.

The Economist. (2021c, September 18). French Covid-19 passports: Le Nudge.

The Economist (2021d, September 18). Vaccinations: Biden's Bidding.

Thomas, C. (2020). *Resilient health and care: Learning the lessons of COVID-19 in the English NHS*. Institute of Public Policy Research.

Tran, B. X., Hoang, M. T., Pham, H. Q., Hoang, C. L., Le, H. T., Latkin, C. A., Ho, C. S., & Ho, R. C. (2020). The operational readiness capacities of the grassroots health system in responses to epidemic: Implications of Covid-19 control in Vietnam. *Journal of Global Health, 10*(1).

Trevisan, M., Le, L. C., & Le, A. V. (2020). The Covid-19 pandemic: A view from Vietnam. *American Journal of Public Health (AJPH), 110*(8).

Trivedi, P. (2020). India's response to coronavirus pandemic: Nine lessons for effective public management. *American Review of Public Administration, 50*(6–7).

Troianovski, A. (2020, May 7). As local health systems buckle, Russian oligarchs take charge. *New York Times*.

Tyson, A., Johnson, C., & Funk, C. (2020, September 17). U.S. public now divided over whether to get Covid-19 vaccine, Pew Research Centre. *Science and Society*.

UK House of Commons. (2021, October 12). *Coronavirus: Lessons learned to date*.

Vicentini, G., & Galanti, T. (2021). *Italy, the sick man of Europe: Political reactions across the Centre and the peripheries, experts and public opinion in the Covid-19 crisis.* South European Society and Politics.

Ward, J. K., Alleaume, C., & Perretti-Watel, P. (2020). The French public's attitude to future COVID-19 vaccine: The politicization of a public health issue. *Social Science and Medicine, 265.*

Wei, S.-J. (2022, December 6). Life, liberty, and lost output. *Project Syndicate*, The Zero Covid Revolution?

Wilson, S. (2020). Pandemic leadership: Lessons from New Zealand's approach to Covid-19. *Leadership, 16*(3).

Wright, L. (2021). *The plague years: America in the time of covid* (p. 243). Alfred A. Knopf.

Yamey, G., & Gonsalves, G. (2020). Donald Trump: A political determinant of covid-19. *British Medical Journal.*

Yong, E. (2020, September). How the virus won: Anatomy of an American failure. *The Atlantic.*

Zakaria, F. (2020). *Ten lessons for a post-pandemic world.* W.W. Norton and Company.

Zhuang, Y. (2022, February 7). A Sudden Jolt in Covid Policy. *New York Times.*

PART III

Global Cooperation

CHAPTER 5

Leadership Challenges to Global Cooperation (A.S. Bhalla and Colin Mackerras)

If great power rivalries and how well or poorly they were managed, shaped much of the history of the past few centuries, the current era is more likely to be defined by how well or poorly the world addresses them.
—Richard Haass, *President, Council on Foreign Relations*

COVID-19 has affected the relationships between and among states, and vice versa. This chapter describes how an emphasis on the bilateral relationship between rising China, where the virus was first directly recorded, and the world's top superpower, the United States, have influenced COVID-19 outcomes. Besides US–China rivalry, a major challenge to international cooperation and coordination in fighting the pandemic is the growing nationalism and populism in many countries, which is also addressed.

Several factors characterized international relations on the eve of the Coronavirus outbreak. Some of the most important ones are the following:

1. The rise of the social media in an age when the Internet had become the main source of information as well as a major source of communication.
2. The rise of China, including its potential to overtake the United States economically and in other ways.

A. S. Bhalla, *National and Global Responses to the COVID-19 Pandemic*, https://doi.org/10.1007/978-3-031-29521-8_5

3. The rise of various forms of nationalism, for example, in the Russian Federation, the United States, China, India, Turkey and parts of Europe.
4. Deglobalization, but to some extent counteracted by China's outreach, especially exemplified by its Belt and Road Initiative.
5. Passionate popular concern about the deterioration of the world environment and the fear of extinction within the next few decades unless immediate remedial action is taken.
6. The Russian invasion of Ukraine (February 2022), which had many follow-on effects including the revival of NATO, with the United States assigning no troops but armaments to Ukraine to fight against the Russians.
7. Severe diminution of food security in parts of Africa and Asia, failure to solve absolute poverty in many countries, economic problems such as inflation in many parts of the more developed countries, including a rise in the price of fuel.
8. Ongoing decline in the US dollar as the internationally accepted traded currency.
9. Continued struggle against Islamist terrorism, including the rise of the Islamic State in Syria and Iraq in 2014 and, despite military defeat, its continued influence into the 2020s.
10. The United States-led attempt to isolate China and Russia.
11. The growth of an anti-West axis comprised especially of China, Russia and Iran.
12. An ongoing United States-led international feminist movement opposing sexual violence against women and affirming women's rights to consent and exercise control over their own bodies, a major expression being the MeToo movement.
13. An ongoing anti-racist movement, Black Lives Matter, and the simultaneous growth of white nationalist/supremacist sentiment.
14. Anti-democratic sentiment symbolized by the attack on the Capitol Building (Congress) in Washington DC on 6 January 2021 by Trump supporters claiming the election had been "stolen" from Trump. Contrary to democratic tradition, this movement was accompanied by legislation to restrict voting rights in Republican-controlled states with potentially dangerous long-term consequences for democracy.

Sino-American Relations and Challenge to Global Cooperation on COVID-19

The most crucial bilateral relationship for leadership challenges to global cooperation over the handling of COVID-19 is undoubtedly that between the United States and China. A period of cooperation between China and the United States, beginning in the early 1970s, came to an abrupt end in 2017–2018. In 2001, with American agreement, China joined the World Trade Organization (WTO). Its consequent economic participation in the world, and the West in particular, led to an acceleration of overall economic growth rate.

Trump seriously damaged global cooperation by pointing the finger of blame at China for the virus. Biden has given more emphasis to vaccinating the American public and combating the virus within his own country. While he has not tried to be conciliatory towards China, he has at least taken his focus away from blame. In the meantime, Xi has done his best to avert blame and emphasize cooperation against the virus. But there has been no response from the American side. A retired US diplomat is right to see *competition* as to which country will dominate the twenty-first century as the crucial issue (Freeman, 2021, May 9). However, that does not preclude the possibility of *cooperation* in some areas, such as tackling the COVID-19 pandemic.

There are several specific ways in which bad Sino-American relations damaged cooperative leadership vis-à-vis the pandemic four of which deserve special attention. These are discussed below.

Views Over the Origin of the Virus

The rights and wrongs of the origins of the virus are extremely complex. Controversy raged over this matter from the start. Numerous versions emerged, some based on science, but all too many on blind prejudice and conspiracy theories. The World Health Assembly of May 2020 called for "a stepwise process of impartial, independent and comprehensive evaluation response to COVID-19." (WHO, 2020, May 19). A committee of scientists visited Wuhan early in 2021 and issued a report, while a WHO-commissioned report by an Independent Panel was released about the same time (IPPPR, 2021a, 2021b).

This report's key finding was that the initial outbreak developed into a pandemic for a lack of preparedness for, and response to, COVID-19.

Although the Panel abstained from pointing the finger of blame at individual countries for these failings, it did comment that "too many countries took a 'wait and see' approach rather than enacting an aggressive containment strategy," and that "coordinated, global leadership was absent. Global tensions undermined multilateral institutions and cooperative action (IPPPR, 2021a, p. 2).

This was especially clear in the attitude Trump displayed. In notes for a meeting on 20 March 2020, he replaced the word "corona" before "virus" by hand with the word "Chinese". When pressed about this change, which many regarded as stereotyping individual nations and even racist, Trump replied: "It's not racist at all, no, not at all. It comes from China, that's why. I want to be accurate." (Cilizza, 2020).

An obvious political move, it was designed to embarrass China and was a very clear demonstration of *conflictual leadership* between the US and China over the pandemic. Unfortunately, Trump persisted in this attitude, attempting to weaponize the pandemic against China at just the time he should have been taking concrete measures to fight the virus (see Chap. 4). The pandemic was a crucial issue in the US Presidential election of 2020, one that harmed Trump because the Democrats blamed him for inaction.

Although the Biden Administration has been less direct and obvious in its castigation of China for its role in the pandemic, its attitude is fundamentally the same as its predecessor's. It has continued to criticize China for withholding information about the origins of the virus, drawing harsh reactions from Chinese spokespersons. Neither Biden nor Secretary of State Blinken has shown any sign of wanting to cooperate with the Chinese leadership to discover the origins of the virus.

Throughout 2020, a theory rumbled that the virus came from the Wuhan Institute of Virology, and that the Chinese had used it deliberately as an instrument of biological warfare. The United States has itself been secretive about whether its biotechnology research in its own labs, which shared their results with other countries including China, may have contributed to COVID-19. Despite calls for an independent inquiry about this, the US National Institute of Health refused to set up an independent investigation of this issue which was requested by many virologists (Maxmen, 2021). In a recent article, Harrison and Sachs (2022, May 27) have again reiterated the need for a bipartisan government inquiry.

As for the Chinese leadership, it was at all times very defensive about the charge that, because the first reported cases of COVID came from

Wuhan, China was automatically responsible for the virus. Chinese spokespersons repeatedly hurled denials, especially against the United States.[1]

Yet to be fair, Xi Jinping consistently called for international cooperation to defeat the virus under WHO leadership. In his speech to the World Health Assembly in May 2020, he said that "China calls on the international community to increase political and financial support for WHO so as to mobilize resources worldwide to defeat the virus." He also offered US$2 billion over two years "to help with the COVID-19 response and with economic and social development in affected countries, especially developing countries." (Xinhua, 2020, May 18). He was considerably more cooperative and generous in his approach than his American counterpart.

Attitudes Towards the WHO

The United States was definitely hostile to the WHO, which is responsible for the global management of health. In May 2020, Trump decided to stop funding the Organization and announced his intention to withdraw from it altogether. According to the Congressional record, the Trump Administration believed that the WHO had "mismanaged its response" to the pandemic and was displaying an "alarming lack of independence" from China (CRS, 2020, October 21). Considering that the WHO is the internationally recognized body responsible for health matters, and that the Chinese leadership had been working closely with it from the start, there could scarcely be a move more calculated to insult China than this. No move could better illustrate division among world leaders in handling COVID-19 or Trump's hostility to globalization.

Trump's decision was very unwise. WHO's functions (providing medicines, vaccines and health advice to the developing world) are generally beneficial in the global management of health (see Chap. 6). It facilitates scientific exchange, compiling and distributing the results of international research, which is especially important in countries that do not have their own pharmaceutical industry. Moreover, Trump's moves made Chinese international influence grow in the field of health at the expense of American influence. As Anne Applebaum (2020, November) reported, "America will lose yet another battle in an ideological war that most of us don't even know we are fighting."

As it turned out, American withdrawal from the WHO was aborted. Because of the process of withdrawal, it was not due to take effect until

July 2021, by which time the Biden administration had taken over. In January 2021, it halted the process Trump had begun. This was one respect in which Biden showed himself less hostile to China than Trump and his leadership more cooperative in dealing with COVID-19.

Policy Responses to the Pandemic

From the outbreak of the pandemic the American and Chinese leaderships adopted different policies towards handling it. Also, there were various approaches to the virus in the United States. State governors came from both major parties, while shutdowns were quite common, even though Trump did not favour them. Moreover, the federal political system in the United States meant that the States could undermine the federal government's authority unlike the centralized control of the Chinese system. Overall, both sides saw advantages in their respective political systems. In particular, China emphasized that the United States had been harder hit by the virus than any other country, while it survived very well. Chinese spokespersons saw evidence of the superiority of their own system.

As discussed in Chap. 4, Trump suppressed scientific data, delayed testing, mocked and blocked mask wearing and convened mass gatherings where social distancing was impossible. The context of mass gatherings is that during the 2020 election Trump played to as many crowds as he could, in the correct belief that making speeches to large crowds was his strength. He made no attempt to limit mass gatherings and poured scorn on Biden for doing so.

Trump had his supporters for his COVID-19 policy. For instance, some believed that the best way to combat COVID-19 was to develop immunity against the disease from the start by taking drugs such as hydroxychloroquine, rather than developing vaccines. Indeed, Trump openly defended the anti-malaria drug even though most scientists had rejected the notion that it provided protection against COVID-19. Trump supporters also believed that the economic effects of shutdowns outweighed the harm COVID-19 caused.

But the reality is that the effects of the virus on the American economy and society were devastating. Regarding health, the following is a serious indictment: "In the final year of Donald Trump's presidency, more than 450,000 Americans died from Covid-19, and life expectancy fell by 1.13 years, the biggest decrease since World War II." (Bor et al., 2021, March 5). As of 31 August 2022, the overall number of COVID deaths in the

United States were over one million compared to about 15,000 in China. The United States ranked fifth in terms of deaths per million (3105) compared to China, which had the lowest rate in the world (see Chap. 2, Table 2.4).

Among ordinary Americans, attitudes towards China were highly negative as a result of COVID-19. A Pew Research survey (July 2020) found historic highs in unfavourable views of China among Americans. "Around two-thirds of Americans (64%) say China has done a bad job dealing with the coronavirus outbreak. Around three-quarters (78%) place a great deal or fair amount of the blame for the global spread of the coronavirus on the Chinese government's initial handling of the COVID-19 outbreak in Wuhan" (Silver et al., 2020, July 30).

As for China, its policy was to go into forced lockdown completely as soon as the severity of the virus was known. This was actually very effective in containing the virus much earlier and more thoroughly than in other countries. It meant that infections and deaths in China were quite low by comparison with most other countries (see Chap. 2).

The disparity with the United States raises the question of what ordinary Chinese think. Clearly, they increasingly resent the way the American leadership continues to treat them as inferior and to castigate and isolate them on human rights grounds. According to some researchers, "Increasingly negative U.S. attitudes toward China may only boost Chinese citizens' positive attitudes toward their own political system," (Feng, 2021, September 23) even to the extent of seeing it as superior to that of America, especially in dealing with crises.

Vaccine Diplomacy

Competition between the United States and China over vaccine diplomacy is another case in point. There has been a clear divergence between the two approaches to vaccine distribution. China's advanced vaccine diplomacy stands in contrast to the "me first policies" of the United States and the European Union. With the shortfall in supplies, US and EU leaders faced high infection rates and death tolls at home and felt the need to inoculate their domestic populations first. This left the world's poorest and most vulnerable people without vaccine supply although the situation has gradually improved. China has not faced these problems as much and could afford to send vaccines abroad.

To his credit, Biden, quickly changed Trump's approach to the pandemic by vaccinating as many Americans as possible against the virus. He said initially that his aim was to have 100 million people vaccinated within 100 days. Then on 21 April 2021, he announced that 200 million Americans had received the jab, double his original aim, which he claimed as "an incredible achievement for the nation," especially since his term in office had not yet quite reached 100 days (Naylor, 2021, April 21). However, apart from initial success in expanding vaccinations, Biden was poor in messaging and slow in rollout of masks and tests. He underestimated stiff opposition to his COVID policy from political opponents (Krugman, 2022, January 20).

On 7 May 2021, the WHO gave formal emergency approval to the Chinese Sinopharm vaccine, first for one produced by a non-Western country. Earlier, it had approved the joint American-German Pfizer/BioNTech, the British AstraZeneca and the American Johnson & Johnson and Moderna. China developed several of its own vaccines and pursued a diplomacy it called the Health Silk Road. The implication was that China had become competitive with the West in vaccine diplomacy. China administered to its own people a total of 2.9 billion doses, nearly one-fourth of the total compared to 520 million doses in the United States (*Our World in Data*, 2022, January 10). China's vaccination rate (91%) was much higher than that of the United States (67%) (see Chap. 2, Table 2.5).

Another participant in vaccine diplomacy and competition was the Quad, a grouping of four countries, viz. the United States, Japan, India and Australia, which united as "like-minded" countries against China. The Quad launched "a joint vaccine distribution initiative in the Indo-Pacific, challenging China's 'vaccine diplomacy efforts by agreeing to cooperate to produce and distribute one billion vaccines for the region." (Rudd, 2022, p. 210). They also took other measures such as the establishment of a vaccine expert working group.

In the light of America's strong belief that China was to blame for the pandemic, the following comment by Zhao Suisheng (2021, April 29) of the University of Denver is of particular interest. "Rolling out of vaccines to developing countries, Beijing has framed itself as a solution to the pandemic rather than the origin of the coronavirus."

Nationalism and COVID-19

Nationalistic sentiments and the "me first" national and local attitudes mentioned above preceded the coronavirus pandemic. So did inward-looking protectionist state policies. But the concepts such as the nation state and national sovereignty as well as protectionism have become much stronger in the course of the pandemic. The world is still experiencing the fallout from the "America First" policies of the Trump era, which have been imitated by many nationalist/populist regimes.

Although there are different shades of nationalism, the concept/practice is based on two major guiding principles, namely the nation state and national sovereignty and self-determination. A violation of the principle of congruence of state and nation offends the nationalist sentiment. Nationalists believe that one-state one nation idea ensures peace and harmony. In multi-nation states/societies, some (ethnic) groups that do not find recognition may protest and lead to social strife and conflict.

Both populist nationalism and absolute national sovereignty can pose serious challenges to global cooperation and conflict resolution. Nation states are often reluctant to cooperate internationally or regionally out of fear that they might sacrifice sovereignty in the process. But such cooperation need not diminish their importance. At any rate, absolute national sovereignty is curbed not only by international agreements/treaties but also by arrangements within states, such as a federal structure of governance, which involves the sharing of responsibility between the centre and states/provinces. It is not easy to reconcile the concepts of "national sovereignty of states" and self-determination of peoples. Indeed, it may be impossible to do so, as Mayall (2000) argues.

Nationalism has been described as "a seductive and corrosive force." (Brown, 2021, p. 369). It is likely to survive even if Sino-American rivalry discussed above is somehow checked. Combined with a surge of populism, it becomes a more powerful force. Populism is generally defined as a political strategy to consolidate power by sowing seeds of social, class and even racial divisions and hatred. It pits ordinary people against the elite who may be rich and privileged, as well as against scientific and medical experts and health professionals. Even before Brexit and Trump, populist tendencies were fuelled by several forces: people's growing distrust of the elites and public institutions, erosion of ethnic identity through mass immigration and deprivation through rising inequalities in income and wealth (Eatwell & Goodwin, 2018; Williams et al., 2020).

There are several causes of rising nationalism and populism across the world, including economic and social insecurity, feeling of losing one's cultural identity and social and political exclusion. Unless these causes are addressed, their undesirable consequences will become even more widespread, leading to further restrictions to international cooperation for COVID-19. Gordon Brown (2021, pp. 389–403) proposes four Rs (Redistribution, Recognition, Representation and Reform) to respond to the rise in populist nationalism. Economic insecurity can be overcome only through better income and employment opportunities for the poor. And better skills and retraining as well as educational opportunity can help narrow the gap between the haves and have-nots.

Populists/nationalists blame globalization, free trade and immigration ("foreign workers") for the loss of jobs and declining real wages in the West. Chap. 4 discusses how economic and social inequalities have hurt minorities and immigrants particularly badly. The anti-immigrant sentiments of populist/nationalists have only made matters worse. Debate about the reasons for job losses, whether it is trade or technology or another factor, continues to rage. Populists tend to underestimate the role of technology and pin most of the blame on trade-induced globalization. They believe that the solution lies in deglobalization, the relocation of offshore manufacturing, trade protection and national self-reliance.

The demonization of immigrants and ethnic minorities is not confined only to Western countries where right-wing conservatives have exploited immigration to achieve electoral successes. In India also, the conservative and nationalistic BJP government singled out Muslims as the main super spreader of COVID-19, particularly following a large number of deaths associated with a regional religious gathering in the country. The Hindu nationalists in India politicized the pandemic in ways not very different from Trump's conservative Republican supporters who vilified immigrants, African Americans and minority groups such as the Chinese and other Asians for spreading COVID-19.

Cultural and racial discrimination can breed social alienation and hate, which needs to be overcome through family and community ties at the local level, and by inculcating a sense of patriotism at the national level. A sense of local identity and loyalty can be restored through recognition and local participation.

Finally, it has become clear that global challenges like COVID-19 cannot be solved with the primacy of the nation state. As we demonstrate in Chap. 6, a number of global and regional initiatives are under way to check and mitigate the devastating effects of COVID-19 despite the rising tide of nationalism.

The rapid spread of the deadly new variants shows that the world today is more interconnected than ever before. What happens in one country can very rapidly affect the rest of the world with immediate and dire consequences. COVID-19 spread quickly throughout the world because of globalization.

Nationalism and populism in times of COVID-19 raise several relevant issues and questions. For example, what is the precise nature of the relationship between nationalism and the coronavirus pandemic? Is there a reinforcing link between the two? Will the pandemic, by exacerbating pre-existing inequalities, trigger ethnic conflicts, and how will the pandemic either erode or reinforce the nation state? (Woods et al., 2020). These issues pose a major challenge to global cooperation on COVID-19, as briefly discussed below.

Impact of Nationalism on the Management of COVID-19

One of the distinguishing features of the current pandemic is the populist/nationalistic sentiments which have deeply influenced how several governments have been responding to it. These forces were much weaker previously (especially during the 2009 pandemic of H1N1).

There was little difference in the nature of the pandemics in 2009 and 2020. However, the responses in the forms of lockdowns, banning of all travel and closure of borders were quite different. So were the political landscapes in the world. Several countries politicized the COVID-19 pandemic to suit narrow populist/nationalistic ends. Nationalist leaders like Bolsonaro and Trump, discussed in Chap. 4, responded to the pandemic on partisan and political lines and challenged scientists and scientific evidence. They downplayed the severity of the virus despite warnings by experts. Political divisiveness in Brazil is similar to that in the United States where the more liberal democrats took the pandemic far more seriously than their Republican counterparts.

Many nationalist leaders in the West (mainly the United States) blamed other countries (China) and other social groups (minorities, Asians and Blacks) for the virus, as noted above. An online reporter recorded 1135 cases of COVID-related discrimination against the Chinese over a two-week period (19 March-1 April, 2020) (Jeung, 2020).

Cases of racism against African Americans (often politically motivated) sometimes occur because of the mistaken belief that they are unhygienic carriers of COVID-19. Aggressive and violent behaviour of COVID-deniers and vaccine-sceptics has been on the rise in a number of countries. While anti-Asian and anti-African American sentiments are often racially and politically motivated, social stigma against unvaccinated or infected persons, stems more out of fear of catching the virus (Ergler et al., 2021; Gardner et al., 2022).

The world today is divided between nationalist and globalist leaders and populist versus globalist, inward-looking and outward-looking governments. For example, countries such as Brazil, India, Turkey, the United Kingdom and the United States are associated with populism/nationalism in one form or another. They have also fared rather poorly in managing the pandemic as shown in Chap. 2.

However, opinions differ regarding the precise ways in which nationalism affected a country's response. According to Greenfeld (2020) of Boston University, "the course of the pandemic was certainly affected by the ways it was handled in different countries, and the way it was handled, ... was a direct function of nationalism, specifically of the national conflict between China and the United States." (Woods et al., 2020).

The following are several concrete examples of the influence of nationalism on the management of COVID-19:

- In the summer of 2020, the United States bought up virtually all the supplies of Remdesivir, one of the first drugs proven to work against COVID-19, leaving none for the United Kingdom, the EU or most of the rest of the world for three months.
- During the Trump presidency, the United States did not join the UN/WHO COVAX Facility.
- The EU imposed import restrictions on the export of PPEs. However, it was soon forced to scale down or drop them, realizing that it would hinder the flow of required parts from such non-EU members states as Norway and Switzerland.

- In Hungary, Orban used the health pandemic to strengthen his authoritarian rule by sidelining parliament and governing by decree. But despite the centralization of power, he made no effort to control the pandemic. The death toll per capita in his country was the highest in the world as of 31 August 2022 (see Chap. 2, Table 2.5).
- The United States did not supply biobags to India in which vaccines are made because it preferred to give priority to its domestic firms under the Defence Production Act. This prevented the Indian Serum Institute from expanding its vaccine production.
- India banned the export of vaccines following a surge of cases in the country in early 2021.
- A pharmaceutical company in South Africa, producing vaccines in partnership with Johnson and Johnson of the United States shipped them to Europe despite the fact that more than 90 per cent of the local population was not vaccinated at all.
- Pfizer denied African clinical trial (Drugs for Neglected Diseases Initiative) access to its antiviral drug, ***Paxlovid***, to use in a large study in ten African countries. Denying access, it had its own plans to conduct similar trials without providing any details (Ledford & Maxmen, 2022, April 4).

The above examples are a clear indication that nationalism can be a stumbling block to global cooperation on COVID-19. It contributes to the primacy of the state which weakens global governance. Nationalists are afraid of losing sovereignty if they get involved in solving global problems such as the current health crisis. The discussion of vaccine nationalism is a case in point. Vaccine-producing countries have failed to share vaccine supplies with poor developing countries, resulting in their low vaccination rates, which makes the goal of herd immunity a distant dream. They fear that doing so will prevent them from looking after their own populations.

Vaccine Nationalism

As the pandemic advances into its third year, it showed no signs of easing up, nor do the leadership challenges to global cooperation appear to be lessening. If the dominant news of 2020 was the pandemic's spread throughout the world, that of 2021 and 2022 has been the attempt to slow or end it through vaccine distribution. Yet the central theme of vaccine distribution has undoubtedly been inequity, with the high-income wealthy countries hogging available vaccines at the expense of poor ones.

The vaccine-producing countries (e.g. the United Kingdom and the United States) bought millions of doses which are several times in excess of their domestic requirements. Low-income countries had to wait several months to make their first vaccine deals.

Macron's proposal for Europe and America to donate 4–5 per cent of their vaccine supplies to developing countries was rejected by Biden who preferred to fund COVAX instead. The United Kingdom, which had already obtained 4.5 million vaccine doses from the Indian Serum Institute, sent an envoy to try to secure another 5.5 million (*The Economist*, 2021a, April 3). It is the smaller countries, like New Zealand and Spain, which have been more generous in pledging to donate 7.5 and 1.6 million doses, respectively (*The Economist*, 2021b, May 15). Lack of political commitment, even among the globalists, to share vaccines has been described by the WHO Director-General as "a moral failure."

Shortages of vaccine supplies in Europe forced a number of EU member countries (Italy, Serbia, Hungary, Poland and the Czech Republic, for example) to approve and accept the use of Chinese and Russian vaccines. This turnaround in the face of dire necessity suggests that downgrading of the Russian and Chinese vaccines only months earlier may have been partly politically motivated. Countries like Italy have agreed to produce the Russian vaccine within its territory given the production bottlenecks in Russia which prevent the rapid expansion of the vaccine supply. Scaling up of production in Russia is being hampered by the lack of biotech equipment which the country does not produce. In India, the Serum Institute could not expand vaccine production for lack of biobags (containers in which vaccines are made), tubing and filters. The United States failed to supply biobags because it preferred to give priority to domestic firms (*The Economist*, 2021b).

The use of Russian and Chinese vaccines (because the West would not supply them their vaccines) showed no adverse effects. Doubts about these vaccines seem to arise from a general perception in the West against authoritarian states. Results published in the *Lancet* on Sputnik V, the Russian vaccine, indicate its high efficacy. But some questions remain about its effectiveness (Jones & Roy, 2021; Logunov et al., 2021; Cohen, 2020; Mallapaty, 2021). Similar issues concern Western vaccines.

Twenty-five deaths of Norwegian patients, who received the American/German Pfizer vaccine, alarmed people in Australia and elsewhere.

In issuing its report in May 2021, Independent Panel (IPPPR, 2021b) made a few recommendations to end the pandemic. The first was that richer countries provide “at least 1 billion” vaccine doses to poor and middle-income nations. This was to help overcome the inequities of the vaccine system, which requires overcoming two major hurdles. One is the kind of vaccine nationalism that prevented the rich countries from distributing their own vaccines to anybody but their own people or those of allies who were prepared to pay. The other is the reluctance of vaccine-producing countries to release rights of intellectual property over their vaccines for fear that others could manufacture them without due payment to the companies that had created them. This is an issue of great importance in terms of cooperative leadership.

As the major vaccine developers, the G7 countries are well placed to transfer vaccine technology to poor developing countries. Yet Europe opposed the demands (until recently, see Chap. 6) of developing countries like India and South Africa (*People's Vaccine Alliance*) for a temporary waiver of vaccine patents so that they could create/expand their own manufacturing facilities. So has Big Pharma, which argues that a waiver will discourage innovation, and that developing countries lack the skills to manufacture vaccines based on new technologies. On the other hand, developing countries argue that waivers were also allowed in the past for anti-retroviral drugs, that taxpayers funded the development of many of the vaccines, that they should enjoy sovereignty over pathogens and share the benefits of research and development, technology and knowledge for generic production (Fidler, 2020).

The Serum Institute in India and Aspen Pharmacare in South Africa faced no notable manufacturing problems. Russia and China shared technology and knowledge. CEPI has identified 250 companies which could manufacture vaccines (Stiglitz & Wallach, 2021). On 5 May 2021, Biden reversed US policy sharply on the question of intellectual property. His trade representative, Katherine Tai, said in a statement that, though the Administration believed in intellectual property protections, it would support a waiver “in service of ending this pandemic.” (Office of the US Trade Representative, 2021, May 5). Although this was a step in the right direction, it did not overcome the shortfall of vaccine doses in 2021.

Negotiations for a patent waiver in the WTO are time-consuming, and associated measures of sharing technology and know-how will be required. And then there is the question of funding which was not even on the agenda of the G7 summit. The American approval of the waiver has been described as "at best an empty gesture and at worst a cynical one." (*The Economist*, May 15).

On the eve of the summit, over 100 former world leaders had called for the G7 summit to contribute two-thirds of the $66 billion for a comprehensive global vaccination programme. The vaccine-producing wealthy countries bear major responsibility for failing to respond *quickly*, withholding deliveries of vaccine supplies to where they are most needed, and thus allowing the emergence of new, more infectious variants.

It would be impossible to eradicate the global coronavirus without globally-coordinated action. But efforts in this direction through the Access to COVID-19 Tools (ACT) accelerator have not made much progress for lack of adequate funding and unwillingness of some major donors to participate (see Chap. 6). Neither have regional bodies such as the European Union (EU) succeeded in coordinating the purchase, distribution and delivery of vaccines to members and non-members. The EU had entered into an agreement with vaccine producers for purchases on behalf of member states to ensure equitable distribution to poorer members (see Chap. 6). But it was not particularly well-equipped to deal with the public health issues, and its slow response to Italy, a badly affected member, was exploited by nationalist leaders and Eurosceptic parties. Vaccine shortages led many individual member states to strike bilateral deals with vaccine suppliers (such as China and Russia and the United States) outside the EU framework, which undermined the bloc's solidarity. Besides, bidding against one another for vaccines resulted in raising the prices of the vaccine doses and of related material inputs.

Bollyky and Bown (2020) have proposed a COVID-19 trade and investment agreement to promote global health cooperation. But for this kind of agreement to help raise vaccine production and supplies, it requires an investment fund to purchase the vaccines. To be effective, such an agreement also needs to recognize the interests, contributions and responsibilities of different groups of countries.

It is ironic that the development of global supply chains for medical goods and equipment, labelled as "solidarity chains," is being relocated in response to greater protectionism and disruptions to trade and commerce.

More than two years into the pandemic, the response of most countries to match production with rapidly growing demand has been woefully slow due to slow procurement through imports, resulting from a partial breakdown of global supply chains.

To conclude, there is a growing trend towards national self-reliance and regionalization of trade and supply chains following Trump's "America-first policy" and its tariff war with China (Enderwick & Buckley, 2020). Some countries (e.g. Japan and the United States) have already made attempts to relocate offshore production, but with mixed results. And Trump's attempts to bring back US firms from China have also not succeeded (Erchi et al., 2020).

In this climate, a proposal for a vaccine certification system to jumpstart international travel and revive the tourism sector would be fraught with implementation problems (Blair et al., 2021, September 1). To make such a system work globally would require a massive amount of data sharing, acceptance and willingness of countries to exchange information and support a dual structure of the vaccinated and unvaccinated. National vaccine regulatory bodies will need to cooperate and coordinate their actions, which is most unlikely in the current environment of going it alone. The certification system will fail without synchronizing between domestic regulatory approval and its recognition globally of at least a minimum number of vaccines. For example, after two years since the rollout of the AstraZeneca vaccine, the FDA still has not approved it. The recent debates in Europe over national vaccine certificates and vaccine passports, and the failure of many countries to adopt them does not show much promise for a global system. Major stumbling blocks include concerns about individual data privacy and discrimination against the unvaccinated.

Will COVID-19 Lead to More Populism and Nationalism?

The rise of nationalism might also be a consequence of states' responses to the pandemic (Rachman, 2020; Tisdall, 2020). De-globalization, relocation of global supply chains, anti-immigration policies and public sentiments, as discussed above, point in that direction. Anti-Chinese (Asian) hate crimes in the wake of Trump's labelling of the coronavirus as a Chinese virus in the United States, Australia and elsewhere and condemnation of Muslims in India as COVID super spreaders are clear indications of the interplay of these forces.

The pandemic health emergency necessitated restrictions on individual privacy and freedom for health protection, besides tracking of people's whereabouts through intrusive surveillance. Many populist/nationalist leaders exploited these measures to strengthen their authoritarian power and control. Autocrats may see nationalism and health emergency measures as an opportunity to act against their opponents as has happened in Hungary under Orban. The weakening of democratic and representative institutions is an inevitable consequence of a toxic mix of nationalism and authoritarianism (Bieber, 2020; Eatwell & Goodwin, 2018). The existence of such a mix suggests that the two phenomena are mutually reinforcing (Bonikowski, 2017; Jenne, 2018). For example, the growth of autocratic regimes in the EU has hurt the bloc's solidarity and effectiveness to respond to the pandemic with one voice.

The pandemic has had other negative impacts such as rising economic and social inequalities (see Chap. 4). These effects may be further exacerbated following the expiry of economic and social relief measures adopted by various governments. The greater the widening of inequalities, the larger is the probability of social discontent among those groups which will suffer the most, notably minorities and immigrants, who are usually at the bottom of economic and social ladder (Sedik & Xu, 2020, October).[2] But whether these inequalities by themselves will trigger intra-state strife and conflict is an open question to which there are no easy answers. Although there may not be any direct causal relation between COVID-19, protests and nationalism, political leaders are more likely to arouse nationalist sentiments during civil unrest than in peace times.

Protests and demonstrations against COVID-19 restrictions are common to both low-income and high-income countries. In the former, they are more likely to be triggered by economic hardships in the wake of prolonged lockdowns, stay-at-home orders and low rates of vaccination. In rich countries, they are due to a mixture of other causes, notably, vaccine hesitancy, and a fight for civil liberties and individual freedom.

As discussed above, inter-state rivalries and tensions have arisen over supplies of medical equipment and vaccines. Sino-American rivalry, which dates back to the pre-pandemic period, became worse during COVID-19. It turned into open confrontation involving trade and tariff barriers besides the imposition of economic sanctions.

Will COVID-19 further reinforce nationalistic/populist forces in the post-pandemic period? A priori, there are three possible scenarios.

Firstly, the restrictive public health measures, besides people's fears of disease and death, are likely to turn people towards their local community for moral support. These forces are likely to strengthen nationalism in future (Rachman, 2020, March 23; Tisdall, March 28). The return of the nation-state has been explained by its greater financial and organizational strengths during an emergency such as the pandemic, fragility of global supply chains discussed above and political trends such as protectionism, localization of production and stricter border controls.

Secondly, the opposite scenario may also be plausible, that is, people and governments may believe that COVID-19 is not engineered by another nation, state or social group. After all, some global and regional cooperation continues to take place despite the existence of nationalistic tendencies (see Chap. 6).

Finally, the outcome may turn out to be indeterminate. The strength of nationalistic forces will depend on the relative importance of nationalistic, political and ideological views of leaders, institutions (governments) and followers. The trend towards political divisions and polarization in a number of countries, particularly in the United States (see Chap. 4), suggests that all the followers do not necessarily support populists. For example, extremely conservative Republicans led by the former president are nationalistic, but liberal Democrats are not. The latter's ideological beliefs are generally more globalist. Nationalistic tendencies may be neutralized as long as there are a sufficient number of people with countervailing beliefs. A study, which examined whether ideological beliefs affect individuals' support for nationalistic policies during COVID-19 in the United States, concluded: "When states' nationalist policies contradict their ideology, people tend to withdraw their support." (Su & Shen, 2021, p. 183). The effect of COVID-19 will most likely be a rise in nationalism when nationalistic and ideological beliefs coincide. However, nationalism may not rise in situations in which liberal beliefs countervail and neutralize the conservative nationalist view.

To conclude, it is difficult to determine what shape nationalism will take in the post-pandemic world. However, it is clear that the COVID-19 health emergency has laid bare the limitations of existing global institutions such as the G7and G20. It took eight months for the G20 to meet in 2020 in the midst of the biggest health and economic crisis. Global action discussed in the following chapter would have been far better coordinated and more effective if the political leaders and the above groups had adopted a global plan of action for COVID-19.

Conclusion

One principal conclusion stands out from this chapter, which is, that the Independent Panel was right to suggest that coordinated global leadership was absent in the handling of COVID-19. The Panel observed that "this pandemic has shaken some of the standard assumptions that a country's wealth will secure its health. Leadership and competence have counted more than cash in pandemic responses." (IPPPR, 2021b, p. 11). It underlined the need for "stronger leadership and better coordination at national, regional and international level, including a more focused and Independent WHO, a Pandemic Treaty and a Senior Global Health Threats Council." (Ibid., p. 45).

No effort was made to prepare a global plan to fight the pandemic. Neither was there any global coordination nor harmonization of policies and measures concerned with vaccinations and international travel. On the contrary, when many countries reopened their borders after lockdowns, chaos and confusion ensued from contradictory measures introduced by different countries. Countries like the United Kingdom appeared to make arbitrary choices who would be allowed into the country. For example, Indian nationals who were fully vaccinated with AstraZeneca produced in the United Kingdom and India were not allowed. The absence of reciprocal arrangements led to retaliation by the victimized countries.

This leads us to the following questions. Is it possible to coordinate global leadership better? Is it possible to reduce global tensions and increase cooperative action? The answer to both is yes, but only to a certain extent. It is unlikely that Biden will wish for a full economic or political recoupling with China, though in our opinion this would help in dealing with the COVID-19 pandemic. However, there are still ways in which the United States and China could cooperate, for example, in meeting challenges of future pandemics, developing a better system of distribution of vaccines to poor countries, climate change and arms control negotiations (Rudd, 2022, p. 222). There may be room for more global cooperation in waiving intellectual property rights to defeat the pandemic. The signing of a detailed statement on climate change by the American and Chinese envoys in Shanghai is an encouraging sign.[3] But any bilateral cooperation is most unlikely in the current situation of mutual distrust and acrimony.

The new variants increase the difficulty of making a universally effective vaccine. Competition to produce vaccines proliferates, which is partly driven by nationalism. Rich countries have so far been stingy in their contributions to the international COVAX, through which vaccines are produced worldwide and distributed equitably. Indeed, they buy up available vaccines disproportionately, making equity more difficult (see Chap. 6).

Some world leaders are keen to sign an international treaty to combat the pandemic as discussed in Chap. 6. Such a treaty could facilitate global leadership cooperation. However, there are problems. Stoked by nationalism, expressed in particular in the war in Ukraine, global tensions show no sign of easing, let alone disappearing. This makes world cooperation to defeat the virus very difficult.

The post-recovery phase of the pandemic requires a global attack on several fronts: promotion of health for all, economic revival of national economies and the global economy, humanitarian responses, global and equitable distribution of vaccines and global research cooperation. The above pessimistic outlook should not detract from the fact that despite road blocks described above, efforts at some international collaboration and coordination are under way, as discussed in the following chapter.

Notes

1. In March 2020, the famous "wolf warrior diplomat," Zhao Lijian "raised a suspicion on his personal Twitter account that it might have been the US army representatives to the Military World Games who brought the novel coronavirus to Wuhan in October 2019." Never proved, this suggestion remained in the realm of conspiracy theory (see Leng & Wan, 2020).
2. The Sydney-based Institute of Economics and Peace (IEP) estimated a 10 per cent rise in civil unrest in 2020, which may not all be due to COVID-19. But it also "counted 5000 instances of pandemic related violence in 158 countries." (*The Economist*, 2021c, July 31).
3. For instance, on 17 April 2021, special climate envoys for China and the United States, Zhenhua Xie and John Kerry signed a detailed statement in Shanghai, which emphasized the necessity for the two countries to cooperate to preserve the climate (see U.S. Department of State, 17 April 2020).

References

Applebaum, A. (2020 How China outsmarted the trump administration: While the U.S. is distracted, China is rewriting the rules of the global order. *The Atlantic*.

Bieber, F. (2020, April). *Global nationalism in times of COVID-19 pandemic*. Nationalities Papers.

Blair, T., Bell, J., & Agus, D. B. (2021, September 1). We need to start travelling again. Here's how. *New York Times.*

Bollyky, T. J., & Bown, C. P. (2020, September–October). The tragedy of vaccine nationalism. *Foreign Affairs.*

Bonikowski, B. (2017). Ethnonationalist populism and the mobilization of collective resentment. *British Journal of Sociology, 68.*

Bor, J., Himmelstein, D. U., & Woolhandle, S. (2021, March 5). Trump's policy failures have exacted a heavy toll on public health. *Scientific American.*

Brown, G. (2021). *Seven ways to change the world.* Simon & Schuster.

Cilizza, C. (2020, March 20). Yes, of course Donald Trump is calling coronavirus the 'China virus' for political reasons. *CNN Politics.* The Point.

Cohen, Jon 2020 Russia's claim of a successful COVID-19 vaccine doesn't pass the 'smell test,' critics say. *Science.*

Congressional Research Service (CRS). (2020, October 21). *U.S. withdrawal from the World Health Organization: Process and implications.* CRS Report, Prepared for Members and Committees of Congress, R46575.

Eatwell, R., & Goodwin, M. (2018). *National populism: The revolt against liberal democracy.* Pelican.

Enderwick, P., & Buckley, P. (2020). Rising regionalization: Will the post-COVID-19 world see a retreat from globalization? *Transnational Corporations, 27*(2).

Erchi, Z., Tong, Q., & Yelin, M. (2020). *Despite attempts to lure them away, multinationals aren't leaving China.* Caixang Global Business Tech.

Ergler, C., Huish, R., Georgeou, N., Simons, J., Eyles, O., Li, Y., Deng, T., & Tame, L. (2021). COVID-19 stigma in New Zealand: Are we really a 'team' of five million? *New Zealand Geographer, 77*(3). Although the article is mainly about New Zealand, the issues of Covid-19 stigma and 'slow violence' are of much wider applicability.

Feng, E. (2021, September 23) As U.S. views of China grow more negative, Chinese support for their government rises. *NPR.*

Fidler, D. P. (2020). Vaccine nationalism's politics. *Science, 369*(6505).

Freeman, C. W. (2021). Washington is playing a losing game with China—Analysis. *Eurasia Review, News & Analysis, East Asia Forum.*

Gardner, D. M., Briggs, C. O., & Ryan, A. M. (2022). It is your fault: Workplace consequences of anti-Asian stigma during COVID-19. *Equality, Diversity and Inclusion, 41*(1).

Harrison, N. H., & Sachs, J. D. (2022). Did US biotechnology help to create Covid-19? *Project Syndicate.*

IPPPR (Independent Panel for Pandemic Preparedness and Response). (2021a, January). *COVID-19: Make it the last pandemic—A summary.*

IPPPR (Independent Panel for Pandemic Preparedness and Response). (2021b, May 12). *COVID-19: Make it the last pandemic—The main report.*

Jenne, E. K. (2018). Is nationalism or ethno-populism on the rise today? *Ethnopolitics, 17*(5).

Jeung, R. (2020, March 19–25). *Incidents of coronavirus discrimination.* A Report for A3PCON (Asia Pacific Policy & Planning Council) and CAA (Chinese for Affirmative Action).

Jones, I., & Roy, P. (2021). Sputnik V COVID-19 vaccine candidate appears safe and effective. *The Lancet, 397.*

Krugman, P. (2022, January 20). Biden vs Friends of Covid. *New York Times.*

Ledford, H., & Maxmen, A. (2022). African clinical trial denied access to key COVID drug Paxlovid. *Nature.*

Leng, S., & Wan, L. (2020, March 25). US urged to release health info of military athletes who came to Wuhan in October 2019. *Global Times.*

Logunov, D. Y., Dolzhikova, I. V., Shcheblyakov, D. V., Tukhvatulin, A. I., Zubkova, O. V., Dzharullaeva, A. S., Kovyrshina, A. V., Lubenets, N. L., Grousova, D. M., Erokhova, A. S., & Botikov, A. G. (2021). Safety and efficacy of an rAd26 and rAd5 vector-based heterologous prime-boost COVID-19 vaccine: An interim analysis of randomized controlled phase 3 trial in Russia. *The Lancet.*

Mallapaty, S. (2021). China's COVID vaccines are going global—But questions remain. *Nature.*

Maxmen, A. (2021). Divisive COVID 'lab leak' debate prompts dire warnings from researchers. *Nature, 594.*

Mayall, J. (2000). *World politics: Progress and its limits.* Polity Press.

Naylor, B. (2021). *Biden says goal of 200 million COVID-19 vaccinations in 100 days has been met.* NPR.

Office of the United States Trade Representative. (2021, May 5). *Statement from Ambassador Katherine Tai on the Covid-19 TRIPS waiver.*

Our World in Data. (2022). Figures as of January 10.

Rachman, G. (2020, March 23). Nationalism is side effect of the coronavirus. *Financial Times.*

Rudd, K. (2022). *The avoidable war: The dangers of a catastrophic conflict between the US and xi Jinping's China.* Public Affairs.

Sedik, T. S., & Xu, R. (2020, October). *A vicious cycle: How pandemics lead to economic despair and social unrest.* IMF Working Paper, no. WP/20/216.

Silver, L., Devlin, K., & Huang, C. (2020). *Americans fault China for its role in the spread of COVID-19.* Pew Research Center Global Attitudes & Trends.

Stiglitz, J., & Wallach, L. (2021). Will corporate greed prolong the pandemic? *Project Syndicate.*

Su, R., & Shen, W. (2021). Is nationalism rising in times of the COVID-19 pandemic? Individual-level evidence from the United States. *Journal of Chinese Political Science, 26.*

The Economist. (2021a, April 3). Vaccines: Spreading the needle.

The Economist. (2021b, May 15). Producing more vaccines: The insufficient miracle.

The Economist. (2021c, July 31). Protests and Covid-19: It's catching.

Tisdall, S. (2020, March 28). Power, equality, nationalism: How the pandemic will reshape the world. *Guardian*.

WHO Health Assembly. (2020, May 19). SEVENTY-THIRD Session. *COVID-19 Response*.

Williams, C. R., Kestenbaum, J. G., & Meier, B. M. (2020). Populist nationalism threatens health and human rights in the COVID-19 response. *American Journal of Public Health (AJPH) Perspectives, 110*(12).

Woods, E. T., Schertzer, R., Greenfeld, L., Hughes, C., & Miller-Idriss, C. (2020). COVID-19, nationalism and the politics of crisis: A scholarly exchange. *Nations and Nationalism, 26*(4).

Xinhua. (2020, May 18). Full text: Speech by President Xi Jinping at the opening of 73rd World Health Assembly. *Global Times*.

Zhao, S. (2021, April 29). Why China's vaccine diplomacy is winning. *East Asia Forum*.

CHAPTER 6

Global and Regional Action

If any issue is a candidate for multilateral global action, then it must be our response to this pandemic. The health of each depends on health of all.
—Gordon Brown, *former British Prime Minister*

A worldwide pandemic of COVID-19 cannot be managed by any one single country. Therefore, world leaders need to launch a concerted and coordinated attack on a common enemy regardless of whether it is black, brown or white. In this chapter, we discuss a number of global and regional initiatives that are underway despite many hurdles outlined in Chap. 5. The world will continue to remain interdependent in the foreseeable future.

Many political leaders discussed in Chap. 4 are proven globalists. They form a hard core to push through global initiatives to control COVID-19 within the framework of the UN, WHO, G20 and G7, and the regional bodies (e.g. the EU, ASEAN and SAARC). The chapter explores whether the rhetoric of global action has been matched by reality.

A. S. Bhalla, *National and Global Responses to the COVID-19 Pandemic*, https://doi.org/10.1007/978-3-031-29521-8_6

Global Action

Four examples of global action discussed below are (1) UN response and recovery fund; (2) ACT Accelerator and vaccine global access facility; (3) Global task force for coronavirus and (4) global research cooperation.

United Nations Response to COVID-19

In April 2020, the United Nations (UN) Secretary-General, Antonio Gutteres, launched COVID-19 Response and Recovery Fund with an appeal for $2 billion dollars (requiring $1 billion initially) "to help support low- and middle-income countries," which suffered from economic and social hardships in the aftermath of the pandemic. These countries have the weakest health care systems. Then there are the refugees and the war zones which are ideal breeding grounds for spreading infections. The UN call for global solidarity and action has three main aims: (1) tackling of the health emergency by assisting in the provision of required medical supplies and payment of salaries of healthcare workers, (2) focusing on social and economic impact and recovery by enhancing social protection mechanisms, meeting children's food and educational needs and promoting digital innovations that boost employment and support livelihoods and (3) helping countries recover better by strengthening their disease and community-based surveillance, health care systems and workforce (UN, 2020).

The Fund is designed to complement WHO's Strategic Preparedness and Response Plan and the UN Office for the Coordination of Humanitarian Affairs (OCHA)'s Consolidated Global Humanitarian Appeal for COVID-19. The WHO appeal has raised funds to the tune of $220 million. OCHA has raised a little over $1 billion, which is well below the requirement of $10 billion for humanitarian support to countries in Asia and Africa whose national health systems are extremely weak. The UN Secretary-General has already launched an appeal for an additional funding of $4 billion to support the needs of over 60 countries in dire need of emergency funding.

While the appeal has its merits, its timing was bad. It is not only a global health crisis but also a global economic crisis when many developed economies were either shrinking or nearly collapsing under the weight of prolonged shutdowns. National governments faced competing demands on limited and shrinking resources.

Global Task Force for Coronavirus

The G20 was called upon to promote global cooperation in the distribution of medicines and medical supplies worldwide (Cockburn, 2020, March 26).[1] Global health institutions such as the WHO and the Global Fund already exist, but there is no single supranational watchdog for their effective coordination (Brown & Erik, 2020, April 7). A pledging conference for research funding co-hosted by the European Union and Norway (May 2020) was attended by a large number of countries except the US, Russia and India. Pledges at the conference amounted to 7.5 billion euros (or $8 billion), to be earmarked as 4 billion euros for vaccine development, 2 billion euros for treatments and 1.5 billion euros for the manufacture of test kits. At a Gavi COVAX summit (April 2022), $4.8 billion pledges to ACT were made and at the Second Global Summit on COVID-19 (May 2022) $1 billion pledges. Despite these commitments, a funding gap of $11.2 billion still remains (WHO, 2022a).

The focus of the Task Force has gradually shifted to a fair and equitable vaccine distribution throughout the world. Gordon Brown (Brown, 2020; Brown & Erik, 2020) who proposed the Task Force has renewed his appeal for global vaccination to overcome emerging vaccine apartheid discussed in Chap. 5 (Brown, 2021a, 2021b). He urged the G7 meeting in June 2021 to exercise vaccine diplomacy and "lead a herculean mobilization to bring together the proven skills of global pharmaceutical and logistic companies, national militaries and local health workers."

The experience of COVAX Act-Accelerator partnership discussed below suggests that the real shortage is not of vaccine supplies so much as that of funds to pay for their distribution and delivery to low-income countries. There are different ways to provide such financing through (1) a special levy on member states similar to the one agreed to for the eradication of smallpox, (2) the IMF's SDRs, (3) World Bank and multilateral development banks and (4) greater development assistance and donations by charitable and corporate institutions. However, there is little appetite for aid, which has considerably declined.

Economic benefits from a global equitable access to COVID-19 vaccines are significantly larger than the donors' contribution to the ACT Accelerator.[2] An equitable distribution of vaccines to low-income countries is not an act of charity but that of enlightened self-interest of high-income countries. COVID-19 cannot be eliminated as long as the bulk of the world is not fully vaccinated. The rapid spread of the new Omicron more infectious variants is a clear indication of this stark truth. There are other non-economic arguments as well in favour of fair and equitable distribution of vaccines such as humanitarianism and good governance.

There is an uneven vaccine rollout across the world, vaccine hesitancy and the delayed arrival of vaccinations for children (Aschwenden, 2021). Therefore, world leaders need to consider global action for an immunization programme as a multi-year effort, perhaps something similar to influenza shots.

The ACT Accelerator and Vaccine Global Access Facility

Access to COVID-19 Tools Accelerator (ACT Accelerator) coalition was launched by the UN and WHO with the European Commission, France and the Bill and Melinda Gates Foundation in response to a call by the G20 leaders (UN, 2020). It brings together governments, scientists, businesses as well as global organizations such as the Coalition of Epidemic Preparedness (CEPI) and the Global Alliance for Vaccine and Immunization (GAVI), the Global Fund, Wellcome and the World Bank. Its objectives are diagnostic tests and training for health care professionals, to prevent infections, to promote the development, manufacture and fair and equitable distribution of vaccines and to strengthen national capacity for health care. Its targets include (a) supply of 2 billion vaccine doses to low-income countries by the end of 2021 to vaccinate up to 20 per cent of their populations; (b) 245 million courses of treatment and (c) 500 million diagnostic tests (WHO, 2021a, 2022b).

ACT aims to raise $38 billion of which initially only $2.6 billion have been raised to achieve the above targets. Additional $5 billion were promised following an appeal at the G7 virtual meeting in early 2021. The above targets have not been met although a number of wealthy countries have donated vaccines. The US was the largest vaccine donor accounting for 41 per cent of the total donations followed by China (12 per cent) and Germany (11 per cent). While many countries have donated through COVAX, many (notably, Russia, China and India) preferred to donate vaccines bilaterally. The US had delivered only 43 per cent of its pledges by the end of 2021. India exported more doses to neighbouring countries (Bangladesh, Nepal and Sri Lanka) and others (60 million) than used at home (44 million). India's generous export of vaccine doses may have come at a high price for its own population. Nearly 13 billion vaccine doses were delivered globally by September 2022. But only 22.5 per cent of low-income countries have at least received one vaccine dose (*The Financial Times* database).

COVAX's target to deliver 2 billion vaccine doses in 2021 could not be met (Banco et al., 2021; Cohen, 2021; Puyvallée & Storeng, 2022). Several reasons accounted for the slow delivery. Firstly, India which had promised 2 billion doses of Covishield vaccine halted its exports following a spike in domestic COVID cases. Secondly, lack of rapid approval of Chinese and other vaccines such as Moderna (approved only on 30 April) by the WHO may have slowed down vaccine delivery. Thirdly, the US vaccines, namely Pfizer and Moderna, encountered production delays, caused inter alia, by the lack of raw materials and the disruption of global supply chains. Finally, many donor countries failed to deliver their full pledges to countries or COVAX in time. As discussed in Chap. 5, diplomatic, political and commercial considerations also applied to vaccine distribution. But supplies and distribution of vaccines, while necessary, are not sufficient. Recipients as well as donors continue to encounter difficulties in their delivery and absorption.

Global Scientific Research Cooperation

Research collaboration has been taking place in the pre-pandemic period (e.g. for Ebola, SARS, and AIDS epidemics), but the urgency for quick results is new. It is perhaps the first time that a pandemic has attacked all corners of the globe including the West where the bulk of research resources are concentrated. When the killer disease is right at your doorstep, you cannot but take serious notice.[3]

There are other ways in which COVID-19 has brought about change in the pursuit of science and greater multidisciplinary cooperation among scientists. For example, priorities have shifted from research on esoteric and abstract subjects to that on viruses. There is also a greater urgency to involve research scientists from different backgrounds and disciplines.

Several significant ways in which new scientific research on the COVID-19 vaccine is different are worth noting. Firstly, knowledge sharing is taking place rapidly across political boundaries and national ideologies. Secondly, secrecy of research findings is being abandoned at least temporarily. Thirdly, scientists are *cooperating* rather than *competing* for research grants. A reason for this sudden shift is that most earlier epidemics were more region-specific and far removed from the Western world. COVID-19 pandemic is truly global. The problems are also more complex. There is a need to gather much information to understand the epidemiology, to develop better treatments for those infected, and ultimately to manufacture vaccines at scale. Scientists understand that a selfish and uncooperative effort, will simply not succeed. Fourthly, public funds are financing research on vaccines, which is not as profitable as other drugs. The private sector is averse to taking risk involved in low-profit projects.

Internet connectivity and global networks of electronic communications have enabled global collaboration in scientific research. Exchange of data, sharing of research results and collaboration in vaccine research have taken place in the past and are expanding further. Examples of this cooperation include (Stein, 2020, p. 270).

- *Scientists' networks* to share information across national borders.
- *Free access to journal articles* which are not yet peer reviewed as well as those that have been.
- *Collaboration among infectious disease specialists* on websites and e-mail chains.
- *Virologists' weekly podcast series, This Week in Virology*, to discuss research results and exchange information on viruses on a regular but informal basis.
- *Defence Advanced Research Projects Agency* (DARPA) in the US developed *Prophecy*, a research programme to study the evolution of viruses and to predict mutations and develop vaccines. The programme collaborated with nine countries around the world including China, Indonesia, Nigeria, Russia and Singapore (Callahan & Poznansky, 2021, June 10).
- *Open Covid-19 Data Working Group* created by scientists from Oxford University and Tsinghua University in China. The Group has already collected detailed records for over 10,000 COVID cases.
- Two other examples of *global cooperation in data sharing* are China's publication of COVID-19 sequence (Fan et al., 2019; Wu et al., 2020) and South Africa's sharing of Omicron sequence. But only a few Western countries (e.g. Denmark and the UK) made good use of the Omicron sequence. Sadly, both countries drastically cut their genome sequencing programmes in early 2022 at a time when the creation of a global early warning and surveillance system is being debated (see below). This will make it more difficult to identify and predict new variants (Zimmer, 2022).

- Moreover, travel bans against Africa were too late to prevent the virus spread. They may discourage countries from sharing information on future variants. They may also slow down research by cutting down lab supplies needed for sequencing.

The example of DARPA's Prophecy programme deserves some discussion in view of its relevance to the COVID-19 pandemic. The *Prophecy* research team developed an alert network with medical doctors working in several hospitals around the world, notably in Jakarta, Singapore and Hong Kong. Collaboration involved the following steps: (1) studying the genome of a dangerous virus to identify where it can mutate, (2) modelling to anticipate viral mutations before they occur and (3) designing of computer models of antibodies: research collaboration around the world enabled obtaining sequencing of newest variants from patients abroad. Sadly, the *Prophecy* programme came to an abrupt end in 2016 with the start of the Trump presidency and subsequent downgrading of scientific projects, budget cuts and lack of funding. Yet step (2) above is highly relevant to the current challenge to control the pandemic.

In addition to the research cooperation among scientists in universities and research institutes, private pharmaceutical companies, which used to compete for drug development, are beginning to cooperate under conditions of lockdowns and disruption of supply chains. Facing difficulties in attracting participants for clinical trials (reluctance on their part to undergo routine and frequent checks and lack of health workers to monitor the trials) has led the companies to consider one of two options: to put trials on hold or to hold remote trials through online consultations and sharing of data and basic trial designs. Several companies have built alliances to share data on basic science and early results on antiviral treatments and designs for clinical trials. Microsoft plans to launch 20 data-sharing groups by 2022, which will include sharing of information on COVID-19 (*The Economist*, 2020, April 25). Whether this global cooperation in drug development is a *temporary* phenomenon or a *permanent* change in the company behaviour remains to be seen.

WHO's Role in Global Health Management

WHO is responsible for the management of global health emergencies such as the coronavirus pandemic. Its role is unquestioned despite its various limitations which are endemic to the entire UN system. We consider three main limitations, namely (1) structural problems, (2) power politics by member states and (3) lack of funding or the tied nature of funding.

Taking the structural problems first, with the exception of the IMF, World Bank and WTO, most other agencies lack any enforcement powers for implementing their regulations, conventions or treaties. This is particularly true of the agencies dealing with social sectors such as health (WHO), education (UNESCO) and labour and working conditions (ILO). These agencies formulate international instruments (e.g. WHO's International Health Regulations and ILO's International Conventions on working conditions and child labour). In theory, they are legally binding meaning thereby that the members states have an obligation to adhere to them by ratifying them. But the agencies cannot take any punitive action against the offenders. This is one of the major structural/organizational limitations of the global health agency. On the other hand, the finance and lending institutions like the IMF, World Bank and WTO carry both sticks (coercive powers through sanctions and refusal to lend) and carrots (persuasion and consensus building). This asymmetrical nature of the mandates largely explains why any future reforms of the WHO and other "social" agencies are unlikely to produce much better results.

The specialized agencies are as good as the member states make them. This brings us to the second major flaw in the governance of the UN system, that is, politicization by the major contributing countries. Invariably, the mandates and priorities of agencies like the WHO are partly a reflection of priorities of the rich countries. This was particularly so until a few years ago when the developing countries led by China, a new economic powerhouse and a rising political power, started making their demands. Criticism of the organization accelerated when the developing countries articulated new initiatives of interest to them (at WHO Assemblies) which were considered inimical to the interests of the Big Pharma (Jarvis, 2020). Three such initiatives were (1) essential drugs and medicines at lower prices, (2) phasing out of breast milk substitutes and (3) campaigns against alcohol and tobacco abuse (Balakrishnan, 2020; Bezanson, 2021; Jha, 2021). A fourth demand during the COVID-19 pandemic was made to the WTO and WHO, for temporarily dropping patents on vaccines so that their manufacturing could be undertaken throughout the world concurrently (see Chap. 5). At the 12th Ministerial Conference of WTO (12–15 June, 2022), member states agreed to temporarily waive property patents on COVID-19 vaccines without the consent of the patent holder for five years. This decision does not fully meet the demands of India and South Africa which also included, besides vaccines, treatments and tests.

The US and many other rich countries were critical of the UN system long before COVID-19. Complaints have been made of unwieldy bureaucracy, duplication and ballooning budgets and programmes. The Trump administration's complaints about WHO's poor performance in handling COVID-19 need to be examined in the light of concrete evidence, early warnings by scholars and business leaders like Bill Gates and the performance of countries themselves. Trump's main criticism of the WHO was its bias in favour of China and its authoritarian methods, delay in informing the world about COVID-19 and spreading of disinformation. As shown below, none of these criticisms are fully justified.

Concerning the timing, the WHO has to wait for the countries to inform it promptly about health emergencies. On several occasions in the past, both democratic and authoritarian states have withheld unpleasant information which may show them in bad light.

WHO has warned the world about COVID-19 since early January 2020. As Inglesby (2020, p. 89) observes: "If one looks at the timeline of WHO's actions and decisions in early January, it is clear that it was quickly communicating what it was learning to the public, and it was rapidly developing and publishing guidance." Compared to this, the timing of action by many Western countries, particularly the US and the UK, was not until early March despite WHO's warnings. Perhaps the organization could have declared a global health emergency earlier, which would not necessarily have elicited any better response from the West.

One American observer refers to WHO's strange mistake in insisting that face masks were not necessary (Applebaum, 2020, p. 226). In the early stages, the United States Centers for Disease Control (CDC) did not insist on mask wearing either. Neither was there any consensus among scientists. For the US to point fingers at the WHO for this when the country's own president (Trump) would not wear a mask or encourage the White House Staff to do so is disingenuous. The Biden administration's introduction of mask wearing in all government departments and public places was a welcome change, but the federal measure has been flouted by the southern Republican states (e.g. Texas) in the midst of rising cases and deaths.

Perhaps, what irritated Trump most about WHO was its praise for China's vigorous and aggressive COVID-19 containment strategy. There is no doubt China as well as many Western countries made many mistakes in the initial stages of the pandemic. However, despite its early missteps, China controlled the virus quickly which enabled its early economic recovery along with Vietnam (also a non-democratic country!), South Korea and Taiwan. China has exploited Western failures to enhance the prestige of its own authoritarian system, which is not surprising (Rudd, 2022).

Independent Western scholars have also praised China's successful efforts. For example, two Cambridge University researchers observe: "What has to be explained ….is not why China followed a particular path, but why other countries in particular the UK, given its history, did not." (Deakin & Meng, 2020, p. 545). They argue that the failure of many Western states has "roots in the transformations of systems of governance which have been occurring since the late 1970s. These changes have been informed by theories of governance which have cast doubts on the effectiveness and legitimacy of public interventions in managing social and economic risks." (Ibid.). They also discuss many trends about COVID-19, one of which "is the widespread mischaracterization of the measures taken to address the pandemic." (Ibid., p. 539). In terms of our analytical framework outlined in Chap. 3, the failure is attributed to lack of cooperation and consensus between leaders, agents and followers.

A decline in the assessed contributions by the major contributors has not helped matters. The share of these contributions in the total budget decreased from 46 per cent in 1990 to 16 per cent in 2020–2021 (WHO, 2021b, 2021c). The major donors have demanded budget and programme cuts, frequent calls for reforms and threats of withdrawal. In particular, they have attempted to downgrade the multilateral system generally and favour bilateral deals on which they have greater control. A gradual retreat from multilateralism has led to loss of moral authority and credibility of leadership which the Western powers had formerly enjoyed. Trade and narrow commercial interests and a transactional approach to diplomacy by the Trump administration.

How the WHO is funded has further implications for global health management during COVID-19. The organization's budget has two components: (1) Assessed contribution of each Member State and (2) voluntary contributions from Member States, international organizations and non-state actors such as Bill and Melinda Gates Foundation. In its early years, assessed contributions were the main source of funding for WHO's programme budget. The voluntary contributions are invariably made to specific programmes, which may not necessarily reflect the major global health challenges. It is for this reason that the WHO requested a 10 per cent increase in its assessed contributions to ensure greater *stability* and *flexibility* of funding.

Although *nominal* assessed contributions remained stable during the past ten years, they declined in *real terms* after adjusting for inflation. This decline adversely affects the implementation of technical programmes since over 50 per cent of these contributions are used to finance them. The largest share of the WHO budget is devoted to universal health coverage followed by country support for building capacity on the ground, emergency operations and health emergencies. It is surprising that the lowest share of the programme budget is allocated to health emergencies, which deserve much greater attention in the post-pandemic period. This paradox is explained by the fact that the priorities are often donor driven.

The much-discussed WHO reforms are unlikely to be implemented as long as donors continue to pursue their own self-interests at the international forums. The founding director of the Munk School of Global Affairs and Public Policy (Toronto) notes that "the reforms (in the wake of SARS did not give the WHO an independent intelligence capability, the power to conduct investigations, or to enforce compliance. Like all other intergovernmental institutions, it is reliant on what member states do." (Stein, 2020, p. 267). It has to depend on member states for information Another Canadian observer remarks: "The WHO can advise but never direct, guide but never govern; lead but never advocate; evaluate but never judge."[4]

WHO is an *intergovernmental* organization (constrained by member states) and not a *supranational* body with legal and enforcement authority. Giving additional powers to the organization involves a loss of national autonomy for which member states are not prepared especially in such matters as national surveillance of health.

In future, priorities will need to be shifted towards major global health challenges and the ways in which future pandemics should be managed. The WHO Budget for 2022–2023 allocates more resources to strengthen countries' national capacity to cope with emergencies. But the proposed allocation for global emergency operations, another priority, remains unchanged (WHO, 2021d). Despite the above limitations, WHO has performed well in the past in a number of areas. The eradication of smallpox through concerted global action by the US, the USSR and other member states was one of its signal achievements. It responded well to the outbreaks of yellow fever, polio, Zika virus disease and Ebola in the Democratic Republic of the Congo (Nay et al., 2020). WHO launched a large *Solidarity Trial* in several hospitals around the world when it became difficult to recruit enough patients in many countries for large trials.

Admittedly, WHO made some mistakes in handling the Ebola epidemic for which it was widely criticized. Three main criticisms were (1) slow response to the disease, (2) failure to challenge official reports and (3) lack of proper coordination between the WHO headquarters and its Regional Office for Africa. It was accused of having been pressured by the pharmaceutical industry to create demand for vaccines. One evaluation concluded that WHO leadership was flawed (Kamradt-Scott, 2018). However, several other investigations (e.g. an independent WHO Panel, the Council of Europe and the *British Medical Journal*) found no evidence of improper conduct.

During the Ebola outbreak, and the earlier Swine flu outbreak in 2009, the WHO used two different frameworks, namely, the *Emergency Response Framework* (ERF) and the *International Health Regulations* (IHRs) to inform the international community, which caused some confusion (Gostin et al., 2015).

WHO's *Health Emergencies Programme,* created in 2016 to eradicate smallpox, had an ambitious mission, inter alia, to promote regional and global alert and surveillance systems, which are now in place. It has been reformed in keeping with the findings of the Oversight and Advisory Committee. It aims to ensure that "1 billion more people are better protected from health emergencies" (WHO, 2019, pp. 22–24).

The IHR (2005), an international health treaty, is legally binding on member states. It was adopted in 1969 and subsequently revised in 2005 to protect against the international spread of disease and public health risks. Under the treaty, member states are obliged to notify the outbreak of disease promptly to the WHO. However, despite its legal status, the Organization can do little if a member state fails to comply. The experience of the 2013 Ebola outbreak in Africa may offer some lessons here. Ebola-affected countries suffer from weak national health systems and lack of adequate resources, which combined with internal political pressures, led to government failures to implement WHO recommendations.

There are other instruments at the disposal of the WHO, for example, *Joint External Evaluation Tool* (JEET), which was first developed in 2005 and revised in 2018. Unlike the IHR, JEET is a *voluntary* instrument. WHO's information exchange with member states on a number of topics, viz. emergencies and epidemics such as COVID-19, results of vaccine research and the distribution and supply discussed above and regular collection and reporting of health and epidemiological data, can be effectively performed without much political interference.

In the context of COVID-19, three new proposals, namely a new *Health Stability Board*, an *International Pandemic Treaty* and a *global fire brigade of experts* deserve some discussion.

A Health Stability Board is proposed as a new body parallel to the WHO similar to the *Financial Stability Board* established by G20 in the wake of the 2008 financial crisis (McGahan, 2020). It is designed to focus on preparedness, response and management of threats to global health. The Board will consist of three committees: (1) *a policy committee* to set global standards; (2) *a vulnerabilities committee* to assess emerging health risks and to alert members with concrete recommendations and (3) *a standards implementation committee* to undertake country reviews to monitor the implementation of standards and to assess gaps in preparedness. A similar proposal was made in 2019 on a multidisciplinary Global Technical Council on Infectious Disease Threats to improve collaboration between different organizations, to fill knowledge gaps in surveillance and R and D needs and to make recommendations for managing global risks associated with pandemics (Bloom & Cadarette, 2020).

In a recent book, Bill Gates (2022) suggests that a global fire brigade of 3000 experts, that is, Global Epidemic Response and Mobilization (GERM) team should be created to act as a permanent standby to respond to any detected outbreak. Experts should be recruited with the following backgrounds: epidemiology and genetics, drug and vaccine development, computer modelling and diplomacy. The functions of GERM will cover data analysis, advice to governments on high-priority drugs and vaccines, funding or lending experts to countries in need, besides distilling findings from simulations to test preparedness, recording of recommendations emerging from them and proposing strengthening of supply chains and improving inter-country coordination.

The case for new bodies remains weak when several similar bodies already exist. Of course, many existing bodies do not perform the functions described earlier. The above proposals are ambitious and are not likely to be implemented without political will and adequate funding. The major donors simply do not have an appetite for setting up new bodies. Besides, many functions which a new Board will perform overlap with those of the WHO and with such mechanisms as the International Health Regulations and the External Evaluation Tool. But a global pool of multidisciplinary experts does not exist either within WHO or anywhere else. It merits serious attention.

Countries and relevant global institutions have underinvested in health systems as well as in early warning systems and anticipatory policies of preparedness (see below). But as discussed above, one of the reasons why the existing bodies do not perform well is that available financial and human resources are inadequate for the tasks assigned.

The proposal for an *International Pandemic Treaty* endorsed by the European Council and WHO has made progress (European Council, 2021; Hannon et al., 2022; *Nature*, 2021). At a special session of the World Health Assembly (29 November–1 December 2021), a consensus was reached to start the process to draft a convention or another instrument. WHO's Intergovernmental Negotiating Body had its third meeting in September 2022 to discuss a concept draft of the new treaty, which is expected to be adopted by May 2024. The Panel for a Global Public Health Convention, which is an independent coalition of health leaders, felt that the draft did not go far enough (*Agence France-Presse*, 2022, December 26).

The treaty needs to be a legally binding instrument to ensure highest political commitment by each country. It is likely to be far-reaching in scope. Besides health, it needs to include such matters as financial mechanisms, economic sectors and global security and solidarity. Therefore, involvement of the UN besides funding agencies such as the World Bank would be crucial.

It would focus on early detection and prevention of pandemics and more active response to future pandemics by ensuring universal and equitable medical solutions. It is hoped that it will provide for a better surveillance of pandemic risks, stronger resilience of national health systems and trust in the international health system.

A case can be made for the above treaty since a precedent exists of *WHO's Framework Convention on Tobacco Control*, which has been widely embraced (WHO, 2021e). Other precedents of similar treaties within the UN system include *UN Framework Convention on Climate Change* and *Protocol on Water and Health*. The existing framework of pandemic alert system of WHO is inadequate to prevent and protect against pandemics (*Nature*, 2021). WHO's *International Health Regulations* do not provide a stand-alone mechanism for monitoring, evaluation and compliance.

There is little chance of success of an international treaty without an endorsement by China and the United States, which are not among the founding members. Secondly, a treaty on its own is unlikely to ensure greater global cooperation and action than is currently forthcoming.

Thirdly, negotiations for a treaty are cumbersome and time-consuming, whereas global action to control any future pandemic would need a rapid and transparent global action. Negotiations for the development of a treaty need to include civil-society groups as well as affected communities besides governments. Finally, there is no guarantee that the WHO, which is expected to administer the implementation of the treaty, will be any more successful in imposing its will without any additional mandate and resources. Establishment of a sustainable financial mechanism is crucial besides an involvement of heads of state at the level of the UN General Assembly instead of a Global Health Emergency Council, which has been proposed by the WHO Director-General (Nikogosian & Kickbusch, 2021).

A Post-Pandemic Global Surveillance System

The existing early warning and surveillance systems suffer from gaps in epidemic/pandemic intelligence. For example, *WHO's Early Warning, Alert and Response System (EWARS)* has a narrow objective of detecting early disease outbreaks in conflict areas or countries affected by natural disasters. Under WHO's IHR (2005), "a global surveillance system for public health emergencies" was considered to be a major advance in global surveillance from what has prevailed in the past (Baker & Fidler, 2006). However, according to the Independent Panel (2021, p. 26), it is a "conservative instrument" which does not facilitate rapid action. It failed to give rapid warning about COVID-19. Neither did any other warning system in the rich countries.[5] For example, in the US, no centralized system exists for disease forecasting and health data, which are scattered throughout the country. Johns Hopkins University epidemiologists have recommended a national system like the National Weather Service to overcome this lacuna (Rivers & George, 2020).

The objective of a truly global surveillance system is to anticipate, identify and prepare for a future pandemic through an analysis of risks related to global health threats and their assessment, management and communication. Risk assessment and management will require sharing of data and its processing in real time.

A critical review of the functioning of existing systems suggests several challenges and deficiencies: (1) inadequacy of health infrastructure; (2) lack of agreement on scientific methods and operation of surveillance; (3) lack of human, technical and financial resources and (4) absence of international political commitment. Furthermore, the world capacity to track viruses and proper sequencing is limited. As noted above, at a time when the success of a global surveillance system depends on strengthening this capacity, countries like Denmark and the United Kingdom have cut back on COVID trackers.

Given the lack of funding, past efforts by the WHO were too inadequate to build such capacity on a mass scale. Wealthy countries did not show any political commitment to early warning systems, which is indicated by the fact that the Global Outbreak Alert and Response Network is not part of WHO's core budget. It is given a relatively low priority by the member states. The non-core ad hoc budget under which it falls is often unpredictable and uncertain. As discussed in Chap. 4, former president Trump disbanded the National Security Council, which was designed to provide early warning. Such structures are considered unnecessary and expensive in a myopic vision of most politicians.

No global surveillance system will ever function effectively without adequate financial and human resources. In the final analysis, its functioning will depend on local and national capacity in low-income countries where it is very weak. In these countries, capacity needs to be built, whereas in high-income ones the existing capacities need to be maintained and strengthened. There is also a need for a systematic documentation and sharing of best practices, innovations and experiences. Finally, the behaviour of national governments and the international community requires change from "short-termism" to a "long view" and anticipatory policy-making.

IMF, World Bank and COVID-19

The financial institutions like the IMF and World Bank on their own or in collaboration with the UN and WHO have contributed significantly to the management of COVID-19, in particular in equitable distribution of vaccines. The initial response by the IMF (March 2020) consisted of emergency financing through Rapid Credit Facility and Rapid Financing Instrument, expansion of existing lending programmes and grants for debt relief to the poorest and most vulnerable countries. A set of guidelines were prepared and a special *Series on Covid-19* (discontinued in December 2021). Initially, the following two areas were accorded high priority in IMF's COVID response, namely (a) health expenditure (outline of principles and guidelines for countries on how to monitor, contain and mitigate the impact of the pandemic) and (b) support for the vulnerable groups (fiscal measures for countries when designing programmes to support vulnerable households and businesses). A study, which assessed IMF's programmes (implemented between March and July 2020), concluded that the IMF did indeed achieve positive results during the early phases of the pandemic (Gallagher & Carlin, 2020). In the past, the IMF's Structural Adjustment programmes had uniformly recommended austerity measures which invariably lowered access to health and raised neonatal mortality (Forster et al., 2020). Therefore, the new emphasis on social spending during the pandemic is out of character.

COVID-19 presented several challenges to the IMF, which had to adapt its traditional role and switch to new activities into uncharted territory of health financing. It raised practical issues involved in switching of resources to new areas in which it did not enjoy particular expertise. In 2020, the IMF launched a funding campaign to raise $100 million to ensure quick delivery of capacity development advice and technical assistance. As of December 2021, the total commitment of funds amounted to no more than about $40 million (IMF, 2021; 2022). The priorities of developing countries also changed towards strengthening health systems and services to minimize the adverse impact of COVID-19. The IMF will need partnership with WHO in the provision of building health capacity and training of health personnel, areas in which the latter has well-established expertise.

The IMF's allocation of $650 billion in SDRs is the largest such contribution to the provision of necessary liquidity to needy countries (IMF, 2022). Such emergency financing is designed to assist the countries, inter alia, to finance the purchase of COVID-19 vaccines.

In June 2021, in partnership with the World Bank, WHO and WTO, the IMF launched a campaign to mobilize support and funding to the tune of $50 billion to accelerate access to COVID-19 vaccines, therapeutics and diagnostics. A target was set of the vaccination of at least 40 per cent of the population in all countries by the end of 2021 and 70 per cent by mid-2022. As of April 2022, only 7 per cent of people in low-income countries compared to 73 per cent in high-income countries were fully vaccinated. Lack of access to oxygen, PPEs and equipment also persisted (Agarwal et al., 2022). The IMF established a COVID-19 Global Tracker as well as country-by-country dashboard to monitor progress towards the attainment of the above target.

The World Bank Group's response to COVID-19 consisted of the following major types of activities: (1) greater financial support to poor- and middle-income countries to fight the health, economic and social shocks and buy needed vaccines, (2) support for strengthening national health systems and capacity, (3) social protection through cash transfers as part of poverty alleviation programmes, (4) protection of the poor and vulnerable through food supplies and employment for households and informal businesses and (5) strengthening of policymaking, institutions and investments to ensure speedy recovery from the adverse impacts of the pandemic (World Bank, 2020, 2022).

The World Bank Group committed over $200 billion from April 2020 to March 2021 to help developing countries to detect, prevent and respond to COVID-19. It has allocated $20 billion to help finance the purchase and distribution of COVID-19 vaccines. The Bank has designed a new financing mechanism, which will enable COVAX to make advance purchases (in addition to their subsidized supply of doses from donors) to raise the level of vaccine supply. It has also entered into partnership with the African Union's Africa Vaccine Acquisition Task Team to help vaccinate up to 400 million people. Oxfam International (2020, pp. 3–4), which reviewed 71 country project documents as of 30 June, came to the conclusion that the World Bank's health funding was strong in disease prevention but it "missed vital opportunities to strengthen public health systems so they can tackle COVID-19." The Bank also failed to address the shortage of health workers. Neither did it recommend the removal of user fee, which particularly hurts the poor. An earlier evaluation of the Bank's health financing had concluded that "support to reduce user payments was limited" and that work to improve financial protection "lacked the necessary fiscal and equity analysis" (World Bank Independent Evaluation Group, 2014, p. xiv). Another assessment (Kilby & McWhirter, 2022) found that the COVID-19 projects were approved without political interference by the major donor (the US) unlike the traditional lending projects, reasons for which are unclear. As the COVID-19 assistance benefits both the donors and recipients, it may have been viewed as an international public good.

Through its Global Health Platform, the International Finance Corporation has provided $4 billion for the local production of vaccines and personal protective equipment, particularly in Africa.

In June 2022, the World Bank established a secretariat at its headquarters, with WHO as the technical partner. Besides undertaking technical work, the secretariat will manage a new financial intermediary fund to "finance critical investments to strengthen pandemic PPR (pandemic prevention preparedness and response) capacities at national, regional and global levels" (*WHO News Release*, 2022c). Commitments of over $1 billion have been made to the new fund by the US, the UK, the European Union, Germany, Indonesia and Singapore, the Gates Foundation and the Wellcome Trust. The fund shall give priority to the strengthening of country capacity in such areas as disease surveillance, laboratory systems, health workforce, emergency communication and community engagement.

Both the IMF and the World Bank have strong economic and financial databases. Therefore, it would be appropriate for them to coordinate (through WHO, which is responsible for health data) the standardization of national health data systems and global sharing of data proposed in Chap. 7. Different sets of standardized data (e.g. on COVID test results, cases and deaths, vaccination rates and viral genome sequences) are needed to facilitate future research and policy analysis. Perhaps the new Secretariat at the World Bank mentioned above can undertake this task.

Finally, as the challenge of COVID-19 has raised the financial needs of the developing countries, it is pertinent to ask whether the lending by the above two major financial institutions has been sizeable enough to make a difference. One study (Duggan et al., 2020, October) concludes that the World Bank's response "is lagging behind its own announced targets," since loan disbursements reached only 50 per cent of the declared goal.

Regional Action

The European Union is in the forefront of regional initiatives on COVID-19. Three such initiatives, viz. (1) a recovery plan, (2) collective vaccination programme and (3) a Health Emergency Preparedness and Response Authority (HERA), are briefly discussed below.

European Union's Recovery Plan

The EU agreed on a Recovery Plan with a package of €750 billion (or $869 billion) divided into 390 billion euros as grants and 360 billion euros as loans. It provides finance to companies, especially SMEs, and temporary worker protection and job creation under a loan-based instrument. It includes the following provisions: (1) boosting of the EU healthcare capabilities, (2) financial support (grants and loans) to the hardest-hit countries and regions (e.g. Italy and Spain) and (3) implementation of sound economic policies by the recipient countries and an ambitious reform agenda. Each country, which wishes to apply for funds, has to submit a national recovery plan. As of September 2022, several countries had received grants or loans under the scheme.

The package is unprecedented in several respects. For the first time, the European Commission was allowed to borrow from the financial markets in the same way as its members do. Secondly, the recovery fund is making grants as well as loans to the worst-affected member countries. Thirdly, a decision on joint borrowing by the Union on an unprecedented scale has strengthened it as a supranational fiscal body. The new measures provide for the combined use of monetary tools (by the European Central Bank) and fiscal ones (by the European Commission) in a complementary fashion.

Rare EU unity was made possible by the prior agreement of its two key members (France and Germany) as well as the four "frugal" members, namely Austria, Denmark, the Netherlands and Sweden during the full negotiations at the EU summit. It shows that what was considered unthinkable in the midst of growing divisions within the EU member states, among nationalists/populists (e.g. Hungary and Poland), and globalists (e.g. France and Germany), can indeed be achieved through strong leadership and political commitment.

The above breakthrough among 27 member countries offers hope for regional cooperation despite challenges discussed in Chap. 5.

European Union's Collective Vaccination Programme

EU's decision to purchase vaccines collectively was to ensure vaccine access to both poor and rich member states. It benefited smaller/poorer countries which would not have been able to negotiate purchases on favourable terms on their own.

The programme did not go as well as expected. The EU wasted time in negotiating a reasonable price while competing countries (UK and the US) mopped up the bulk of vaccine supplies. Delay by the EU regulatory body in approving the vaccines was partly to blame. To make matters worse, the drug companies failed to deliver the promised supplies, allegedly because of unforeseen production bottlenecks, or a pressure by the vaccine-producing countries to divert production to them. Both the EU and vaccine producers underestimated possible glitches in ramping up production.

Another initiative is the EU-Africa Partnership for Vaccine Manufacturing (PAVM) as part of a European Global Health Strategy (Glassman & Yadav, 2022). The EU has announced a contribution of 1 billion euros in cash and expertise to PAVM to support regional manufacturing of vaccines within Africa for the African people. However, such issues as the size of new manufacturers to make vaccine production economically viable, the level of demand for vaccines in sub-Saharan Africa and who will procure and distribute vaccines were not fully discussed.

Health Emergency Preparedness and Response Authority (HERA)

HERA proposes to undertake five types of action: (1) Technological innovation and rapid response to market and regulatory challenges; (2) harmonization of policy development; (3) monitoring, preparedness and response; (4) detection of cross-border threats and hazards (horizon scanning) and (5) education and training of personnel. Under (4) it is planned to establish a joint EU-WHO surveillance system to be managed by the European Centre for Disease Control (ECDC). However, the precise form HERA will take is not yet known (Villa et al., 2021). It will work closely with the existing EU bodies (e.g. ECDC and EMA, European Medicines Agency). The European Commission (2021, September 16) has earmarked €6 billion for 2022–2027. It has already allocated €20 million to finance its key preparatory activities.

In a *Lancet* article, the League of European Universities (LERU) and the European Global Health Research Institutes Network (EGHRIN) outline how Europe should take a leading position globally in developing a comprehensive and timely response to health emergencies. While its focus could be on stockpiling, LERU and EGHRIN outline how HERA should eventually take the form of a complete end-to-end authority which streamlines initiatives in the area of health preparedness and response and builds upon the competences already in place through existing bodies like the ECDC and the EMA.

As noted above, a joint EU-WHO global surveillance system, with capacity to anticipate and identify cross-border threats early, if effectively implemented, can be a major achievement. However, it is unclear how the above initiative will feed into the proposed EU-WHO-HERA proposals. WHO needs to enjoy a coordinating authority and capacity to maximize benefits from different national, regional and global surveillance systems.

National and local capacity on the ground within individual countries are necessary preconditions for the success of any global systems.

Other regional groupings, namely *ASEAN and SAARC*, have also coordinated their COVID-19 responses by pledging additional funds. For example, SAARC member countries have set up a *Covid-19 Emergency Fund*. Similarly, ASEAN has set up a new *Covid-19 Response Fund* and has pledged to share information and strategies to mitigate the impact of the global health crisis on the region.

Concluding Remarks

The present climate of global divisions and competition, nationalist tendencies and trade and tariff wars are not conducive to the launching of global coordinated humanitarian assistance and research cooperation. In addition, there is the ongoing China-US rivalry, which is unlikely to diminish if China bashing continues. Admittedly, in these conditions, *universality* in global action is hard to achieve. But the second-best solution, that of global action by a "coalition of the willing" and like-minded countries, is not only desirable but is already under way as discussed in this chapter.

There are plenty of globalist leaders who believe in international cooperation and action. They are optimistic that adequate global resources would be available for *coordinated* actions. The Biden administration's rejoining the WHO provides hope for the future. On the other hand, pessimists are likely to strike a note of caution that the recent experiences and the current political environment do not augur well. They argue that competition among countries is growing, retreat from multilateralism is real and donor countries are more likely to go-it-alone and take credit for their individual aid to countries.

Whether the optimists or the pessimists will win, and whether global cooperation will score over power rivalry is anybody's guess. But truth may lie somewhere in between. Rivalry between China and the US has been underway for several years and is most likely to continue. Notwithstanding, global research cooperation will survive albeit under financial constraints.

Given the current political and ideological fissures, global action needs to be viewed not only in terms of state-driven intergovernmental partnerships. It is time for some fresh thinking on new types of collaboration and networks which embrace public-private partnerships, involving civil society and informal non-governmental institutions.

There is no shortage of ideas for undertaking such global action as sharing of vaccine supplies in the immediate future. For example, WHO and some academics have proposed that the vaccine-producing countries should delay vaccinating their children in order to share vaccine supplies with poor countries where they are urgently needed (Hoeg et al., 2021). Others have suggested that the same countries could release supplies by delaying the administration of second dose or boosters. But even those Western countries, which believe in the advantages of multilateralism, do not have the political will to share vaccines to control the pandemic globally. Failure to do so may begin to haunt them when more new and deadlier variants circulate freely across national boundaries.

Notes

1. Global leaders demanded that a G20 task force be set up to coordinate coronavirus response (see Brown & Erik, 2020, April 7).
2. Global equitable access to COVID-19 vaccines facility is estimated to generate economic benefits of at least US$153 billion in 2020–2021 and US$466 by 2025 in ten major economies according to new report by the Eurasia Group (2020). Cited in Bassi (2021, February 8). These estimates are based on the expected negative effects of the coronavirus outbreaks in the low- and middle-income countries and the baseline scenarios of the IMF *World Economic Outlook* (October 2020) forecasts.
3. I owe this point to Professor Lindsay Greer, Director of Research Relations (Physical Sciences and Technology) and former Head of School of Physical Sciences, University of Cambridge.
4. The Canadian observer is Steven Hoffman, Professor of Global Health, Law and Political Science at York University, cited in Vanderklippe (2020, June 12).
5. A number of early warning and surveillance systems have been in existence for several years. For a description and assessment of these systems see Hitchcock et al. (2007).

References

Agarwal, R., Farrar, J., Gopinath, G., Hatchett, R., & Sands, P. (2022, April). *A global strategy to manage the long-term risks of Covid-19.* IMF Working Papers WP/22/68.

Applebaum, A. (2020). When the world stumbled: Covid-19 and the failure of the international system. In H. Brands & F. J. Gavin (Eds.), *Covid-19 and world order: The future of conflict, competition, and cooperation.* Johns Hopkin s University Press.

Aschwenden, C. (2021). Why herd immunity for Covid-19 is probably impossible. *Nature, 591.*

Baker, M. G., & Fidler, D. P. (2006). Global public health surveillance under new international health regulations. *Emerging Infectious Diseases, 12*(7).

Balakrishnan, B. (2020, April). WHO's role in the Covid-19 outbreak must be strengthened. *RIS Diary*, 2nd Special Issue on Covid-19.

Banco, E., Cancryn, A., & Paun, C. (2021). Failure to vaccinate poor countries fans fears of uncontrolled outbreak. *Politico.* 23 November.

Bassi, L. L. (2021). Allocating covid-19 vaccines globally: An urgent need. *JAMA Health Forum.*

Bezanson, K. (2021). *Learning from Covid-19: Towards a fit for purpose international health system.* Centre for International Governance Innovation (CIGI).

Bloom, D. E., & Cadarette, D. (2020). Strengthening the global response to infectious disease threats in the twenty-first century, with a COVID-19 epilogue. In S. Benatar & G. Brock (Eds.), *Global health and global ethics.* Cambridge University Press.

Brown, G. (2020, April 28). The deadly urgency of now. *Project Syndicate.*

Brown, G. (2021a, April 12). G7 must push for global vaccination: Here's how it could do it. *Guardian.*

Brown, G. (2021b) *Seven ways to save the world.*

Brown, G. B., & Erik, F. J. (2020, April 7). Now or never for global leadership on Covid-19. *Project Syndicate.*

Callahan, M. V., & Poznansky, M. (2021, June 10). The vaccines we have are good: But they could be so much better. *New York Times.*

Cockburn, H. (2020, March 26). Coronavirus: Gordon Brown calls for new global government to fight impact of Covid-19. *Independent.*

Cohen, J. (2021, December 17). Effort to address global vaccine shortfalls envision a more equitable new year. *ScienceInsider.*

Deakin, S., & Meng, G. (2020). The governance of Covid-19: Anthropogenic risk, evolutionary learning and the future of the social state. *Industrial Law Journal, 49*(49).

Duggan, J., Morriss, S., Sandefur, J., & Yang, G. (2020, October). *Is the World Bank's COVID-19 crisis lending big enough, fast enough? New evidence on loan disbursements.* Centre for Global Development (CGD) Working Paper 554.

European Commission. (2021). *Questions and answers: European health emergency preparedness and response authority.* HERA.

European Council. (2021, March 30). An international treaty on pandemic prevention and preparedness.

Fan, Y., Shi, Z., Zhou, P., & Zhou, K. (2019, March). Bat Coronaviruses in China. *Viruses*.

Forster, T., Kentkelenis, A., Stubbs, B., & King, L. (2020). Globalization and health equity: The impact of structural adjustment programmes in developing countries. *Social Science and Medicine, 267*.

Gallagher, K. P., & Carlin, F. M. (2020). Th role of the IMF in the fight against COVID-19: The IMF Covid-19 recovery index. *Covid Economics, 42*.

Gates, B. (2022). *How to prevent the next pandemic*. Allen Lane.

Glassman, A., & Yadav, P. (2022). *African vaccine manufacturing with EU support: Addressing demand uncertainties is crucial for success*. Centre for Global Development (CGD) Blog.

Gostin, L., DeBartolo, M., & Friedman, E. (2015, November 28). The International Health Regulations ten years on: The governing framework for global health security. *The Lancet*.

Hannon, E., Hanbali, L., Nehtimaki, L., & Schwalbe, N. (2022). Why we still need a pandemic treaty. *The Lancet, 10*.

Hitchcock, P., Chamberlain, A., van Wagoner, M., Inglesby, T. V., & O'Toole, T. (2007). Challenges to global surveillance and response to infectious disease outbreaks of international importance. *Biosecurity and Bioterrorism: Biodefence Strategy, Practice and Science, 5*(3).

Hoeg, T. B., Prasad, V., & Gandhi, M. (2021, May 12). American kids can wait. *The Atlantic*.

IHR. (2005). Revisions of the International Health Regulations, World Health Assembly, WHA.58.3, WHO, Geneva.

IMF (International Monetary Fund). (2021, December). IMF's Covid-19 crisis capacity development. *Report on activities*.

IMF (International Monetary Fund). (2022). *Crisis upon crisis, 2022 Annual Report*.

IMF, Independent Evaluation Office. (2022, July 27). *The IMF and capacity development—Funding issues*. Background Paper by L. Stedman, BP/22–02/13.

Inglesby, T. (2020). Make pandemics lose their power. In H. Brands & F. J. Gavin (Eds.), *COVID-19 and world order: The future of conflict, competition and cooperation*. Johns Hopkins University Press.

IPPPR (Independent Panel). (2021). *COVID-19: Make it the last pandemic*.

Jarvis, L. M. (2020, May 1). How big pharma firms are quietly collaborating on new coronavirus antivirals. *Chemical and Engineering News*.

Jha, A. (2021, March–April). America needs a global health policy for the pandemic age. *Foreign Affairs*.

Kamradt-Scott, A. (2018). What went wong? The World Health Organization from swine flu to Ebola. In A. Kruck, K. Oppermann, & A. Spencer (Eds.), *Political mistakes and policy failures in international relations*. Palgrave Macmillan.

Kilby, C., & McWhirter, C. (2022). The world bank COVID-19 response: Politics as usual? *Review of International Organizations, 17.*

McGahan, A. (2020, May 14). We need a Financial Stability Board for Health. *Financial Times.*

Nature. (2021, April 6). The world must learn from COVID before diving into a pandemic treaty. *Editorial.*

Nay, O., Kieny, M. P., Marmora, L., & Kazatchkine, M. (2020). The WHO we want. *The Lancet, 395.*

Nikogosian, H., & Kickbusch, I. (2021). The case for an international pandemic treaty. *British Medical Journal, 372*(527).

OXFAM International. (2020, December). *From catastrophe to catalyst—Can the World Bank make COVID-19 a turning point for building universal and fair public health care systems?.*

Puyvallée, A. B., & Storeng, K. T. (2022). COVAX, vaccine donations and the politics of global inequity. *Globalization and Health* (Open access).

Rivers, C., & George, D. (2020, June 29). *How to forecast outbreaks and pandemics: America needs the contagion equivalent of the National Weather Service.* Foreign Affairs.

Rudd, K. (2022). *The avoidable war.* Public Affairs.

Stein. (2020). Take it off-site: World order and international institutions after COVID 19. In H. Brands & F. J. Gavin (Eds.), *COVID-19 and world order.* Johns Hopkins University Press.

The Economist. (2020, April 25). The data economy: Tear down this wall.

UN (United Nations). (2020). *Secretary-General's UN Covid-19 response and recovery fund.* United Nations.

Vanderklippe, N. (2020, June 12). Chan reshaped the WHO and brought it closer to China. *Globe and Mail.*

Villa, S., van Leeuwen, R., Gray, C. C., van der Sande, M., Konradsen, F., Fröschl, G., Nord, D. G., Da Costa, C. P., Ramirez-Rubio, O., Abubakar, I., & Bärnighausen, T. (2021). HERA: A new era for health emergency preparedness in Europe? *The Lancet.*

WHO. (2019). *Promote health, keep the world safe, serve the vulnerable.* Thirteenth General Programme of Work, 2019–2013.

WHO. (2021a, October 8). ACT-Accelerator strategic review: *Final Report*—An Independent Report prepared by Dalberg.

WHO. (2021b). WHO's financing dialogue: *A proposal for increasing the assessed contributions.*

WHO. (2021c). *Introduction to WHO budgeting and planning.*

WHO. (2021d, May 19). Programme, Budget and Administration Committee, World Health Assembly (WHA), Proposed Programme and Budget 2022–2023. *Building Forward Better.*

WHO. (2021e, December 1). World Health Assembly agrees to launch process to develop historic global accord on pandemic prevention, preparedness and response. *News Release.*

WHO. (2022a). *ACT Accelerator: Q2 Quarterly update, 1 April–30 June 2022.*

WHO. (2022b, April 26). *The ACT Accelerator: Two years of impact,* June 30.

WHO. (2022c, 30 June). World Bank Board approves new fund for pandemic prevention, preparedness and response (PPR). The World Bank to work together WHO to set up Secretariat at the World Bank, with WHO as lead technical partner. *News Release.*

World Bank. (2020, June). *Saving lives, scaling up impact and getting back on track: World Bank COVID-19 crisis response approach paper.*

World Bank. (2022, August 10). *How the World Bank Group is helping countries address Covid-19 coronavirus pandemic.*

World Bank Group, Independent Evaluation Group. (2014, July). *World Bank Group support to health financing: An independent evaluation.*

WTO (World Trade Organization). (2022, June 12–15). Ministerial Decision on the TRIPS Agreement. Ministerial Conference, Twelfth Session. Geneva (WT/MIN (22)/30, WT/L/1141.

Wu, J. T., Leung, K., & Leung, G. M. (2020). Nowcasting and forecasting the potential domestic and international spread of the 2019-nCoV outbreak originating in Wuhan, China: A modelling study. *The Lancet, 395.*

Zimmer, C. (2022, April 2). Cuts in Britain could cause a covid data drought. *New York Times.*

CHAPTER 7

Lessons for the Future

It is far better to foresee even without certainty than never to foresee at all.
—Henri Poincare, *The Foundations of Science*

Forecasting the future is difficult at the best of times. It is all the more so in conditions of systemic risks, uncertainty and incomplete information or what has been called "predictable unpredictability" (*The Economist*, 2021b, December 18). Given these characteristic features of the pandemic, it may be tantamount to shooting in the dark. Therefore, the precise impact of the pandemic on the future of the national and global economy and society may not be foreseeable. Yet one can guess what the future shape of things may look like based on the past experiences. Indeed, many observers had sounded the warning bells about the pandemic well in advance of the actual reality which a large number of national political leaders ignored. More than two years into the pandemic, many scholars and experts warn that new pandemics will occur in the future as they have in the past at almost regular intervals (see Chap. 1).

Model builders and others have tried different methods—scenario planning, forecasting and early warning systems—to anticipate or forecast the future and to guide political leaders and policymakers in decision-making and policy choices to meet unforeseen challenges. A more pragmatic approach is a combination of best past experiences and practices and

A. S. Bhalla, *National and Global Responses to the COVID-19 Pandemic*, https://doi.org/10.1007/978-3-031-29521-8_7

current/recent experiences of policy successes and failures in the management of COVID-19. It can suggest some key guidelines for what a new normal may/should look like in the post-pandemic world.

Two broad conclusions are worth noting before delving into detailed lessons for the future. The first broad conclusion is that political leaders alone are not fully responsible for the failures or successes in the containment and control of the pandemic. True many world leaders have been irresponsible, unaccountable and incompetent in managing the crisis. But the responsibility for controlling the pandemic also rests on the agents and followers. Even the most competent and dedicated political leaders cannot control/eliminate the coronavirus without the support of public and private institutions and the public. The fact that many high-income countries have performed poorly despite all the scientific and economic benefits stacked in their favour suggests some inadequacies in institutional capacity and behavioural responses.

A number of world leaders including those from the international community have spoken about the role of political leadership and trust in governments. For example, Helen Clark and Ellen Johnson, Co-Chairs of the WHO-sponsored Independent Panel, underlined the need for collective and competent leadership. Dr. Tedros Adhanom Ghebreyesus, the WHO Director-General, who was more directly concerned with the coronavirus pandemic on a daily basis, made the following remarks on 13 July 2020: "Too many countries are headed in the wrong direction. The virus remains public enemy number one, but the actions of many governments and people do not reflect this .... Mixed messages from leaders are undermining the most critical ingredient of any response: trust."

People's Trust in Leaders and Agents

In the book, the role of public trust and confidence in political leaders, government, public institutions and health services and vaccines, besides interpersonal trust and community spirit, form an integral part of the institutional framework developed in Chap. 3 to study responses to COVID-19.

To recapitulate, *relations* between (political) leaders, public and private agents and followers are an important determinant of success or failure in the performance of leaders and agents in controlling the pandemic. Cooperation between all the three stakeholders ensures positive results in terms of a good balance between health and economic goals, whereas competition and conflict will lead to a negative outcome. People's trust and confidence in a leader enhance his or her effectiveness. Public anger and hostility may arise when government leadership fails to meet people's expectations in terms of protection during a health crisis and thus breaches the social contract between the rulers and the ruled (Liu et al., 2021).[1]

People's trust depends on a host of factors, notably, individualism or selfishness or consideration of others' well-being, the existence of social cohesion, faith in science or in traditions and government's performance. It is likely to vary over time depending on the context, government response and its impact on their health and well-being.

Our analysis of government responses to COVID-19 provides the following conclusions:

1. Public trust and confidence and people's perception of risk and their cooperation with leaders and public institutions are interlinked. Government's sincerity and sense of responsibility, participatory approach and timely and accurate information dissemination on the pandemic generated greater trust and cooperation than secretiveness and partisan feuds.
2. When it comes to the issues of personal health and hygiene, followers' individual decisions play a major role during the pandemic as well as in the post-pandemic period. The followers have to depend on different sources of public and private information, for example, government information campaigns, digital and social media, and family and friends. Regular and timely public information campaigns, which dispel misinformation and conspiracy theories, raise people's trust in leaders and government. Good governance and accountable governments in general command greater respect and ensure compliance and enforcement of rules.
3. Disconnect between the public and government leaders is lower when the latter meet people's expectation by delivering public goods and services and providing protection from disease and death during the pandemic.
4. People's compliance with temporary COVID restrictions such as lockdowns and curbing of civil liberties was tolerated more in societies with greater social cohesion and public trust. But the level of trust is not immutable; it may decline if restrictions such as strict lockdowns persist over long periods. The experience of China is a case in point (see Epilogue).[2]

5. Governments, which were transparent and explained to their citizens the need for introducing restrictive COVID measures to protect their health and well-being and provided timely economic and social relief measures, commanded greater public confidence and compliance than others.
6. Responses to the pandemic are much more likely to succeed if they are *people-driven* rather than *government-driven*. A major responsibility for protection against the virus will rest on individuals, support groups and local communities. The Indian experience of innovative *community* response in Dharavi slum (see Chap. 2, Box 2.1) as well as similar community initiatives in South Korea and Vietnam provide valuable lessons for the rest of the world. Local community leaders and support groups as well as community clinics are a useful resource to promote *collective* behaviour and social inclusiveness.
7. In an increasing number of countries, political polarization, party politics and political interference in scientific work hindered the effectiveness of COVID responses. Conflictual or uncooperative relationship emerged between leaders, agents and followers. Lack of people's trust in politicians, leaders and government agents was an inevitable consequence.

With continued uncertainty in the future about the global economy, world order, political and ideological divide between major powers and an unknown evolution of new variants and sub-variants, risk and perceptions of fear on the part of the public may remain important in the future. The relaxation of all restrictions and business as usual may even worsen the situation of risk and uncertainty. This is particularly so given the *unpredictability* of the future evolution of new variants and sub-variants and the degree of their *transmissibility*.

Political leaders and governments in many countries relied on different types of COVID restrictions in their containment and mitigation strategies. Quite a few countries aimed at a complete elimination of the virus till the end of 2022, when new highly transmissible Omicron variants and sub-variants started appearing. More may yet evolve, but it is too early to tell with certainty. This new situation has led to the collapse of the zero-COVID strategy including in China where it was most vigorously implemented (Epilogue).

Almost all countries have now shifted away from the elimination and mitigation strategies to manage the virus. The new normal now is to live with the virus hoping its impact would be less severe, thanks to generally high rates of vaccination (at least in the West), milder forms of some new variants and a milder winter as the Mother Nature's gift to mankind.

Globalization Versus Deglobalization

The above discussion pertains to national-level responses to COVID-19 by the various stakeholders. But global pandemic has a global perspective as well, such as the need for a global response to the pandemic in all countries and economic recovery of the global economy. A shift away from globalization, frequent lockdowns and supply-chain bottlenecks have shattered the global economy. Failure to share COVID-19 data and vaccines, which are largely developed in the high-income countries, with poor low-income countries has left the global health of mankind in danger.

The world is more interconnected today than ever before, and what happens in one country can very rapidly affect the rest of the world with immediate and dire consequences. COVID-19 spread quickly throughout the world because of globalization. Cross-border flows, international travel, business and trade and political rallies spread the virus like wild fires and took most leaders by surprise. The new variants and sub-variants moved around the world with a lightning speed. Two Oxford scholars colourfully describe the phenomenon of associated systemic risks as the "butterfly defect," that is, small flappings of butterfly wings spreading negative ripple effects throughout different dimensions of society. Thanks to globalization, "the butterfly of change has lost its innocence" and has resulted in new forms of risks (Goldin & Mariathasan, 2016).

The post-recovery phase of the coronavirus pandemic requires a global attack on several fronts: health promotion, economic revival of national economies and the global economy, humanitarian response and research collaboration. While the first will need to be both *people-driven* and *government-driven*, the remaining two issues will call for a combined public and private-sector response and the involvement of civil society. National governments, international bodies and the global community need to work together to find *common* solutions.

The process of globalization has suffered from several major shocks, which have slowed its pace: 2008 financial crisis following the collapse of Lehman Brothers in the United States; US-China tariff war and other trade disruptions and Russia's invasion of Ukraine and COVID-19 which brought trade, foreign investment and international travel to a halt. The closure of borders has been damaging for businesses and tourism.

Trade, which flourished in the pre-pandemic period, has suffered as a result of COVID-19 and the disruption of global supply chains. The US tariff and trade war with China may have also had some adverse effect on trade. But the Chinese exports have been rising (especially during the first two years of the pandemic) despite these disruptions. This is not surprising considering that China controlled the pandemic early, which enabled faster economic recovery. But its persistence with a strict enforcement of zero-COVID strategy slowed down the process till early December 2022 when Xi abruptly dismantled it and reopened the economy (see Epilogue for more details).

Other adverse effects of COVID-19 on globalization have been felt in the closing of national borders, greater control of immigration and calls by many national governments for greater self-reliance. Countries ranging from the United States to France and to India and China have set in motion inward-looking policies and measures, such as the creation of domestic supply chains as a matter of national security. These geopolitical considerations and US-China rivalry have upended the logic of global economic cooperation (Rodrik, 2022, May 9).

Under the relief and recovery/stimulus packages during the pandemic, which were introduced by many countries, provisions were made for subsidies to key industries and incentives for the relocation of firms from abroad. But bringing back production of essential goods may lead to national autarky and *dirigisme* at a time when a better balance is needed between national self-reliance and globalization. Globalization is being replaced by regionalization and relocation. But there are considerable costs involved in relocating production, which many multinationals are not prepared to incur. Deglobalization may hurt economic growth especially of small, open and undiversified economies (Rogoff, 2020, June 3). It may also push up prices and interest rates. At any rate, relocation is not a new phenomenon. It has been occurring in response to rising labour costs, with production shifting from China to lower labour-cost countries like Bangladesh and Vietnam. But the nature of this process during the pandemic is different. It is moving production away from low-labour-cost to high-labour-cost locations, which entails a considerable increase in production cost.

The benefits of globalization in the form of economies of scale and supply of cheap consumer goods cannot be achieved through deglobalization, which is a misleading term to describe a reorientation of the global economy towards regionalization and new regional trade agreements (e.g. revised NAFTA, Comprehensive and Progressive Agreement for Trans-Pacific Partnership and the Regional Comprehensive Economic Partnership for the East Asian region). A complete dethronement of globalization would be costly in terms of economic growth, output expansion, job creation and economic efficiency.

There are three ways in which the COVID-19 shock to globalization is different from the earlier shocks. Firstly, complete lockdowns and sealing of national borders during the pandemic have hurt all countries, big and small, rich and poor, which has led to loss of output and jobs. Secondly, the pandemic has created systemic risks and uncertainty, which are likely to last longer than expected. Lingering uncertainty has serious implications for both consumption and investment decisions. Thirdly, there is a lack of *global* coordinated response to the pandemic.

Globalization has always been a double-edged sword. Its negative consequences in the form of widening income and wage inequalities, job destruction through imports and environmental hazards were known in the past but were not adequately addressed by national governments and global institutions (Bhalla, 1998; Haass, 2020; Rodrik, 2011, Stiglitz, 2006, 2019).

Lack of Global Action and Coordination

The world economy will not recover on a sustained basis without global and coordinated action. Neither can better health for all be provided without advance preparedness to anticipate future pandemics and contain them quickly before they become out of control. Therefore, the existing global economic (World Bank), finance (IMF), trade (WTO) and health (WHO) institutions need to be reformed and strengthened, not weakened.

On-the-shelf earlier experiences and best practices highlight the importance of the positive role played by global cooperation and coordination in research as well as in pandemic management and control. For example, SARS was detected early by the Global Public Health Intelligence Network. WHO was effective in containing it despite the adverse effects of its bureaucratic structure and political pressures by Member states. If SARS could be contained through global cooperation, why COVID-19 cannot be controlled especially when vaccines are available to do so?

An answer to this question lies in the changed environment of populism and nationalism. Experts warn of a real possibility of pandemics recurring in the future. The question is not if but when they will strike again. As discussed in Chap. 6, the European Council and the WHO have proposed an International Epidemics Treaty to ensure global cooperation in preparedness and to anticipate and tackle future pandemics. Effective early warning systems at the national levels are also needed to detect pandemics. At present, very few countries are suitably equipped. Also missing are suitable mechanisms for early response such as rapid and mobile medical teams to deal with global emergencies.

The world has missed at least two opportunities for global action to fight the virus, namely global sharing of COVID-19 data sets and equitable sharing/distribution and delivery of COVID vaccines. As discussed in Chap. 5, action on the distribution of vaccines to the poorest countries has been hampered by vaccine nationalism on the part of vaccine-producing countries, lack of required resources and low commitment of major donor countries.

Systematic management of health data on a global basis is also important for future innovations in the field of medicine and health. WHO, which is responsible for health data, may need to manage specific clusters of data especially for particular innovations. But the issues of data privacy and sharing of data will need to be sorted out, perhaps within the framework of the proposed International Pandemic Treaty discussed in Chap. 6.

Related to the above is the need for global sharing of data networks on COVID-19. Policymakers and researchers need different types of data during the pandemic: COVID test results, numbers of cases and deaths, those who have been vaccinated and viral genome sequences to determine the identity of variants. At present, "there is no agreed, trusted mechanism for access" to such data (*Nature*, 2021, June 1). Many countries prohibit access because it may involve risks of people being identified or businesses sharing data with competitors.

A proposal has been made to establish "a Supply Chain Infomediary" with which all different groups of suppliers and purchasers of vaccines share their data, for example, on demand and supply, confirmed purchase orders, supplies of input materials and finished products (Yadav & Weintraub, 2021, May 6). Such information does exist but is dispersed among different organizations (e.g. GAVI, CEPI, WHO and UNICEF) not to speak of individual wealthy countries. Such a depository will need to be neutral to function properly.

Generally, governments and private companies are reluctant to share information although scientists and medical professionals have been sharing research data. For example, genetic sequencing of coronavirus shared by Chinese scientists enabled Moderna company to develop its COVID-19 vaccine. Moderna took only two days to develop a blueprint for the vaccine on the basis of the data provided (Maxmen, 2020; Slaughter & McCormick, 2021). Global data sharing of this kind can also reduce the concentration of economic and political power of giant companies.

Many political leaders are proven globalists and remain so even though nationalists and populists are on the rise. They form a hard core to push through global initiatives to control COVID-19 within the framework of the UN, WHO and the global (G20 and G7) and regional bodies (e.g. the EU and ASEAN). But their commitment or influence has not been as strong as expected.

Political leaders of G7 and G20 countries could have done much more like preparing a global plan of action on COVID-19 and a well-coordinated response. Global leadership and political commitment were lacking when it was badly needed. Global geopolitical tensions between major powers have seriously undermined multilateral institutions. It took G20 eight months to meet, and disunity within the G7 came out into the open in 2018 when Trump refused to sign the joint communiqué. Often priorities on the agenda of the G7 reflect those of the host countries rather than the urgent global issues that need attention.

Similarly, the new systemic risks to environment and health will need to be tackled through *common* solutions. National governments, the international community as well as the private sector and civil society face a major challenge here.

Lessons for the Future

Our review and analysis of Chaps. 1, 2, 3, 4, 5, and 6 point towards several lessons for the future.

Firstly, too much dependence on one or two foreign countries for drugs, vaccines and medical supplies can be suicidal. Building/strengthening of public health capacity needs to be recognized as an issue of economic, social and national security. Essential public goods (e.g. medical supplies) need to be produced within countries even if their production fails the test of profitability. The efforts of most developed countries to match production with rapidly growing demand have been woefully slow.

Too much dependence on imports from abroad from only one or two countries can cost lives especially if procurement is inadequate or slow.

Worldwide shortages of personal protective equipment (PPE) and ventilators during the pandemic led to panic and calls for national self-reliance. But *overconcentration* of supply chains and reshoring are not the solutions as they can raise systemic risks. What is needed instead is their *diversification*. Another solution lies in keeping strategic medical reserves as was done by Finland, one of the few countries to do so. There were others (e.g. the United States) which had some stockpiles could not be used due to damage through neglect.

The theory of comparative advantage and economic specialization would counsel against the setting up of all types of factory units to produce simple medical goods for which the high-income countries have no special advantage. We believe that a healthy combination of a properly managed globalization and some national self-reliance for health and security reasons would be the best way forward.

Secondly, there is a greater role for the government in the provision of public health goods and services. Health services are in short supply even in the richest countries of the world as the stark truth has been laid bare during the pandemic. Market failures in supplying and distributing public health goods and services are well known. Governments need to step in as in France, where a law was passed (March, 2020) to enable the government to control people's movements, manage prices and requisition goods.

However, a worrying question is whether these *temporary* control measures will become a new normal in the future. Some countries led by autocratic/authoritarian leaders (e.g. Hungary and Turkey) used the pandemic as an excuse to grab more power and ignore democratic values and the rule of law. For example, the Hungarian parliament passed a "coronavirus law" without an expiry date, which allows the prime minister to rule by decree. *Reporters without Borders* cite 38 countries that used the pandemic as the pretext to harass the media (*The Economist*, 2020b, April 25).

The large size of government would not necessarily ensure success if much of the government expenditure were wasted on white elephants. Bloated bureaucracy may simply indicate that governments have taken control of too many activities for which they lack competence. Western governments have been overloaded besides being torn apart by vested interests (Micklethwait & Wooldridge, 2020, p. 65). They suffer from several flaws, namely their relative decline compared to the private sector, excessive burden of too many obligations and failure to attract qualified manpower for lack of trust in politics. What matters in managing the health pandemic is not so much the size or *quantity* of government but its *quality*. The latter is embodied in qualified and committed leaders and politicians besides well-trained medical personnel and healthcare workers.

The states/governments are characterized by different criteria, for example, size (large, medium or small), political orientation (Left, Right or Centre), type of governance (federal or unitary) and ideology (democratic, autocratic, authoritarian, monarchical). Western democracies often tout their superiority over authoritarian regimes in managing crises through free and accurate flow of information. However, it is a matter of value judgement whether democracies have promoted free, accurate and timely information on COVID-19. More often, misinformation, fake news and conspiracy theories have crowded out accurate and scientific information, as discussed above.

Table 7.1 summarizes links between the government's size, ideology or political party affiliation and its performance to contain and control COVID-19. The performance is defined *quantitatively* in terms of the number of COVID-19 deaths per capita. The table shows that neither the size of government nor political ideology or regime type matters in explaining country performance. Both democratic and non-democratic governments have performed well or poorly. Therefore, it is safe to conclude that explanations for success in controlling COVID-19 lie elsewhere.

Table 7.1 Government size, political ideology and COVID-19 performance

Government	*COVID-19 performance*	
	High	*Low*
Big government		
Democratic		
– Left (progressive)	X	x
– Right (conservative)	X	x
– Populist	...	x
– Authoritarian	X	x
Small government		
Democratic	X	
– Left	X	
– Right	X	
– Authoritarian	X	x

The failures of democracies can be attributed not so much to democracy per se (or big government) but to the erosion of democratic norms and institutions. For example, in the United States, the fallout from the Trump years—attack on the Capitol (the very symbol of democracy), breakdown of the two-party system and suppression of the voting rights of African Americans—reflects the weakening of a liberal democratic order. COVID-19 did not start this process, only hastened its decline (*The Economist*, 2020c, November 28).

That committed political leadership matters is shown clearly by the relative success of the Biden administration compared to that of Trump. In its first 100 days, the Biden administration took central control and direction since the Trump administration had left the pandemic in a shambolic condition. The speed with which it ramped up vaccine production and distributed the vaccines to the states and districts and administered it (over 300 million doses in the first 150 days) was remarkable. But defiance of public agents (e.g. mainly conservative Republicans) and followers to wear masks or get vaccinated besides overruling of the federal mandate by the courts in some cases led to a spike in cases, hospitalizations and deaths.

A few democratic countries with big governments (e.g. Austria, Germany and Greece) managed the crisis effectively at least in the early stages. However, the best performers were the Southeast Asian countries whose government expenditure as a proportion of GDP was nearly half of that for Western governments in Europe and North America. Although there is no clear-cut evidence on the role of political party affiliation, Chap. 4 showed that conservative populist governments (e.g. Indian, American, Brazilian and British) performed poorly.

Therefore, one can conclude that the *size* of government does not matter as much as its *effectiveness*. In future, *more* government will mean *better* government, that is, better accountability and governance, greater focus, change in priorities and the reallocation of resources to social sectors (public healthcare and education) and better early warning and data systems.

Good governance calls for smart, committed political leaders, accountable and responsive governments, better-qualified public agents, more effective central direction and coordination, greater interagency cooperation and consultation, decentralized decision-making, more popular participation and community involvement.

Capacity will need to be created to anticipate future pandemics, through the establishment of early warning systems. Our review of country experiences shows that the existence of capacity per se does not mean its effective *utilization*, which may depend on competent and decentralized decision-making under a non-hierarchical governance structure.

A welfare or "social" state will need to be brought back in the post-pandemic world. More and better social safety nets are necessary for health protection and human welfare of all individuals in an equitable manner. Social protection has suffered from a long-lasting impact of "the Washington Consensus" under which free markets were considered the dominant paradigm of economic and social development. Added to this, austerity measures, necessitated by the 2008 financial crisis, led to a demise of the welfare model. As discussed in Chap. 2, even in very high-income countries, the well-funded health sectors, which were considered resilient, failed to cope with the peaks of the pandemic. Many countries had to increase funding for healthcare in their relief packages in the face of growing demand for health protection, which will need to be maintained on a *permanent* basis.

Social protections in the form of health insurance, paid sick leave, decent minimum wage and welfare benefits are limited in coverage and are highly inadequate in most countries. For example, the United States does not provide these protections except for the rich. Countries will need to improve health insurance and other social protection measures if they are to prepare themselves adequately to meet the challenge of another pandemic in the future.

Most Western countries were unprepared and reactive and failed to learn lessons from the past experiences. Very few had in place any *anticipatory* policies or early warning systems which were perceived to be expensive and time-consuming (DeLeo, 2016). In future, more proactive and anticipatory measures will be needed to strengthen healthcare systems and services with, inter alia, expanded capacity and qualified health manpower (Bhalla, 1995; Drèze & Sen, 1989, 1995).

Some social groups (e.g. the elderly, minorities and the poor) were worse hit than others, thus exacerbating the existing social, economic and health inequalities (Blundell et al., 2021). National governments, which fail to check/reverse these widening gaps, may face serious social discontent and upheaval in the future. Although enough has been written on income inequalities within and between countries, the implications of non-income inequalities based on ethnicity and race during the pandemic have received much less attention.[3] Less understood also is the effect of poor leadership on inequalities and governance. These are important areas for further research.

Neglect of the low-income and low-status ethnic communities, most of which provide "essential" workers for public health agencies, can worsen the existing inequalities. In future, societies will need to place a much higher value on the productive role of the "essential workers." Their special needs deserve more attention and financial support during any future emergency planning if only to ensure steady supply and support of carers in care homes where a large proportion of COVID deaths in the West have occurred. At the global level, lack of access to new drugs and vaccines, through what is called "ugly vaccine nationalism," will worsen global inequalities in healthcare and economic well-being (Brown, 2020; Bollyky & Bown, 2020).

The COVID-19 experience has underlined the critical importance of *timing*. A quick response saved many lives and hastened economic recovery. Slow and late responses made it impossible to control the virus. Frequent, partial and wholesale lockdowns were a direct consequence of inaction and lack of preparedness. New waves of the virus spread more rapidly in the winter of 2020–2021 and the following Spring, which caused the return of new and stricter lockdowns in a large number of countries. Early economic gains may have already been lost in many countries especially in the absence of any coordination and harmonization of policy responses at least among neighbouring countries (*The Economist*, 2021a, July 3).

Poor enforcement of public health guidelines and lockdowns allowed cases and deaths to grow and new mutants to develop, which largely went undetected in several countries. Vaccines were developed without the knowledge of these more lethal variants. These vaccines are said to be less effective for Omicron and its sub-variants. Therefore, periodic adaptation of vaccines to new variants would be essential. A growing number of experts suggest the need for annual COVID booster similar to influenza shots.

One important lesson for the post-pandemic world is that piecemeal and quick fixes in the name of economic revival can be dangerous. A *premature* reopening of the economy can neutralize all the gains and positive results of pandemic control. The experiences of countries/regions which partially reopened suggest that normalization of economic activity and social interaction can cause fresh spikes in COVID cases unless adequate precautionary measures are put in place.

Another lesson relates to national data systems on healthcare, which are poor in most low-income countries but also in several high-income countries. Lack of adequate and good-quality data hinders cross-country analyses on a comparative basis. There is an urgent need for the processing, standardization and management of data and its timely sharing among different government and non-governmental agencies and the research community. Better management of data systems at the national level will help better modelling, forecasting and policymaking. Quick decisions based on poor detection and reporting for lack of proper facts can lead to wrong policy responses.

Related to data sharing is the role of science and scientists in the post-pandemic world. Their contribution to overcoming the harmful effects of misinformation and conspiracy theories can be significant even though a growing number of politicians have been downplaying their role. Discussion of scientific findings in the public press is an indication of a growing interest in science, an opportunity which scientists can seize to neutralize the above adverse effects (Freedman et al., 2020).

Greater use of information technology and digitization can prevent recurrence of the virus, but IT and digital infrastructure are unevenly distributed. Slow digitization of many government operations in national bureaucracies in many countries prevented the use of high-tech apps for rapid testing and tracing. Although concerns of privacy may be relevant, barriers to the use of high-tech are largely technological. Asian willingness to adopt high-tech to control COVID-19 needs to be seen as a civic duty and recognition of the technology as a public good (Cha, 2020).

Finally, changes in human behaviour, working habits and life style will be necessary. New ways of living and working may increasingly involve keeping physical distance, for example, between people and places of work and learning/teaching.

A few examples of the new types of future distance/remote activities are presented below.

Distance learning: Demand for online courses, remote training of instructors for virtual classes and teleconferences is already growing as a result of frequent lockdowns and closure of schools. Distance learning and working, video conferences and virtual meetings are also on the rise and may become a new normal.

However, distance learning is no substitute for in-person teaching in class rooms. A comparative study of distance teaching in Italy (a centralized system of education) and Switzerland (a highly decentralized system) shows that in the absence of central control, discretion and professionalism (distinctive knowledge and responsibilities) were allowed to flourish in both countries (Malandrino & Sager, 2021). Educational institutions will need to decide on a suitable reallocation of resources between in-person and virtual learning on the basis of an assessment of pros and cons of each type of teaching method.

The existing production and social structures and systems are ill-prepared for changes that have been necessitated by the prolonged lockdowns. For example, online teaching resources (e. g. Zoom, Moodle and virtual classrooms) have become popular, but digital infrastructure is yet to be developed for all students. Teachers will need to be trained in new technology and greater access to the internet by all countries will need to be ensured. There is a shortage of online teaching kits or trained teachers even in high-income countries such as the United Kingdom and the United States. It is estimated that seven million school-age children in the United States cannot access the internet at home (*The Economist*, 2020a, March 21). The situation is similar in South Asian countries where one-third of school students are unable to do remote learning for lack of internet access.

The above types of digital inequalities are less discussed than the economic and social disparities reviewed in the book. It is partly because COVID-19 is the only pandemic that has occurred during the Internet age. The phenomenon of distant teaching and learning is relatively new especially in developing countries.

Teleworking: Working from home may increasingly become popular, particularly in high-income countries. The experience of American companies shows that many employees remained uninterested to return to office despite attractive incentives. More and more employees would like to combine work from home and office. Hybrid working is attractive since it offers flexibility and reduces the need for daily commuting (Goldberg, 2022; Luce, 2020; *The Economist*, 2022a, 2022b, April 9 and May 7).[4]

However, working from home is not without problems. Firstly, teleworking is difficult for essential workers in healthcare services and those engaged in personal services. It will grow mainly in such activities as banking, insurance, data gathering and processing, high-tech and research. Secondly, it may involve prolonged adjustment, drop in productivity and social isolation/alienation. Thirdly, some employers may also be wary about workers not delivering on time.

Startups have expanded telework option into messaging, video conferencing and project management. The global economy could become more integrated since such economic activities as legal accountancy and financial services can be split into discrete semi-skilled tasks, which can be done in low-wage countries (Atchison et al., 2020; Baldwin & Evenett, 2020). Another option is to work from anywhere, which will blur business and leisure. Tourist countries like the Bahamas, Costa Rica and Malta offer visas for "digital nomads" who may work from hotel rooms. But there are practical difficulties (such as legal, tax and payroll ramifications) faced by globe-trotters in working from different locations.

Teleconferencing: Distance learning and remote working will raise the demand for teleconferencing and home delivery of food. Online seminars and virtual meetings create opportunities for younger researchers and scientists to participate actively in discussions with senior colleagues. They are likely to be encouraged to interact more freely in their own personal space and in the absence of cost barriers to participation.

Home Delivery: Food supplies and cooked meals are increasingly provided through orders online by such companies as Smood, Getnow and Instacar. Home delivery of food is growing rapidly in high-income countries although less so in low-income ones at present.

Telemedicine: Like education, healthcare, medical practices may also change in the post-pandemic world. In-person consultations and medical care can be shifted to online care to reduce doctor-patient contact and congestion in hospitals and healthcare facilities. Online medical consultations reduce burden on underfunded and inadequate healthcare services.

Remote medical consultation and monitoring can improve access to health besides lowering costs. Online pharmacy can reduce competition and dominance by Big Pharma and middlemen. However, two conditions will need to be fulfilled to encourage online medical consultations. Firstly, insurance regulations will need to be changed to reimburse online services. Secondly, both in-person and online consultations will need to be reimbursed at the same rate in order not to distort the pricing structure.

The use of medical robots in the management of COVID-19 is taking place in such countries as China, Japan and South Korea (Khan et al., 2020).[5] Applications of robots to healthcare include such wide-ranging activities as cleaning and food preparation especially considered hazardous for human beings (as in China), nursing/caring old people (as in Japan) and pharmacy and laboratory work. In Japan, nurse robots are being used to take care of elderly people, which relieves stress on healthcare personnel.

Digitization and Logistics: Artificial intelligence, machine learning and digitization of freight management are being used to ensure speedy and reliable delivery of goods. For example, California's Flexiport and its platform connect shippers, forwarding agents and distribution centres to improve the monitoring of their supply chains (Laube, 2020).

The next generation of technologies are forecast to be those related to the rapid expansion of the digital economy and digital health platforms. As more and more activities go online, development and scaling up of the uses of artificial intelligence and robotics, for example, will become even more important.

Though welcome, the above activities have their downside as well. They are available only to those who have access to electricity and the internet. The bulk of the poor, who do not enjoy such access, cannot benefit, which will only exacerbate the existing economic and social inequalities between low-income and high-income countries and between rich and poor people within countries.

Conclusion

To conclude, coronavirus has the knack of defying leaders, agents and the public besides the medical profession. It is constantly evolving with new variants and sub-variants at unpredictable intervals. Therefore, it is difficult to foresee whether a new single normal or different normals will be required in the future.

Of course, lessons can be learnt from the past experiences (and best practices) of Ebola, HIV/AIDS, SARS and the 1918 Influenza. Concrete action was taken for Ebola without which a worldwide pandemic would undoubtedly have occurred. In essence, the WHO knew what to do and clearly had blueprints in place. But many national leaders did not become familiar with the on-the-shelf plans to enable them to choose when to implement them. As discussed in this book, very few countries learnt any lessons from either past experiences or previous warnings about the looming pandemic crisis. There is every indication that in the future more pandemics will occur, and both the national and global leaders will need to be better prepared for these new but unpredictable challenges.

Public trust deficit was another stark experience of the past three years of COVID-19. Invariably, but particularly in the West, trust in politics, political leaders and governments has been in short supply. The reasons for this are manifold: disconnect between the citizens and voters and their elected representatives, poor character and performance of politicians and political leaders and lack of government accountability discussed above.

In future, performance, transparency and accountability on the part of leaders and agents will need to be promoted for better public cooperation and compliance (Seijtz et al., 2022). During the pandemic, lack of proper communication by the government institutions, the social media and the press gave rise to wild conspiracy theories and misinformation. All these channels failed to provide the public with timely and accurate information on the uncertainty, risk and social health implications of the pandemic and the vaccines. Often, politicians exploited the media for political purposes.

Information provided on COVID strategies and policies for containment and mitigation were often opaque or complex for people to understand especially in poor regions and rural areas of developing countries. Even in the high-income countries, communication failures or distortions (often by the press, social media and government departments) generated misleading information and conspiracy theories. Public mistrust and non-compliance were undesirable and harmful consequences of miscommunication.

Social media (e.g. Facebook and Twitter) was partly responsible for spreading misinformation about the pandemic to create mistrust of government and political leaders (*The Lancet*, 2020). During lockdowns and self-isolation, people relied heavily on digital media and networks, which often spread misinformation about COVID-19. Unlike traditional media which bears responsibility for verifying information, for lack of specialized knowledge or through clear design, digital media promote falsehood under the guise of a free exchange of information. But right to free speech is not a licence for spreading incorrect and harmful information. In future, sifting facts from fiction will become a real challenge for leaders, public agents, private media companies and providers of health services.

Misinformation and conspiracy theories cause confusion which further diminishes public trust, promotes polarization and prevents consensus-building for collective action. Screening of the content of media information may become necessary to ensure an appropriate balance between free speech and critical debate and the promotion of public health. In the absence of a regulatory framework and minimum standards for content of information to be disseminated through social media, an explosion of more harmful misinformation will await us when another pandemic occurs in the future.

Promoting trust in scientific experts, leaders, policymakers and government agents will be essential to adequately prepare for future pandemics. Regarding scientists, the Biden administration has issued guidelines on upholding the highest standards of scientific integrity within the federal government and ensuring science-based policymaking (*Nature*, 2023, January 12). While this is a step in the right direction, more is needed to protect scientists from political interference that occurred in the past. As discussed above, public trust has been scarce during the past three years of the pandemic. In the future, building of public trust will remain a pipe dream until reliable, credible and accountable scientists, leaders and agents are found.

The responsibility for the pandemic needs to be equitably shared between the key stakeholders. Unquestionably, political leaders are expected to bear the major burden of policy choices, direction and control of events, politics and incentives and disincentives. But leaders of industry, scientific organizations, health departments and centres for disease control and the news and social media also bear responsibility. So do different government departments, public health services and the followers. Behaviour and actions of all the different players involved in COVID-19 will need to change to make the world a better and safer place. It is not a return to normalcy that we may need to seek but a "new normal." (Mazzucato, 2020).

Notes

1. The authors (Liu et al., 2021) undertake a cross-country regression analysis on the basis of global data from the International Coronavirus Survey of 178 countries (March–April 2020) to quantify the impact of public trust and confidence. They show that effective government response in the form of containment and mitigation of COVID-19 was most crucial in winning public trust.
2. Protests against prolonged shutdowns and other COVID restrictions on civil liberties also took place in other countries such as France, Germany, Poland, the UK and the US.
3. See Templeton et al. (2020) and Atchison et al. (2020) for a fuller discussion of the subject.
4. Tata Consultancy Services, one of the largest consulting companies, has already eliminated office work (Luce, 2020).
5. The *International Federation of Robots* predicts the demand for such robots to grow to worth $ 9.1 billion by 2022 and much higher subsequently (Khan et al., 2020).

References

Atchison, C., Bowman, L., Vrinten, C., Redd, R., Pristera, P., Eaton, J. W., & Ward, H. (2020). Perceptions and behaviourial responses of the general public during the Covid-19 pandemic: A cross-sectional survey of UK adults. *medRxiv* (The pre-print server for Health Sciences).

Baldwin, R. E., & Evenett, S. J. (Eds.). (2020). *COVID-19 and trade policy: Why turning inward won't work*. Centre for Economic Policy Research Press.

Bhalla, A. S. (1992). *Uneven development in the third world: A study of China and India*. Macmillan.

Bhalla, A. S. (1995). *Uneven development in the third world: A study of China and India*. Macmillan.

Bhalla, A. S. (Ed.). (1998). *Globalization, growth and marginalization*. Macmillan.

Blundell, R., Dias, M. C., Joyce, R., & Xu, X. (2021). COVID-19 and inequalities. *Fiscal Studies, 41*(2).

Bollyky, T. J., & Bown, C. P. (2020). *The tragedy of vaccine nationalism*. Foreign Affairs.

Brown, G. (2020, April 28). The deadly urgency of now. *Project Syndicate*.

Cha, V. (2020). Asia's COVID-19 lessons for the west: Public goods, privacy and social tagging. *Washington Quarterly, 43*(2).

DeLeo, R. (2016). *Anticipatory policymaking: When government acts to prevent problems and why it is so difficult*. Routledge.

Drèze, J., & Sen, A. (1989). *Hunger and public action*. Oxford University Press.

Drèze, J., & Sen, A. (1995). *India—Economic development and social opportunity*. Oxford University Press.

Freedman, T. S., Headley, M. B., Serwas, N., Ruhland, M., Castellanos, C. A., Combes, A. J., & Krummel, M. F. (2020). Lessons of COVID-19: A roadmap for post-pandemic science. *Journal of Experimental Medicine (JEM), 217*(9).

Goldberg, E. (2022, May 22). The rules of hybrid workers were always made up. *New York Times*.

Goldin, I., & Mariathasan, M. (2016). *The butterfly defect: How globalization creates systemic risks, and what to do about it*. Princeton University Press.

Haass, R. (2020, May 12). Deglobalization and its discontents. *Project Syndicate*.

Khan, Z. H., Siddique, A., & Lee, C. W. (2020). Robotics utilization for healthcare digitization in global COVID-19 management. *International Journal of Environmental Research and Public Health, 17*.

Laube, H. (2020). A whole new world. *Credit Suisse Bulletin, 2*.

Liu, J., Shahab, Y., & Hoque, H. (2021). Government response measures and public trust during the COVID-19 pandemic: Evidence from around the world. *British Journal of Management*.

Luce, E. (2020, May 1). Tata's lessons for the post-Covid world. *Financial Times*.

Malandrino, A., & Sager, F. (2021). Can teachers' discretion enhance the role of professionalism in times of crisis? A comparative policy analysis of distance teaching in Italy and Switzerland during the Covid-19 pandemic. *Journal of Comparative Policy Analysis: Research and Practice, 23*(1).

Maxmen, A. (2020). Why the United States is having a Covid-19 data crisis. *Nature.*

Mazzucato, M. (2020). Capitalism after the pandemic: Getting the recovery right. *Foreign Affairs, 99*(6).

Micklethwait, J., & Wooldridge, A. (2020). *The wake-up call. Why the pandemic has exposed the weakness of the west—And how to fix it.* Short Books, Chapter 3 on the 'Overloaded state'.

Nature. (2021, June 1). Wanted: rules for pandemic data access that everyone can trust. *Editorial.*

Nature. (2023, January 12). Plan to "Trump-proof" US science against political meddling, by Jeff Tollefson.

Rodrik, D. (2011). *The globalization paradox: Democracy and the future of the world economy.* W.W. Norton.

Rodrik, D. (2022, May 9). A better globalization might rise from hyper-globalization's ashes. *Project Syndicate.*

Rogoff, Kenneth (2020, June 3). Deglobalization will hurt growth everywhere. *Project Syndicate.*

Seijtz, G., de Clercy, C., & Miller, R. (2022). Character and trust in crisis leadership: Probing the relationships among character, identification-based trust, and perceptions of effectiveness in political leadership during the COVID-19 pandemic. *Journal of Applied Behavioral Science.*

Slaughter, M. J., & McCormick, D. H. (2021, May–June). Data is power: Washington needs to craft new rules for the digital age. *Foreign Affairs.*

Stiglitz, J. (2006). *Making globalization work.* W.W. Norton & Co.

Stiglitz, J. (2019). *People, power and profits.* W.W. Norton & Co.

Templeton, A., Guven, S. T., Hoerst, C., Vestergren, S., Davidson, L., Ballantyne, S., Madsen, H., & Choudhary, S. (2020). Inequalities and identity processes in crisis: Recommendations for facilitating safe response to the Covid-19 pandemic. *British Journal of Social Psychology, 59.*

The Economist. (2020a, March 21). COVID-19 and school closures.

The Economist. (2020b, April 25). Covid-19 and autocracy.

The Economist. (2020c, November 28). The resilience of democracy.

The Economist. (2021a, July 3). The economics of lockdowns: Lives vs. livelihoods.

The Economist. (2021b, December 18). The legacy of a pandemic: the new normal.

The Economist. (2022a, April 9). Bartleby The secret of hybrid working.

The Economist. (2022b, May 7). Bartleby Work from anywhere.

The Lancet. (2020). Building trust while influencing online COVID-19 content in the social media world, 2.

Yadav, P., & Weintraub, R. (2021). 4 strategies to boost the global supply of Covid-19 vaccines. *Harvard Business Review.*

Epilogue

Since the completion of the book manuscript in October 2022, China, the last bastion of the zero-COVID policy, abruptly announced its dismantling in early December 2022. The main components of the policy, namely strict lockdowns of large cities, quarantines in government-run facilities, and mass testing and tracing have been abandoned. Mass testing in public centres is no longer required. Neither are those affected by COVID virus required to be isolated in government-run facilities. People with mild symptoms can stay at home. An electronic pass is no longer required to enter public places.

The suddenness of the decision and its timing have come to most observers as a surprise especially in the midst of winter when the virus is likely to spread more rapidly (Dyer, 2022). It sounds even more so since the strict lockdowns were highly successful in controlling COVID-19 for nearly three years. So why abandon the policy now.

Reasons for a sudden shift in policy are complex and manifold. First, it has been obvious for some time now that the zero-COVID policy is hard to sustain indefinitely. President Xi may have realized that the highly transmissible Omicron variant and sub-variants would make it extremely difficult if not impossible to prolong it. But he may have waited for a face-saving exit. Widespread protests in major cities (Beijing, Chongqing, Guangdong and Shanghai), which started spreading to smaller cities, may have

A. S. Bhalla, *National and Global Responses to the COVID-19 Pandemic*, https://doi.org/10.1007/978-3-031-29521-8

provided an opportunity to change course of action. Mass protests demonstrated that people had reached the end of their tethers. The lockdown fatigue had become intolerable, and people wanted freedom of movement and travel, work and livelihoods. Xi was able to claim that he respected people's will. In no other country did people demonstrate such capacity for prolonged hardships for a national and humanitarian cause of saving lives from the pandemic. But capacity to suffer has its limits even in a very nationalistic and authoritarian country such as China. The economic cost which the Chinese as well as the global economy suffered during the past three years may have also weighed heavily on President Xi.

Many other countries/regions (e.g. Australia, Hong Kong, New Zealand, Singapore and Vietnam) which had also followed the elimination strategy, abandoned it in 2022, realizing that it was politically and economically untenable, following the emergence of new highly transmissible variants and sub-variants. But unlike Australia, New Zealand and Singapore, China's health system and infrastructure are quite weak despite their gradual improvement. Indeed, the rationale for Xi's policy of strict lockdowns and mass testing was based on full recognition of this context of the state of Chinese health services. The low capacity of intensive care units (ICUs), poor rural health infrastructure and inadequate community health care platforms, may have been among the main reasons to maintain zero-COVID policy for so long. The rationale of prolonged lockdowns in China as well as elsewhere (e.g. India) was to allow public agents time to strengthen the capacity of the limited health infrastructure.

One welcome feature of the new policy response is a much higher priority to the vaccination of the elderly and vulnerable population. Many observers have criticized the Chinese policymakers for neglecting this target group, and for concentrating too much on the working-age population. Political leaders and public agents bear some responsibility for this failure.

Relatively low vaccination rates among the elderly in China as elsewhere are also due to vaccine hesitancy and fear of the risks involved and possible adverse side effects of vaccines. Besides, the Chinese people have serious misgivings about Western vaccines and medicines. They prefer traditional Chinese medicines which the government has vigorously promoted. Elderly people tend to be more easily swayed by the arguments of anti-vaxxers and conspiracy theorists. In the past, the Chinese public health authorities had warned elderly people with pre-existing conditions (e.g. diabetes and high blood pressure) against getting vaccinated, which may have also contributed to vaccine hesitancy and perception of fear.

According to *Our World in Data*, China's rate of vaccination of people aged 70+ is 6 per cent, compared to 3 per cent in India, 5 per cent in Sri Lanka, 7 per cent in Singapore and 5 per cent in Brazil. These vaccination rates are rather low even in such high-income countries as Ireland (9%) and Greece (10%) compared to Japan (18.5%) and Germany and Italy (16%). Some countries may show low rates simply because of a lack of adequate supplies of vaccines.

By the end of 2022, only 40 per cent of people aged 80+ have had three vaccine shots of inactivated Chinese vaccines which are less effective than the mRNA vaccines. The WHO recommends three shots for people over the age of 60 years, and the Chinese scientists are engaged in developing several mRNA vaccines one of which was approved by Indonesia. (Dyer, 2022). China's negotiation with Moderna for the rights to produce such a vaccine within the country fell through.

Since the end of 2022, China has been making serious efforts to raise the vaccination rate for the elderly. According to *Caixin* (a Chinese business magazine), the new policy is to achieve the target of 90 per cent rate of vaccination (at least one shot) for this group of people by the end of January 2023 (*The Economist*, 2022, December 10, p. 52). Whether the target can be achieved remains to be seen. State Council's joint prevention and control mechanism has released data, which indicate that 66 per cent of those over 80 had been fully vaccinated by late November 2022 (Lewis, 2023).

Xi and the Chinese public health authorities faced a real dilemma of reopening the economy and at the same time, expecting local authorities to control infections and deaths. Reopening of travel and family gatherings related to celebrations of the Chinese New Year at the end of January 2023 as well as other outdoor activities spread the virus at an accelerated pace. At a press conference in the middle of January 2023, a medical official of the National Health Commission of China announced that COVID-related deaths in hospitals were nearly 60,000 between 8 December 2022 (when restrictions were lifted) and 12 January 2023. Of these, over 5500 deaths were due to respiratory failures and the remaining were due to COVID as well as other underlying diseases such as cancer and cardiovascular diseases. Previously, China used to report COVID deaths as those who died of respiratory failure (*CNN*, 2023, January 15).

A modelling expert on infectious diseases, Shengji Lai (University of Southampton, UK) has undertaken a preliminary analysis of the number of infections in China and travel between cities. His suggests that the massive COVID-19 outbreak may have already peaked in late December 2022 (Lewis, 2023). According to an international repository of viral genetic information (GISAID), China provided 15 sequences from two regions in the 17 days since lifting restrictions. By 9 January 2023, it had made available 880 sequences covering 11 provinces, regions and cities, which showed no evidence of any new variants (*The Economist*, 2023, January 10).

A sudden dismantling of all COVID restrictions and the reopening of the economy put pressure on weak public health services. Although Xi has claimed that the dismantling of zero-COVID was in response to the people's will, he and his government might not tolerate more protests or riots. The government is likely to act firmly if the COVID situation deteriorates and blame it on protestors or the local authorities. Many social media platforms, which were used in organizing the protests, have already been banned. Local authorities can also be blamed for failing to do their job of fulfilling vaccination and other targets.

People's trust in the Chinese leader and the government, which kept them safe from COVID-19, may be eroded. As shown in the book, the Chinese people largely escaped the virus for nearly three years, for which many were grateful to their political masters. Now that all COVID restrictions have been lifted, people are afraid to go out for fear of catching the virus. Many are now seen wearing special masks in public. The followers' behaviour, to self-isolate and take other precautions (like wearing masks and keeping social distance) when required would be welcomed by the Chinese authorities. It should reduce pressures on public/private health services following the reopening of the economy.

Public trust may have sustained the zero-COVID policy for as long as it did. It would have been extremely difficult for Xi to justify its dismantling earlier since people might not have accepted it. After all, the government had praised the policy for keeping people safe and COVID-free. The strategy allowed China to raise vaccination rates, develop health capacity at various levels and train community health workers. Singapore's experience in shifting policy from COVID elimination to living with it suggests that it can be done in stages and through a sound transitional plan of action. It is unclear whether China has developed such a plan or has prepared for possible massive increases in cases and deaths following the reopening of the economy and lifting of all the remaining restrictions regarding domestic and international travel. COVID infections and deaths have been rising elsewhere as well following the detection of new variants and sub-variants.

It is clear that China has begun to converge with the rest of the world and has now accepted to live with COVID infections and to restore economic growth and jobs, which are important for the legitimacy of the Chinese Communist party (CCP), perhaps with one difference, however. Chinese leaders and policymakers are known for their pragmatism. If the COVID situation becomes alarming, they will not hesitate to reintroduce COVID restrictions, albeit on a targeted basis. In fact, many counties and districts in China have continued to impose lockdowns as a means to keep the virus under control despite a shift in national policy. In future, lockdowns will be targeted at high-risk areas and buildings instead of entire districts and cities (Burki, 2022).

The shift in Chinese policy has implications for both China and the rest of the world. China has borne heavy economic cost in terms of loss of output and employment for saving lives through zero-COVID policy. The Chinese economic growth (according to the IMF estimates in Table 2.7, Chap. 2) was reduced from over 8 per cent in 2021 to a little over 3 per cent in 2022. High growth and job creation (youth unemployment is high) are the main sources of Xi's legitimacy and popularity, which he would like to restore as soon as possible. Having been confirmed by the 20th CCP Congress in 2022, he naturally felt more confident and powerful to take a bold step to reopen the economy which had stalled during the zero-COVID period. Consumer confidence and private consumption as well as exports, which contribute to economic growth, had also badly suffered.

The Chinese people are optimistic about the future economic prospects and feel confident that eventually, after a few hurdles during transition, the reopening of the economy will restore normal life as in the pre-pandemic period. The Chinese are known to be quite entrepreneurial, and the economy has bounced back. Although consumer confidence may take time to return, the Chinese New-year celebrations and family gatherings as well as domestic and international travel is triggering a rise in consumer demand.

Reopening of the economy also offers opportunity to manufacturers to step up production in response to rising demand. But for production to pick up and exports to expand, it is necessary for the authorities to remove supply-chain bottlenecks.

China is the second largest economy in the world. It can significantly contribute to the growth of the global economy when it rebounds following the dismantling of the zero-COVID policy. Much of the rest of the world depends on China as a major supplier and buyer of finished goods and raw materials. Spending by Chinese abroad can boost other economies like those of Hong Kong, Thailand and western countries. Some economists predict that it can boost Hong Kong's GDP by as much as 8 per cent over time (*The Economist*, 2023, January 7). China's imports of such materials as oil (almost 20%), refined copper (about 50%) and iron ore (60%) will also contribute to economic growth of other countries. But there will be negative effects as well. For example, China's economic recovery, depending on how fast it grows, may contribute more to higher inflation than economic growth.

In a highly polarizing world and a growing political and ideological divide between the West and the East (Foa et al., 2022), it is not surprising that opinions diverge on the sudden shift in the Chinese zero-COVID policy and its aftermath. The Western press declares the old policy as a failure while portraying a doomsday scenario for China in the post-COVID era.

The Western modellers predicted millions of deaths in China in the near future, which have not occurred (Dyer, 2022). Forecasts of political chaos, threats to Xi's position and social upheaval also turned out to be untrue. Therefore, we avoid citing these forecasts, recalling how wrong the past modelling forecasts were. Indeed, China's rapid economic recovery has already proved how inaccurate the most recent predictions turned out to be. Only two countries today, India and China, are driving the world economy.

The Chinese version of events lays the blame squarely on the Western world for failing to do much to control the virus during the past three years, while China was largely COVID-free. A Chinese scholar based in Beijing (Liu, 2022) has this to say: "In early 2020, China's aggressive lockdowns effectively brought COVID-19 under control, buying time for the rest of the world to implement similarly firm policies and stem the spread of the virus. Unfortunately, the world did not seize the opportunity. So, in 2020 and 2021, countries suffered from wave after wave of variant-fueled outbreaks."

Within Asia, a few countries (e.g. India, Japan and South Korea) required Chinese nationals to provide a negative COVID test on arrival. The United States and many Western countries have introduced similar restrictions to which the Chinese authorities strongly objected. One Chinese observer, based in the United States (Huang, 2022), has described these restrictions as anti-Asian and smacking of racial discrimination. To quote: "Troubling reports of debilitating long-covid symptoms and multiple reinfections have done little to influence policy, but as soon as China reopened to the world, the administration mobilized …The official narrative cites concern that a surge of infections in China could spawn a more dangerous variant, even though the newest Omicron subvariant, XBB.1.5 … is spreading in the United States without triggering nationwide mask mandates or alarm." The new variants and sub-variants are no more likely to come from China than other countries.

Countries such as Thailand welcome the Chinese tourists with open arms being fully conscious of their fat purses. Switzerland has also been missing them since they were among the biggest spenders during the pre-pandemic period. In January 2023, the Swiss authorities appointed Roger Federer, the Swiss tennis maestro, its ambassador to attract the Chinese tourists back to the country.

As is usually the case, the truth will probably lie somewhere between the above divergent opinions. However, one thing is already clear to scientists and health experts: the above travel restrictions are unlikely to be effective since the contagious virus is already spreading throughout many countries. Such restrictions need to be universally applied in order to be effective.

References

Burki, T. (2022, December 16). Moving away from zero COVID in China. *The Lancet.*

Dyer, O. (2022, December 9). Covid-19: Winter surge feared as China lurches away from zero Covid. *British Medical Journal.*

Foa, R. S., Mollat, M., Isha, H., Romero-Vidal, X., Evans, D., & Klassen, A. J. (2022, October 20). *A world divided: Russia, China and the West.* Centre for the Future of Democracy, University of Cambridge.

Huang, F. (2023, January 5). America's Covid test requirement for Chinese travelers is a farce. *New York Times.*

Lewis, D. (2023, January 16). China's COVID wave has probably peaked, model suggests. *Nature.*

Liu, Q. (2022, December 7). China after zero-COVID. *Project Syndicate.*

The Economist. (2022, December 10). China: Vaccinating the vulnerable.

The Economist. (2023, January 7). China-Covid-19. The tsunami.

The Economist. (2023, January 10). Covid is complicating China's efforts to re-engage with the world.

Bibliography

Barry, John (2018). *The Great influenza: The story of the deadliest pandemic in history* (revised ed.). Penguin Books.

Beschloss, M. (2018). *Presidents of war*. New York: Broadway Books.

Bhalla, A. S. (Ed.). (1998). *Globalization, growth and marginalization*. Macmillan.

Bhalla, A. S. (2019). *Asia's trouble spots: The leadership question in conflict resolution*. Rowman & Littlefield International.

Brands, H., & Francis, J. G. (Eds.). (2020). *Covid-19 and world order: The future of conflict, competition, and cooperation*. Johns Hopkins University Press.

Brown, A. (2015). *The myth of the strong leader: Political leadership in the modern age*. Vintage Books.

Brown, G. (2021). *Seven ways to save the world: How to fix the most pressing problems we face*. Simon and Schuster.

Case, A., & Deaton, A. (2020). *Deaths of despair and the future of capitalism*. Princeton University Press.

Christakis, N. A. (2020). *Apollo's arrow: The profound and enduring impact of coronavirus on the way we live*. Little, Brown & Co.

Deaton, A. (2013). *The great escape: Health, wealth and the origin of inequality*. Princeton University Press.

Deakin, S., & Meng, G. (2020). The governance of Covid-19: An anthropogenic risk, evolutionary learning and the future of the social state. *Industrial Law Journal, 49*(4).

Diamond, J. (2005). *Guns, germs and steel*. Vintage, Random House.

Friedman, T. (2020, March 17). Our new historical divide: B.C. and A.C.—The world before Corona and the world after. *New York Times*.

Gates, B. (2022). *How to prevent the next pandemic*. Knopf and Allen Lane.

A. S. Bhalla, *National and Global Responses to the COVID-19 Pandemic*, https://doi.org/10.1007/978-3-031-29521-8

Greer, S. L., King, E. J., Massard da Fonseca, E., & Peralta-Santos, A. (Eds.). (2021). *Coronavirus politics: The comparative politics and policy of COVID-19*. University of Michigan Press.

Haass, R. (2018). *A world in disarray: American foreign policy and the crisis of old order*. Penguin Books.

Horton, R. (2020). *The Covid-19 catastrophe: What's gone wrong and how to stop it happening again*. Polity Press.

IHR. (2005). Revisions of the International Health Regulations, World Health Assembly, WHA.58.3, WHO, Geneva.

Ji, Y., Shao, J., Tao, B., Song, H., Li, Z., & Wang, J. (2021). Are we ready to deal with a global COVID-19 pandemic? Rethinking countries' capacity based on the Global Health Security Index. *International Journal of Infectious Diseases, 106*, 289–294.

Kagan, R. (2012). *The world America made*. Alfred A. Knopf.

Kissinger, H. (2014). *World order*. Penguin Books.

Kupchan, C. A. (2002). *The end of the American era: US foreign policy and the geopolitics of the twenty-first century*. Alfred A. Knopf.

Lahariya, C., Kang, G., & Guleria, R. (2020). *Till we win: India's fight against the Covid-19 pandemic*. Penguin Books.

Lincoln, Martha. (2020). Study the role of hubris in nation's CVID-19 response. *Nature* 585.

Mahbubani, K. (2020). *Has China won?* Public Affairs.

Masciulli, J., Molchanov, M. A., & Knight, W. A. (Eds.). (2009). *The Ashgate research companion to political leadership*. Ashgate Publishing Ltd..

Mazzucato, M., & Quaggiotto, G. (2020, May 19). The big failure of small government. *Project Syndicate*.

McChrystal, G. S., Eggers, J., & Mangone, J. (2018). *LEADERS: Myth and reality*. Portfolio/Penguin.

Micklethwait, J., & Wooldridge, A. (2020). *The wake-up call: Why the pandemic has exposed the weakness of the west, and how to fix it*. Short Books.

Pamuk, O. (2022). *Nights of plague*. Penguin Books.

Patrick, S. (2020, July–August). When the system fails: Covid-19 and the costs of global dysfunction. *Foreign Affairs*.

Pietraszewski, D. (2020, April). The evolution of leadership: Leadership and followers as a solution to the problem of creating and executing successful coordination and cooperation enterprises. *Leadership Quarterly*.

Rachman, G. (2022). *The age of the strongman: How the cult of the leader threatens democracy around the world*. Bodley Head.

Rodrik, D. (2020, May 12). Making the best of a post pandemic world. *Project Syndicate*.

Rudd, K. (2022). *The avoidable war: The dangers of a catastrophic conflict between the US and xi Jinping's China*. Public Affairs.

Shergold, P., Broadbent, J., Marshall, I., & Verghese, P. (2022). *FAULT LINES: An independent review into Australia's response to COVID-19*. e61 Institute.
Steytler, N. (Ed.). (2022). *Comparative federalism and Covid-19: Combating the pandemic*. Routledge.
Stiglitz, J. (2002). *Globalization and its discontents*. W.W. Norton & Co.
Stiglitz, J. (2006). *Making globalization work*. W.W. Norton & Co.
Stiglitz, J. (2010). *Free fall: America, free markets and the sinking of the world economy*. W.W. Norton & Co.
Stiglitz, J. (2019). *People, power and profit*. New York: W.W. Norton.
Stiglitz, J. E. (2016). *The great divide: Unequal societies and what we can do about them*. W.W. Norton & Co.
Taylor, S. (2020). *The psychology of pandemic*. Cambridge Scholars Publication.
The Economist. (2022, December 10). China: Vaccinating the vulnerable.
The Economist. (2023, January 7). China-Covid-19. The tsunami.
The Economist. (2023, January 10). Covid is complicating China's efforts to reengage with the world.
WMO (World Meteorological Organization). (2021, March 18). Review of meteorological and air quality factors affecting the Covid-19 pandemic. *First Report of the WMO Covid-19 Task Team*.
Wright, L. (2021). *Th plague year: America in the time of covid*. Knopf.
Zakaria, F. (2020). *Ten lessons for a post-pandemic world*. W.W. Norton &.

Index[1]

[1] Note: Page numbers followed by 'n' refer to notes.

A. S. Bhalla, *National and Global Responses to the COVID-19 Pandemic*, https://doi.org/10.1007/978-3-031-29521-8

T

FSC
www.fsc.org
MIX
Papier | Fördert gute Waldnutzung
FSC® C083411

Kolibri 360 GmbH
Ferdinand-Jühlke-Straße 7
99095 Erfurt, Deutschland
produktsicherheit@kolibri360.de